AF505764

CORRUPTION AS A
LAST RESORT

CORRUPTION AS A LAST RESORT

Adapting to the Market in Central Asia

Kelly M. McMann

CORNELL UNIVERSITY PRESS   ITHACA AND LONDON

First published 2014 by Cornell University Press

Printed in the United States of America

Library of Congress Cataloging-in-Publication Data

McMann, Kelly M., 1970– author.
   Corruption as a last resort : adapting to the market in Central Asia /
Kelly M. McMann.
      pages cm
   Includes bibliographical references and index.
   ISBN 978-0-8014-5327-4 (cloth : alk. paper)
   1. Corruption—Asia, Central.   2. Political corruption—Asia, Central.
3. Post-communism—Economic aspects—Asia, Central.   4. Asia,
Central—Economic conditions—1991–   5. Asia, Central—Politics and
government—1991–   I. Title.

   HV6771.A783M36 2014
   381.3—dc23
                                                                    2014006949

Cornell University Press strives to use environmentally responsible suppliers and materials to the fullest extent possible in the publishing of its books. Such materials include vegetable-based, low-VOC inks and acid-free papers that are recycled, totally chlorine-free, or partly composed of nonwood fibers. For further information, visit our website at www.cornellpress.cornell.edu.

Cloth printing   10 9 8 7 6 5 4 3 2 1

To Gregory York

Map 1. Kazakhstan, Kyrgyzstan, and Uzbekistan

Contents

Tables

Acknowledgments

The idea for this book came from discussions at kitchen tables in the former Soviet Union. While conducting earlier research, I lived with families who regularly described the struggles they faced as a result of the demise of the Soviet welfare state and, in many countries, the smaller economic roles that their new, market-oriented governments played. No longer did their governments guarantee them employment, housing, higher education, and other necessities. While the families celebrated the political freedoms that the collapse of the Soviet Union brought, they lamented the loss of economic guarantees. After researching the political changes brought about by the collapse, I turned to an examination of how people were coping with the economic transformation. I am grateful to these dear friends and welcoming families for sharing their daily experiences with me.

I also extend my thanks to the 266 individuals who shared their experiences more formally through interviews and observational studies that I conducted, and to the 4,500 Central Asians who participated in mass surveys that a team and I completed.

The coleader of that survey team was Pauline Jones Luong. I am grateful that she too was concerned about the paucity of data about Central Asia and enthusiastic about conducting surveys to help rectify that. We both appreciate the assistance of the Kazakhstani research firm BRIF in administering the surveys.

Two additional colleagues were instrumental in this project. Henry Hale suggested corruption as a frame when he read a conference paper I wrote early on. As the title of the book indicates, this was a recommendation that stuck. I am indebted to Andrew Barnes for many suggestions about different parts of the project over time and for comments on an early version of the complete manuscript.

I also appreciate suggestions from those who read parts of the book or the papers that preceded it: Laura Adams, Catherine Boone, Allen Hicken, Kathryn Hochstetler, Michael Johnston, Pauline Jones Luong, Marcus Kurtz, Joel Migdal, Jessica Pisano, Susan Stokes, Daniel Treisman; and colleagues at Case Western Reserve University, Karen Beckwith, Justin Buchler, Brian Gran, Samantha Hill, Kathryn Lavelle, Pete Moore, Elliot Posner, and Joseph White. Justin Buchler provided helpful statistical advice repeatedly and enthusiastically as well. I appreciate the useful suggestions that two anonymous reviewers and the Cornell University Press faculty Board of Editors provided in the final stages.

I also received valuable feedback when I presented my research at numerous institutions, including Cornell University; the Havighurst Center at Miami University; Harvard University; Indiana University; the Kennan Institute; the Norwegian Institute of International Affairs; Ohio State University; University of Illinois, Urbana-Champaign; University of Wisconsin, Madison; Yale University; and conferences of the American Political Science Association; the Association for Slavic, East European, and Eurasian Studies; and the Central Eurasian Studies Society.

Providing feedback, in addition to assisting with research and editing, were a talented set of Case undergraduates: Philip Kehres, Alexandra Klyachkina, Bhavani Raveendran, Sarah Tremont, Andrew Wolf, and—two students who provided many hours of assistance these past few years—Brandon Mordue and Andrew Slivka.

This book would not have been possible without the generous support of the International Research & Exchanges Board, the National Council for Eurasian and East European Research (NCEEER), the National Endowment for the Humanities, the Social Science Research Council, and Case Western Reserve University. NCEEER's support was particularly essential as it provided significant funding to complete the mass surveys. None of these organizations is responsible for the views expressed here. I also thank SAGE Publications for permission to reproduce information from my article "Market Reform as a Stimulus to Particularistic Politics," *Comparative Political Studies* 42, no. 7 (2009): 971–94.

This book would also not have been possible without the support of Cornell University Press Executive Editor Roger Haydon. I am grateful for the interest he took in the manuscript and the time he devoted to reading it carefully and making numerous helpful suggestions.

The support of my family was also invaluable. My husband's parents, Theodore and Penelope York, have consistently expressed an interest in my research and have always been understanding when I have disappeared from family gatherings to squeeze in some extra work. For a decade, my parents, Ellen and John McMann, have made a monthly trek to Cleveland to play with their grandchildren and thus provide me with additional time to work. And those grandchildren, my daughter Marie and my son Henry, helpfully broadened my perspective. Their own growing interests in foreign countries and politics have been powerful reminders that my work can resonate with nonscholars. My greatest debt of gratitude is to my husband, Gregory York, who has provided me with space to work, insights during challenging times, and accolades during moments of success. I dedicate this book to him.

Note on Transliteration

I transliterated Kazakh, Kyrgyz, and Uzbek names and words from their Russified forms using the Library of Congress system of Russian transliteration. I also relied on the Library of Congress system for transliterating Russian names and words. For all of the languages I used a more common spelling, if one existed, for well-known names and words (for example, oblast instead of *oblast'*).

Acronyms

BEEPS: Business Environment and Enterprise Performance Survey
CPI: Corruption Perceptions Index
CSO: Civil society organization
EBRD: European Bank for Reconstruction and Development
FINCA: Foundation for International Community Assistance
GDP: Gross domestic product
IJU: Islamic Jihad Union
IMU: Islamic Movement of Uzbekistan
NGO: Nongovernmental organization
PSU: Primary sampling unit
UNDP: United Nations Development Programme
USD: U.S. dollar
USSR: Union of Soviet Socialist Republics

Glossary

aiyl okmota: village council in Kyrgyzstan

akim: leader

akimat: administrative office

aksakals: respected male leaders

fitr: a payment to religious institutions or leaders during or at the end of *uraz*, the month-long feast concluding in the Uraz-Bayram celebration in the Islamic faith

jamiyats: neighborhood Islamic charities

kolkhoz: collective farm in the Soviet era

mahalla: a subdivision of an urban neighborhood, particularly in predominantly Uzbek neighborhoods

mazar: shrine

oblast: province

oblast akimat: provincial administrative office

oblast kenesh: provincial representative body in Kyrgyzstan

oblast maslikhat: provincial representative body in Kazakhstan

raion: district

raion akim: district leader

raion akimat: district administrative office

sadaq: voluntary contributions in the Islamic faith

shaar bashchylar: mayors in Kyrgyzstan

sovkhoz: state farm in the Soviet era

uraz: the month-long feast concluding in the Uraz-Bayram celebration

waqf: religious endowments in the Islamic faith

zakat: an annual obligatory welfare contribution of surplus wealth in the Islamic faith

AN ABSENCE OF ALTERNATIVES

A New Framework for Understanding Corruption

"I do not like to give bribes," Marzhan, a villager in Kazakhstan, said to me. She was explaining why she avoids seeking assistance from government officials. Instead, when she needs money, credit, or employment, she relies on her uncle Kanat, a successful private farmer.[1] Her experience illustrates a fundamental point about corruption: individuals contemplate *alternatives* before deciding to engage in corrupt behaviors. Government officials' demands, ineffective laws, cultural norms, or economic needs do not automatically propel ordinary citizens into illicit exchanges with officials, as studies of corruption have implied. Rather, citizens consider whether relatives, groups in society, the market, or formal government programs can provide them with the resources they need.

From this insight about alternatives to corruption, this book makes two arguments about its causes. First, when essential goods and services are not available from alternative sources, individuals engage in corrupt behaviors to try to acquire what they need from government officials. Second, market reform—policies to decrease state economic intervention—can limit these alternatives and thus encourage corruption. The first argument reveals the absence of alternative goods and services as a cause of corruption, and the second argument offers an explanation for why the absence exists. Together, the arguments constitute an "absence-of-alternatives framework" for studying corruption.

---

1. Marzhan and Kanat are pseudonyms used in order to protect the individuals' privacy. Their comments and descriptions of their experiences appear throughout the book. Other ordinary Central Asians who appear multiple times in the book also have pseudonyms. I refer to others by their positions or other descriptors. Author's interview (#161), Kazakhstan, July 22, 2001.

The corruption this book examines is petty corruption—ordinary citizens' use of bribes, personal connections, and promises of political support to try to secure small quantities of goods or services from low-level government officials. My focus on petty corruption is a departure from existing studies, most of which examine grand corruption, or illicit exchanges of large quantities of goods and services between high-ranking officials and businesspeople. Although the book examines petty corruption, its arguments are also relevant to grand corruption. Through the absence-of-alternatives framework, this book provides a new way to understand, and ultimately reduce, both types of corruption.

The Absence-of-Alternatives Framework

The absence-of-alternatives framework emphasizes that citizens' decisions about whether or not to offer bribes and favors to government officials are as important as officials' calculations about whether to demand them. Existing theories of corruption have focused on government officials' incentives and capacity, over-looking citizens—the other half of corrupt exchanges. The absence-of-alternatives approach also highlights the importance of family, societal, and market resources—not simply state resources—in citizens' decisions. Earlier theories have examined the availability of state resources for corruption but ignored the fact that, from a citizen's perspective, the value of goods and services from the state depends, in part, on the possibility of obtaining them from other sources.

An additional advantage of the absence-of-alternatives framework is its ability to solve two puzzles concerning corruption. The book's first argument provides an answer to a puzzle neglected by prior studies of corruption: why do some individuals in countries where corruption is rampant rarely or never engage in illicit exchanges? It demonstrates that some individuals within a country have greater access than others to alternative resources, and this enables them to avoid corruption. The first argument also accounts for variation in corruption across countries—the puzzle that corruption studies typically tackle. Specifically, in countries where alternative sources of essential goods and services are more limited, corruption is more common.

Under what conditions are alternative resources scarce? While numerous factors may contribute to this scarcity, a leading cause in many countries is market reform; this is the book's second argument. Market reform can undermine the ability of markets, societal groups, and families to provide essential goods and services when two conditions are present: (1) states have previously exerted significant economic control, and (2) reforms have failed to create institutions to strengthen markets, such as credit registries, judicial systems, and antimonopoly policies. When market reforms are introduced under these two conditions, market actors and societal groups start from scratch with few resources and limited opportunities to increase them. At the same time, market reform reduces many families' resources: price liberalization results in higher prices that drain families' savings, and economic restructuring closes or downsizes inefficient enterprises that once employed family members. Under this set of circumstances, essential goods and services are not readily available from markets, societal actors, and extended family. Simultaneously, market reform, regardless of the two conditions, eliminates formal government programs, so the state provides fewer needed goods and services. Unable to readily obtain essential goods and services from markets, societal actors, extended family, or formal government programs, most citizens try to acquire them illicitly from government officials. Yet some individuals have relatives who have benefited from market reform, so they can rely on assistance from kin and avoid corruption. Market reform under the two conditions accounts for both resource scarcity in a country and some individuals' greater access to those resources that do exist.

These circumstances have existed in many countries of the world. The two conditions, a legacy of significant state economic intervention and weak or absent market-enhancing institutions, were very common as market reform spread around the world in the late twentieth century. The socialist, and to a lesser extent the state-led capitalist development, programs of the mid-twentieth century resulted in states with substantial control of their economies. And the version of market reform championed in the 1980s and 1990s emphasized the reduction of states' economic roles rather than the creation of support institutions to ensure market competition. Individuals in such settings are often unable to obtain the goods and services they need either through the state or from private actors. In these circumstances, they turn to corruption—it is their last resort.

By trading bribes or favors for essential resources, individuals can survive trying economic circumstances, but these illicit exchanges can also be harmful to society. These behaviors can reduce government legitimacy and effectiveness and increase economic inequality and inefficiency. Although these exchanges constitute "petty" corruption because they involve small amounts of goods and services, they are not inconsequential.

From the absence-of-alternatives approach it follows that a reduction in petty corruption requires attention to citizens, rather than just to government officials. Anticorruption strategies commonly call for a reduction in the resources available to government officials, a decrease in their discretion, and an increase in their accountability, but these approaches do not address citizens' incentives to engage in corruption. Ordinary citizens must be able to acquire essential resources through means other than illicit exchanges with government officials. Substitute resources have to be available from the market, groups in society, and extended family in order to stem corruption.

Existing Approach: The State as the Cause of Corruption

To underscore the novelty of this book's arguments, consider how corruption and its relationship to market reform have been understood to date. A large portion of corruption studies has concentrated on how characteristics of the state can enable government officials to engage in corruption.[2] This body of work is valuable because it has illuminated the government side of corrupt exchanges, even though it has neglected the citizen side.[3] Studies have found that an overbearing state, one with myriad responsibilities, provides officials with many opportunities to dole out government resources for personal gain.[4] Works have also documented that a state with weak capacity cannot constrain officials from distributing resources in return for bribes and favors.[5]

Policymakers and scholars saw market reform first as an antidote to an overbearing state and then as a cause of weak state capacity. As the economies of over-

---

2. Besides the two institutional theories examined here, there are two others—those that focus on democratic institutions and those that examine decentralization. Subsequent chapters examine them as well as economic and cultural theories of corruption.

3. A new wave of this research provides additional value by distinguishing between politicians and their subordinates, either brokers or bureaucrats. See Susan C. Stokes, et al., *Brokers, Voters, and Clientelism: The Puzzle of Distributive Politics* (Cambridge: Cambridge University Press, 2013); Daniel W. Gingerich, *Political Institutions and Party-directed Corruption in South America: Stealing for the Team* (Cambridge: Cambridge University Press, 2013). One of the few scholars to examine both sides of the exchange is M. S. Alam, who has studied how ordinary citizens can counter government officials' demands and attempts to benefit personally from their positions. Yet, this approach also does not explore citizens' incentives. M. Shahid Alam, "A Theory of Limits on Corruption and Some Applications," *Kyklos* 48, no. 3 (1995): 419–35.

4. Classics on the overbearing state include: Frances Hagopian, *Traditional Politics and Regime Change in Brazil* (Cambridge: Cambridge University Press, 1996); Robert E. Klitgaard, *Controlling Corruption* (Berkeley: University of California Press, 1988), 74–75; Gordon Tullock, *The Rent-Seeking Society*, ed. Charles K. Rowley, vol. 5, *The Selected Works of Gordon Tullock* (Indianapolis: Liberty Fund, 2005).

5. A few of the many works that make this point include Klitgaard, *Controlling Corruption*, 74–75; Susan Rose-Ackerman, *Corruption and Government: Causes, Consequences, and Reform* (Cambridge: Cambridge University Press, 1999), 12; Carolyn M. Warner, *The Best System Money Can Buy: Corruption in the European Union* (Ithaca, NY: Cornell University Press, 2007). Capacity refers to the ability of the state to implement official goals despite social group opposition or challenging socioeconomic circumstances. Theda Skocpol, "Bringing the State Back In: Strategies of Analysis in Current Research," in *Bringing the State Back In*, ed. Peter B. Evans, Dietrich Rueschemeyer, and Theda Skocpol (Cambridge: Cambridge University Press, 1985), 3–39, here 9.

bearing states failed to meet growth expectations, market reform became the standard solution. Overbearing states had developed in the twentieth century in many regions, including Africa, Asia, the Middle East, the Eastern bloc, and Latin America. Some overbearing states had their roots in colonial policies of granting governments broad powers and developing expansive civil services. Later in the twentieth century many countries adopted socialist and state-led capitalist development programs that further increased state responsibilities. In the 1980s, market reform began to spread to most regions of the world, largely through training of these countries' economists in Western universities and through programs of international lending institutions such as the World Bank and the International Monetary Fund. The market reforms that countries adopted were not identical, but they share enough similarities to make them a useful concept for my purposes. Market reforms were consistently characterized by withdrawals of states from their economies and the implementation of some or all of the following policies: privatization of state property, deregulation of industries, liberalization of trade, reduction of welfare expenditures, and increases in labor market flexibility. The reforms were meant to generate economic growth, in part, by reducing political corruption.[6] The thinking was that a cutback in states' responsibilities and resources would reduce opportunities for government officials to exchange state goods and services, such as contracts and licenses, for bribes, favors, and political support. States would simply not be involved in these activities, and economies would instead be driven by market competition.

In practice, however, because implementing market reforms was itself an additional responsibility for government officials, it could promote corruption. Research has shown that market reform initiatives generated new opportunities for government officials to exchange state goods and services for personal benefits.[7] Privatization enabled government officials to receive bribes in exchange for access to property sales and price reductions. Officials also provided this access to members of their ethnic groups and particular individuals in society in order to maintain their political support.[8] Government efforts to liberalize foreign

---

6. Bela A. Balassa et al., *Toward Renewed Economic Growth in Latin America* (Washington, DC: Institute for International Economics, 1986), 30–31; John Williamson, "What Washington Means by Policy Reform," in *Latin American Adjustment: How Much Has Happened?* ed. John Williamson (Washington, DC: Institute for International Economics, 1990), chap. 2, here 8.

7. Pranab Bardhan, "Corruption and Development: A Review of Issues," in *Political Corruption: Concepts and Contexts*, ed. Arnold J. Heidenheimer and Michael Johnston (New Brunswick, NJ: Transaction, 2002), 331–32; Gulnaz Sharafutdinova, *Political Consequences of Crony Capitalism inside Russia* (Notre Dame, IN: University of Notre Dame Press, 2010); Andrew Hall Wedeman, *Double Paradox: Rapid Growth and Rising Corruption in China* (Ithaca, NY: Cornell University Press, 2012).

8. In other words, this is the maintenance of ethnic and clientelist networks. See, for example, Leslie Holmes, *Rotten States? Corruption, Post-Communism, and Neoliberalism* (Durham, NC: Duke University Press, 2006), 189–90, 200; Rose-Ackerman, *Corruption and Government*, 35–38; Yan Sun,

trade and to permit private credit-lending enabled officials to illicitly sell licenses.[9] Government officials also could profit from business people's attempts to shape the new legislation that market reform required.[10]

Studies have demonstrated that market reform can also weaken state capacity to prevent and combat corruption.[11] Market reform focused on downsizing the state and overlooked the importance of developing regulatory institutions, such as legal frameworks and independent judiciaries, for emerging markets. Research has shown that government officials had new responsibilities to promote market reform, but not the regulatory institutions to constrain themselves. By scaling back the state, market reform could also weaken state capacity overall,[12] contributing to, among other problems, contradictory laws, ineffective law enforcement, powerless judiciaries, poor tax collection, and inadequate welfare provision, each of which further encouraged corruption.[13] Scholars now argue that creating regulatory institutions prior to market reform can prevent the growth of corruption.[14] In practice, however, these regulatory institutions were not established in advance of reform. Moreover, some people still advocate fighting corruption primarily by downsizing states.[15]

Scholarship that focuses on state strength has provided a useful yet partial explanation for corruption. In describing government officials' incentives and

---

Corruption and Market in Contemporary China (Ithaca, NY: Cornell University Press, 2004), 60; Morris Szeftel, "Misunderstanding African Politics: Corruption and the Governance Agenda," *Review of African Political Economy* 25, no. 76 (1998): 221–40, here 233; Warner, *The Best System Money Can Buy*, chap. 4.

9. Rasma Karklins, *The System Made Me Do It: Corruption in Post-Communist Societies* (Armonk, NY: M.E. Sharpe, 2005), 22; Sun, *Corruption and Market in Contemporary China*, 60–62.

10. This lobbying has been labeled "state capture," and it has generated numerous studies. For an overview, see Joel S. Hellman and Daniel Kaufman, "The Inequality of Influence," in *Building a Trustworthy State in Post-Socialist Transition*, ed. János Kornai and Susan Rose-Ackerman (New York: Palgrave Macmillan, 2004), 100–118, here 100.

11. Quentin Reed, "Corruption in Czech Privatization: The Dangers of 'Neo-Liberal' Privatization," in *Political Corruption in Transition: A Skeptic's Handbook*, ed. Stephen Kotkin and Andrâas Sajâo (Budapest: Central European University Press, 2002), 261–86; Szeftel, "Misunderstanding African Politics," 233.

12. Alena V. Ledeneva, *How Russia Really Works: The Informal Practices That Shaped Post-Soviet Politics and Business* (Ithaca, NY: Cornell University Press, 2006); Szeftel, "Misunderstanding African Politics," 233–34.

13. According to this line of thought, the motivation for government officials and citizens to engage in illicit acts may be not only to take advantage of, but also to compensate for, weak state capacity. Ledeneva, *How Russia Really Works*, 24–25.

14. Rose-Ackerman, *Corruption and Government*, 42–44; Susan Rose-Ackerman, "Democracy and 'Grand' Corruption," *International Social Science Journal* 48, no. 3 (2008): 365.

15. For example, Anders Åslund writes that after privatization, "The next step [to combating corruption in the former Eastern bloc] is to deprive the state apparatus of material resources by cutting public expenditures." Anders Åslund, *How Capitalism Was Built: The Transformation of Central and Eastern Europe, Russia, and Central Asia* (Cambridge: Cambridge University Press, 2007), 252.

resources, it overlooks citizens' incentives and resources. Yet, corruption involves two parties: a state actor and a private actor. This book examines why individual citizens decide to engage in corruption.

Lessons from Central Asia, Implications for the World

To illustrate how individuals consider alternatives to corruption and how market reform affects those alternatives, I begin with an analysis of Central Asia and then extend the investigation to other regions of the world. Central Asia presents a critical case for the argument because it includes countries where, according to some observers, alternative sources of support might be expected to exist despite the implementation of market reform. The proliferation of Islamic organizations and secular charities in many Central Asian countries since independence has suggested to some region-watchers that citizens could turn to these organizations and charities for assistance instead of to the state. Especially in countries where the states' economic roles have shrunk as a result of market reform, these groups could be critical to citizens' economic survival. However, data I have collected in the region demonstrate that Islamic institutions and secular charities do not provide the type and scope of assistance citizens need. Instead, people use bribes, personal connections, and promises of political support to try to obtain help from government officials, especially when relatives cannot assist them. The nearly twenty years of evidence from the region also emphasizes the staying power of corruption: citizens continue to engage in illicit practices because alternatives remain limited.

Within Central Asia, I focus on Kazakhstan and Kyrgyzstan and draw a contrast with Uzbekistan. Since emerging as independent countries from the Soviet Union in 1991, the governments of Kazakhstan and Kyrgyzstan have undertaken market reform, but the government of Uzbekistan has not. The governments of Kazakhstan and Kyrgyzstan have privatized small firms, land, and pensions; deregulated wages; and "liberalized" or reduced restrictions on the conversion of currency, trade, and the movement of interest rates and prices.[16] In Uzbekistan, by contrast, "the government continues to rule out fundamental market-oriented reform."[17] In fact, according to one regional expert, "Uzbekistan's economic

---

16. World Bank and International Finance Corporation, *Doing Business in 2004: Understanding Regulation* (Washington, DC: World Bank and Oxford University Press, 2004); European Bank for Reconstruction and Development, "Transition Report 2004: Infrastructure" (London, 2004).

17. European Bank for Reconstruction and Development, "Transition Report 2005: Business in Transition" (London, 2005).

reform program has been distinguished by the effort to retain the state as the key actor and manager in the Uzbekistan economy."[18] Details about Kazakhstan's and Kyrgyzstan's market reforms and Uzbekistan's lack of them appear in chapter four.

While the causal factor, market reform, exists only in Kazakhstan and Kyrgyzstan, the two conditions—a legacy of significant state economic intervention and weak or absent market-enhancing institutions—are present in all three countries, as indicated in Table 1.1. As former Soviet republics, each country experienced substantial state economic intervention. The Soviet party-state owned the means of production, distributed capital, set prices, directed labor, and produced goods and services. Since the countries have become independent, none of the three governments has created effective institutions to strengthen markets.

As the argument predicts and the later evidence shows, citizens in Kazakhstan and Kyrgyzstan are more likely than their counterparts in Uzbekistan to compete for state goods and services to meet their basic needs, and this competition is characterized by bribery, favoritism, and clientelism.[19] Individuals in Uzbekistan have typically received basic state provisions without competing. This finding does not mean that corruption does not exist in Uzbekistan,[20] but simply that corruption to meet everyday needs has been less common in Uzbekistan, where market reform has not been implemented. Nor should the reader conclude that Kazakhstan and Kyrgyzstan were free of corruption in the Soviet era. Corruption did exist in the Soviet era, but market reform reshaped who engages in illicit practices and why. These independence-era economic policies have had a more significant effect than Soviet experiences have had on citizens' decisions about whether to engage in corruption to meet basic needs.

---

18. Gregory Gleason, *Markets and Politics in Central Asia: Structural Reform and Political Change* (New York: Routledge, 2003), 119.

19. Clientelism is "the proffering of material goods in return for electoral support, where the criterion of distribution that the patron uses is simply: did you (will you) support me?" Susan C. Stokes, "Political Clientelism," in *The Oxford Handbook of Comparative Politics*, ed. Carles Boix and Susan C. Stokes (New York: Oxford University Press, 2007), 604–27.

20. For a discussion of illicit practices in Uzbekistan other than corruption to meet everyday needs, including firms' experiences paying bribes related to customs, taxes, licenses, regulations, government contracts, and adjudication as well as personal enrichment by high-ranking officials, see World Bank, "Trends in Corruption and Regulatory Burden in Eastern Europe and Central Asia" (Washington, DC: International Bank for Reconstruction and Development/World Bank, 2011); Alisher Ilkhamov, "Neopatrimonialism, Factionalism and Patronage in Post-Soviet Uzbekistan," in *Neopatrimonialism in Africa and Beyond*, ed. Daniel Bach and Mamoudou Gazibo (New York: Routledge, 2012), 186–96; Alisher Ilkhamov, "Neopatrimonialism, Interest Groups, and Patronage Networks: The Impasses of the Governance System in Uzbekistan," *Central Asian Survey* 26, no. 1 (2007): 65–84; Lawrence P. Markowitz, "Unlootable Resources and State Security Resources in Tajikistan and Uzbekistan," *Comparative Political Studies* 44, no. 2 (2011), 156–183.

TABLE 1.1. Conditions and causal factor

	COMPARABLE CASES		CONTRASTING
	KAZAKHSTAN	KYRGYZSTAN	UZBEKISTAN
Causal factor: Market reform	yes	yes	no
Condition 1: Legacy of significant state economic intervention	yes	yes	yes
Condition 2: Weakness or absence of market-enhancing institutions	yes	yes	yes

Examining Kazakhstan, Kyrgyzstan, and Uzbekistan also makes my finding more generalizable. Although they are both market reformers, Kazakhstan and Kyrgyzstan are in many other ways quite different. As the information in Table 1.2 indicates, Kazakhstan is considerably wealthier, more urbanized, and richer in natural resources than Kyrgyzstan. It is also larger and more populous. Uzbekistan, not a market reformer, falls in-between Kazakhstan and Kyrgyzstan on many of these socioeconomic measures. The exceptions are urbanization, wealth, and population size. The percentage of Uzbekistan's population living in urban areas is nearly identical to that of Kyrgyzstan, as noted in Table 1.2. Poverty figures for Uzbekistan and Kyrgyzstan are similar, and both countries are considerably poorer than Kazakhstan. Uzbekistan's population is larger than Kazakhstan's and Kyrgyzstan's.

To examine the effect of the two conditions, I extend the analysis beyond Central Asia. Statistical analysis of economic and political data from ninety-two countries around the world allows me to explore the importance of historical state economic intervention and institutions that strengthen markets. Whereas the set of Central Asian countries provides variation only in terms of market reform, the group of ninety-two countries provides variation on these two conditions as well, thus enabling closer consideration of them. This analysis offers support for the argument; it suggests that countries with weaker legacies of state economic intervention and more effective institutions to strengthen markets have less corruption.

Conceptualization, Measurement, and Data

What constitutes corruption has generated considerable scholarly debate. I have opted to follow the lead of ordinary Central Asians in describing as corruption the use of irregular payments, personal connections, and promises of political

TABLE 1.2. Socioeconomic characteristics

	MARKET REFORMERS				NONMARKET REFORMER	
	KAZAKHSTAN		KYRGYZSTAN		UZBEKISTAN	
	2003	2012	2003	2012	2003	2012
GDP (nominal per capita, USD)	2,068	11,935	381	1,160	396	1,717
Percentage of the population living on less than 2 USD per day	22[a]	1[a]	67[a]	22[a]	76[a]	NA[a]
Urban population (percentage of total population)	55	54	35	35	37	36
Energy production (thousand tons of oil equivalent)	101,918	160,148[b]	1,290	1,620[b]	56,416	57,268[b]
Territory (square kilometers)	2,724,900	2,724,900[c]	199,950	199,949[c]	447,400	447,400[c]
Population (number of people)	14,909,019	16,797,459	5,043,300	5,582,100	25,567,650	29,776,850

Source: All data are from World Bank, "World Databank," http://databank.worldbank.org/ddp/home.do (accessed November 2013), unless otherwise noted. Data are provided for the most recent year and for the time period I conducted surveys.

[a] This statistic is called the "Poverty headcount ratio at $2 per day," and it is expressed in U.S. dollars at 2005 international prices. Poverty statistics are from 2002 and 2009; 2009 is the most recent year for which data are available for Kazakhstan and Kyrgyzstan. The latest year for Uzbekistan is 2003. The statistic is not available for Kyrgyzstan in 2003. The 2002 figure for Uzbekistan is only one percentage point lower than the 2003 number. The statistic for Uzbekistan was accessed from the database in 2011. Poverty statistics no longer appear in the online Databank for Uzbekistan. A comparable statistic, 71.7 percent for 2000, appears in a spreadsheet titled "WDI Uzbekistan," provided by the World Bank and available from the author.
[b] The latest energy production data are from 2011. According to the World Bank, "Energy production refers to forms of primary energy—petroleum (crude oil, natural gas liquids, and oil from nonconventional sources), natural gas, solid fuels (coal, lignite, and other derived fuels), and combustible renewables and waste—and primary electricity, all converted into oil equivalents."
[c] The latest territory data are from 2011.

support to try to obtain goods and services from government officials. Adhering to local interpretations underscores that my use of the label "corruption" does not represent a normative critique of these societies, but merely a line of inquiry. Also, local citizens' interpretations of what is corrupt is preferable to legal definitions, which may not exist in new or developing states, and international norms, which may conflict with local ones. Interestingly, these Central Asians' conceptualizations of what constitutes corruption do, in fact, resemble those in much of the scholarly literature and international development community.

Petty corruption,[21] the focus of this book, is especially interesting to study because of the ubiquity of market reform policies in the late twentieth and early twenty-first centuries. A key aspect of market reform is the reduction of citizens' reliance on the state, yet existing studies have not investigated reform's effect on individuals' relationships with government officials, as this book does.[22]

This book also departs from earlier work by examining a variety of informal techniques. Many studies focus exclusively on bribes,[23] personal connections,[24] or selling electoral support.[25] Studying a variety of techniques is important to understanding the citizen side of corrupt exchanges. Government officials' positions may enable them to engage in only one or two types of corruption. For example, only elected officials and their subordinates can trade goods and

---

21. I opted to use the standard term *petty corruption*, even though it falsely implies that the corruption is insignificant, because it more readily relates my argument and findings to existing work than a new term would.

22. Studies have provided insights into how market reform has reshaped groups' interactions with the state.

23. A bribe is a payment to a government official to circumvent a rule "with the goal of obtaining a benefit or avoiding a cost." Rose-Ackerman, *Corruption and Government*, 9. Ernesto Dal Bó, Pedro Dal Bó, and Rafael Di Tella, "'Plata o Plomo?' Bribe and Punishment in a Theory of Political Influence," *American Political Science Review* 100, no. 1 (2006): 41–53.

24. This is also termed *nepotism*, "the instrumental use of positions of power to distribute jobs, goods and other public decisions . . . [to family members and close friends] to maintain and strengthen positions of political power." Simona Piattoni, ed., *Clientelism, Interests, and Democratic Representation: The European Experience in Historical and Comparative Perspective* (Cambridge: Cambridge University Press, 2001), 6, esp. note 7. Alena V. Ledeneva, *Russia's Economy of Favours: Blat, Networking, and Informal Exchange* (Cambridge: Cambridge University Press, 1998); David L. Wank, "Business-State Clientelism in China: Decline or Evolution?" in *Social Connections in China: Institutions, Culture, and the Changing Nature of Guanxi*, ed. Thomas Gold, Doug Guthrie, and David L. Wank (Cambridge: Cambridge University Press, 2002), 97–116.

25. This is also referred to as *clientelism*. See, for example: Javier Auyero, *Poor People's Politics: Peronist Survival Networks and the Legacy of Evita* (Durham, NC: Duke University Press, 2000); Herbert Kitschelt and Steven Wilkinson, "Citizen–Politician Linkages: An Introduction," in *Patrons, Clients, and Policies: Patterns of Democratic Accountability and Political Competition*, ed. Herbert Kitschelt and Steven Wilkinson (Cambridge: Cambridge University Press, 2007), 1–49; Piattoni, *Clientelism, Interests, and Democratic Representation*; Susan C. Stokes, "Perverse Accountability: A Formal Model of Machine Politics with Evidence from Argentina," *American Political Science Review* 99, no. 3 (2005): 315–25.

services for votes. By contrast, if needed goods and services are available from different types of government officials, citizens can use a range of techniques. As chapter three describes, an individual's economic position, as well as the characteristics of the government official, influences the choice of technique. To understand citizens' calculations, I thus examine a variety of forms of corruption. I do not, however, study citizens' use of informal techniques where they are not trying to meet everyday needs, such as when they pay bribes to traffic officers who have pulled them over. In addition, I exclude corruption that does not involve government officials, such as bribing to enter a private university.

Regardless of how the phenomenon is defined, a key challenge in studying political corruption is that individuals may not want to admit that they have engaged in such practices, which they and their peers consider illegal, unethical, or socially unacceptable. Individuals may also be wary of revealing such behavior if they perceive that the researcher disapproves of it.

Confronting these problems, most scholars either rely on media, police forces, and judiciaries to document incidents of political corruption or they use existing survey data sets.[26] Many data sets claim to be measuring people's experiences with corruption but actually ask respondents to report on the experiences of people like them in reality or hypothetically. In other cases, the respondents are experts asked to evaluate corruption in a country. Their judgments are also perceptions of corruption.

A smaller number of scholars generate new data,[27] most of which originates from indirect measures of political corruption. For example, an approach to understanding clientelism is to ask respondents from which political parties they received goods and for whom they voted.[28] Another approach, common among economists, is to estimate levels of corruption by calculating differences between

---

26. For examples of the first approach, see: Sun, *Corruption and Market in Contemporary China*; Warner, *The Best System Money Can Buy*; Wedeman, *Double Paradox*. A couple of examples of the many scholars using existing survey data sets include: Hellman and Kaufman, "The Inequality of Influence"; Jong-Sung You and Sanjeev Khagram, "A Comparative Study of Inequality and Corruption," *American Sociological Review* 70, no. 1 (2005): 136–57. Others combine these two approaches. For example, see: Karklins, *The System Made Me Do It*; Szeftel, "Misunderstanding African Politics."

27. Giorgio Blundo and Jean-Pierre Olivier de Sardan, eds., *Everyday Corruption and the State: Citizens and Public Officials in Africa* (New York: Zed, 2006); Gingerich, *Political Institutions*; Holmes, *Rotten States?*; Ledeneva, *How Russia Really Works*; William Lockley Miller, Åse B. Grødeland, and Tatyana Y. Koshechkina, *A Culture of Corruption? Coping with Government in Post-Communist Europe* (Budapest: Central European Universtiy Press, 2001); Sharafutdinova, *Political Consequences of Crony Capitalism inside Russia*; Stokes, et al., *Brokers, Voters, and Clientelism*; Vineeta Yadav, *Political Parties, Business Groups, and Corruption in Developing Countries* (New York: Oxford University Press, 2011). For descriptions of a few studies that have generated data through direct observation, see Benjamin A. Olken and Rohini Pande, "Corruption in Developing Countries," *Annual Review of Economics* 4 (2012): 479–505.

28. See, for example, Stokes, "Perverse Accountability."

funds designated for and actually spent on public goods and services or between bureaucrats' incomes and consumption.[29] Anthropologists do gather direct evidence. Their approach has been to collect a small number of accounts of political corruption from participants by living with them for extended periods.[30] However, these ethnographies of corruption are not common, in part because anthropologists have been reluctant to study corruption;[31] they began to do so only in the mid-1990s. Moreover, anthropologists have examined discourses and representations of everyday corruption, not causes.[32]

Unlike the many studies that rely exclusively on indirect measures of corruption, this book also includes direct measures, and, by combining the two, illuminates both the extent and character of petty corruption. In research spanning 1994 to 2013, I conducted mass surveys, observational studies, and in-depth interviews, and I analyzed existing economic and corruption data sets and news reports. The observational studies and in-depth interviews provide direct evidence of corruption, whereas the other research offers indirect evidence.

The surveys were administered in Kazakhstan, Kyrgyzstan, and Uzbekistan in November and December 2003. They were conducted in Kazakh, Kyrgyz, Russian, or Uzbek as face-to-face interviews lasting approximately an hour. In each country the mass survey questionnaire was administered to 1,500 individuals ages eighteen and older.[33]

Consistent with many earlier studies, my survey questions asked respondents indirectly about corruption; respondents were not asked to reveal their own corrupt practices. Instead they described from whom they sought assistance and

---

29. For a review of these studies, see Olken and Pande, "Corruption in Developing Countries."

30. Jakob Rigi, "Corruption in Post-Soviet Kazakhstan," in *Between Morality and the Law: Corruption, Anthropology and Comparative Society*, ed. Italo Pardo (Aldershot, Hampshire, UK: Ashgate, 2004), 101–19; Daniel Jordan Smith, *A Culture of Corruption: Everyday Deception and Popular Discontent in Nigeria* (Princeton, NJ: Princeton University Press, 2007).

31. Cris Shore and Dieter Haller, "Introduction—Sharp Practice: Anthropology and the Study of Corruption," in *Corruption: Anthropological Perspectives*, ed. Dieter Haller and Cris Shore (London: Pluto, 2005), 1–26.

32. Giorgio Blundo, "Corruption in Africa and the Social Sciences: A Review of the Literature," in Blundo and de Sardan, *Everyday Corruption and the State*, 15–68.

33. The sample for the mass survey in each country was a multistage stratified probability sample of the country. In each country, macroregions were defined—fourteen for Kazakhstan, eight for Kyrgyzstan, and fourteen for Kazakhstan, including the capital cities as macroregions. Strata were distributed among the macroregions based on each macroregion's proportion of the total population. Primary sampling units (PSUs) were administrative districts. PSUs were selected randomly using probability proportional to size. Within each PSU, households were randomly selected. One respondent was randomly chosen from each household. If a potential respondent declined to participate, another was selected randomly from the PSU. The estimated response rate in the three countries ranged from 60 percent to 80 percent. Pauline Jones Luong and I shared space on the questionnaire, including questions for our different projects. BRIF, a research and marketing firm in Almaty, Kazakhstan, administered the survey.

characterized citizen–government interactions, such as citizen competition for state resources. These indirect questions provide more valid answers than direct questions would. Survey respondents are more likely to answer indirect questions honestly because they are not reporting on their own behavior nor is there a stigma attached to these behaviors. At the same time, the concept of competing to possess state resources encompasses the behaviors of interest in this study: ordinary citizens' use of bribes, personal connections, and promises of political support to try to secure goods or services from government officials.

Survey respondents spoke openly about seeking assistance and about interactions between citizens and officials. At the time of the survey, Uzbekistanis were more reluctant than Kazakhstanis and Kyrgyzstanis to publicly discuss one topic—Islamic institutions not approved by the state. This wariness was due to the brutal persecution of these organizations by the government of Uzbekistan. To reduce the apprehension of respondents in Uzbekistan, a question asking those who indicated that they had sought assistance from religious institutions whether these institutions were approved by the state was dropped from the questionnaire. It was evident from the survey pretest and interviewers' assessments that Uzbekistanis were otherwise willing to speak frankly and did not fear describing competition for state resources.

The survey data reveal differences among countries in terms of the frequency with which people seek government assistance and the nature of interactions between citizens and government officials generally. The data also reveal differences in the goods and services sought from government officials across countries. Differences across individuals—members of various ethnic groups, rural versus urban dwellers, and the employed and unemployed—are also evident. These differences provide support for the argument that market reform with a legacy of significant state economic intervention and absent or weak market-enhancing institutions promotes corruption.

Direct evidence of corruption came from the nine observational studies and 266 in-depth interviews that I conducted from 1994 to 2009 in Kazakhstan and Kyrgyzstan. Because these countries are the market reformers in the study and the argument examines market reform's effect, it was important to collect more in-depth information in these countries. For the observational studies, I lived for extended periods of time with local families, taking note of their interactions with relatives, market actors, societal groups, and government officials. I interviewed average citizens; village, district, provincial, and national government officials; and market and societal actors who may have provided substitutes for state services. These market and societal actors included bankers, heads of private employment agencies, directors of university placement offices, religious leaders, representatives of local and foreign charities, heads of professional associations, and wealthy businesspeople. I used Kazakh, Kyrgyz, and Uzbek for introductions and culture-specific words, but mostly conversed with people in Russian. Because of Soviet education policies, peoples of all ethnic backgrounds and social statuses are comfortable speaking Russian. In fact, elites, such as government officials, were often more comfortable speaking Russian.

The observational studies and interviews took place in rural and urban areas of northern, central, and southern Kazakhstan and Kyrgyzstan. I worked in households and communities where I had ties so that I could discuss the sensitive topics of corruption with members of the household and their networks. I did this first by making connections with different households and communities in the mid-1990s during the course of research for another project. I then returned to these households and locations and added a few new ones with the assistance of old acquaintances who could vouch for me. It would not have been helpful to have randomly selected households, since the purpose of this portion of the investigation was to prepare the survey questionnaire and then to elaborate on the survey data, which were representative of the population. I also did not randomly select market actors, societal groups, or government officials, but instead interviewed those to whom members of households reported turning for assistance or to whom they could potentially turn for assistance.

Interviews began with questions about everyday problems that people faced and where they turned for assistance. Ordinary citizens provided firsthand accounts; market and societal actors and government officials described problems that people approached them about and whether and how they could solve them. Many interviewees brought up the subject of corruption in response to these questions. Otherwise, near the end of the interview, I posed specific questions about corruption, but ones that did not implicate the interviewee. For example, of a credit lender I would ask to what extent applicants for loans believed they needed to offer a bribe or have a personal connection in order to obtain credit. These questions typically initiated extended discussions of corruption. Based on this information, I describe different forms of corruption, the government officials targeted by citizens for corrupt exchanges, and the resources available to government officials to use in these exchanges. When I found inconsistencies in different people's accounts, I continued to conduct interviews to clear up the discrepancies. Consistent evidence on a topic enables me to make generalizations, which I illustrate with accounts from specific interviews.

Of the interviewees, government officials were most likely to provide firsthand accounts of engaging in corrupt exchanges. Typically, the officials viewed practices like taking bribes or buying votes as so commonplace that they were not embarrassed to reveal their involvement, or they were officials whom I knew well. Average citizens were more likely to describe how friends and acquaintances had used bribes, personal connections, and promises of political support to try to obtain benefits from government officials. However, people I knew well provided firsthand accounts of decisions about corruption. Moreover, in the households where I lived I directly witnessed some decision making. Journalists I interviewed also described specific illicit exchanges that they had uncovered. In presenting the information from these interviews and observations, I do not include details that would make it possible to identify individuals. In order to save space, I provide background information for each interviewee, but I footnote only direct quotations.

Finally, socioeconomic data and news reports, from 1994 to 2013, were helpful to the project. Sources of socioeconomic data include the national statistical agencies of the countries and international organizations such as the World Bank. From print and online media outlets, I found useful news articles.

Together the mass surveys, observational studies, in-depth interviews, existing economic, political, demographic, and corruption data sets, and news and historical reports provide support for the argument that market reform promotes petty corruption. This is clear from Table 1.3, where the types of evidence used to support each point of the argument are documented.

In addition to the analytical leverage they provide, the data collected here substantially increase our knowledge of the world, especially Central Asia. Unlike most prior works on corruption, this book draws primarily on original data, including in-depth interviews from rural areas—a large segment of developing countries—which most studies do not include.[34] The breadth of research allows the book to answer questions often overlooked by corruption studies: Which goods and services do people seek and why? Which government officials do they target and why? From where do the officials obtain the resources to exchange? The survey data I collected are unusual for the region in that they are both nationwide and comparable across multiple countries.[35]

---

34. See, for example: Judith Chubb, *Patronage, Power, and Poverty in Southern Italy: A Tale of Two Cities* (Cambridge: Cambridge University Press, 1982); Donatella Della Porta and Alberto Vannucci, *Corrupt Exchanges: Actors, Resources, and Mechanisms of Political Corruption* (New York: Aldine de Gruyter, 1999).

35. Besides these surveys, other surveys that are nationwide and comparable across countries include "Asiabarometer," https://www.asiabarometer.org (accessed December 19, 2013); Beth Kolko et al., "The Effect of the Internet on Society: Incorporating Central Asia into the Global Perspective," National Science Foundation, http://www.nsf.gov/awardsearch/showAward.do?AwardNumber=0326101 (accessed December 19, 2013); Scott Radnitz, Jonathan Wheatley, and Christoph Zürcher, "The Origins of Social Capital: Evidence from a Survey of Post-Soviet Central Asia," *Comparative Political Studies* 42, no. 6 (2009); Michael Swafford et al., "General Social Survey of the Russian Federation and Central Asia, October–December 1992," Inter-University Consortium of Political and Social Research, 1992, http://www.icpsr.umich.edu/icpsrweb/ICPSR/studies/06499 (accessed December 19, 2013).

TABLE 1.3. Summary of evidence and data

CENTRAL EVIDENCE	DATA (CHAPTER NUMBER)
Market reform, a legacy of significant state economic intervention, and absent or weak market-enhancing institutions exist in Kazakhstan and Kyrgyzstan.	• Economic data sets (4)
Because of absent or weak market-enhancing institutions, market actors are not an alternative to corruption in Kazakhstan and Kyrgyzstan.	• Survey data (4) • Interview data (4) • News reports (4)
Individuals tend not to turn to market actors for assistance in Kazakhstan and Kyrgyzstan.	• Survey data (4) • Interview data (4)
Market reform has limited state goods and services and thus legal means to obtain them in Kazakhstan and Kyrgyzstan.	• Interview data (4) • News reports (4)
Governments' market-reform messages in Kazakhstan and Kyrgyzstan discourage use of state goods and services.	• Interview data (4) • News reports (4)
Because market reform under a significant state economic legacy and absent or weak market-enhancing institutions has limited resources of societal actors, they are not an alternative to corruption in Kazakhstan and Kyrgyzstan.	• Interview data (5) • Historical reports (5) • News reports (5)
Individuals tend not to turn to societal actors for assistance in Kazakhstan and Kyrgyzstan.	• Survey data (5) • Interview data (5)
Individuals compete to obtain state goods and services in Kazakhstan and Kyrgyzstan.	• Survey data (4)
Individuals use corruption to try to secure state goods and services in Kazakhstan and Kyrgyzstan.	• Interview data (3) • Observational studies (3)
Individuals with family members who can meet their needs avoid corruption in Kazakhstan and Kyrgyzstan.	• Interview data (6) • Observational studies (6)

CORROBORATING EVIDENCE	
In rural areas, where market alternatives are more limited, people are more likely to seek state assistance.	• Survey data (4)
Individuals' demands of the state match challenges brought about by market reform in Kazakhstan and Kyrgyzstan.	• Survey data (4) • Interview data (4) • Economic data sets (4)
Those most affected by market reform are those most likely to seek state assistance.	• Survey data (4)
Competition for basic state resources is not as common in the nonmarket reformer Uzbekistan.	• Survey data (4) • Economic reports (4)
Uzbekistanis are no more likely to turn to market and societal actors for assistance than Kazakhstanis and Kyrgyzstanis.	• Survey data (4)
Alternative explanations do not explain the differences among the three Central Asia countries.	• Survey data (4) • Economic data sets (4) • Political data sets (4) • Demographic data sets (4)
The argument applies outside of Central Asia.	• Economic data sets (4) • Global corruption data set (4)
Citizens in Kazakhstan and Kyrgyzstan are not averse to religious organizations and charities.	• Interview data (5) • News reports (5)

Combined, the different types of data provide an important window into how citizens in Central Asia have coped with the economic upheaval caused by the collapse of the Soviet economy and implementation of market reform. In particular, they highlight the role (or lack of a role) of family, market actors, societal groups, and the state in individuals' survival strategies. The findings also challenge preconceived notions, such as the idea that Islamic organizations and foreign charities have become citizens' main sources of support and thus are threats to Central Asian states. The nearly twenty-year span of the data allows me to comment on change, or lack of change, over time. The book's arguments indicate that an increase in alternative sources of essential goods and services, as a result of new or strengthened market-enhancing institutions, should reduce corruption. Unfortunately, the latest evidence shows that market-enhancing institutions continue to be weak in Kazakhstan and Kyrgyzstan, and corruption remains rampant.

Structure of the Book

Why is corruption more common in some countries, and yet why do some individuals in these countries rarely or never engage in illicit exchanges? The absence-of-alternatives framework provides answers in chapter two. The reader will also find definitions of the arguments' core concepts—basic needs, market reform, legacy of significant state economic intervention, and market-enhancing institutions. In addition, this chapter elaborates on how the absence-of-alternatives approach is distinct from existing theories of corruption and offers advantages over them.

Chapter three describes the specific corruption this book seeks to explain—petty corruption in Kazakhstan and Kyrgyzstan. The interview, observational, and survey data reveal that citizens use bribes, personal connections, and promises of political support to try to obtain money, credit, and employment, mostly from village and other low-level officials.

What are the causes of this corruption? Chapters four and five show how market reform coupled with a legacy of significant state economic intervention and weak or absent market-enhancing institutions have promoted corruption by limiting alternative resources. Chapter four demonstrates how these three factors have restricted income, credit, and employment from market actors and formal government programs. This is not the case, however, in Uzbekistan, where market reform has not been undertaken. The absence-of-alternatives framework can account for the difference between Uzbekistan and the market reformers, Kazakhstan and Kyrgyzstan, whereas other theories of corruption cannot. The ninety-two-country statistical analysis provides additional support for the argument. Shifting to societal actors, chapter five shows how market reform under the two conditions has also limited the ability of religious institutions and secular charities to meet basic needs in Kazakhstan and Kyrgyzstan. The goods and services of other societal actors, including foreign charitable organizations, foreign companies, local companies, labor unions, *aksakals* (respected male elders), and educational establishments have also not become substitutes for state resources.

Despite the widespread corruption in Kazakhstan and Kyrgyzstan, how have some people managed to rarely or never engage in it? Chapter six demonstrates that they have family members who can help meet their needs. Yet, not all families can provide the credit, employment, and money that their kin require. Market reform has made only some family networks resource-rich. This chapter describes factors that account for these families' financial success in the new economies.

Finally, chapter seven uses these insights about corruption to offer policy prescriptions more in tune with the socioeconomic reality of developing countries than previous advice has been. In particular, anticorruption strategies should include the expansion of nonstate sources of assistance for average citizens. This book highlights that corruption, despite its negative societal implications, is a sound survival strategy for individuals. Loosening government policies that limit the activities of societal groups, such as religious organizations, as well as actively developing institutions to increase market competition, such as credit registries, would provide individuals with survival alternatives that have fewer social costs. In addition to reforming government, providing citizens with alternatives to corruption is likely to be an effective anticorruption strategy. Unfortunately, little evidence indicates that Central Asia is on this path.

ALTERNATIVES TO CORRUPTION AND THE EFFECT OF MARKET REFORM

The Arguments and Their Theoretical Implications

"Workers who gave money to the sovkhoz received goods," Marzhan, the woman in the village in Kazakhstan, recounted to me.[1] In the late 1990s when the sovkhoz (state farm) in the village collapsed, workers who gave bribes to the local authorities received goods from it, Marzhan and other village residents explained. Former sovkhoz workers needed these essential agricultural inputs for the new farms they were establishing; their limited income and access to credit made it difficult for them to obtain the goods elsewhere. Yet some villagers, like Marzhan and her family, opted not to pay bribes and thus not to receive the inputs.

This story underscores that not all individuals engage in corruption. Earlier studies of corruption have examined the puzzle of why it is more common in certain countries, but they have neglected the question of why some individuals in countries where corruption is rampant rarely or never engage in it.

The absence-of-alternatives explanation presented in this book solves both puzzles. First, it shows that corruption is more common in countries where alternative sources of essential goods and services are more limited. Second, even within a single country some individuals have greater access to alternative resources than others, and this enables them to avoid corruption. Market reform can account for individuals' differing access to resources as well as the paucity of resources in a country. By enriching some families and impoverishing others, market reform leads individuals whose relatives have not prospered to engage in corruption to meet their everyday needs. When market reform limits the resources

---

1. Author's interview (#161), Kazakhstan, July 22, 2001.

that formal government programs, market actors, and societal groups can provide to individuals, it increases the prevalence of corruption in a country. To elaborate on these arguments and demonstrate the benefits of the absence-of-alternatives framework, I begin with some fundamental observations about seeking assistance.

Seeking Assistance

Central to the absence-of-alternatives framework are the ideas that individuals have basic needs to meet and that they prefer not to use illicit means to meet them. These *basic needs* include employment, credit, money, food, clothing, and shelter. Employment and credit both provide money—employment does so through income, and credit does so by enabling people to initiate profitable entrepreneurial ventures. Individuals may also receive money as a direct handout. Regardless of the source, money enables individuals to purchase food, clothing, and shelter. People may also receive these goods directly as charitable donations. This definition of basic needs is supported by the accounts given by Central Asians. As the data in chapter three reveal, Central Asians seek employment, credit, and money in order to ensure that they have food, clothing, and shelter.

The claim that individuals prefer to avoid illicit exchanges with government officials to meet these needs reflects reality: studies of countries in Africa, Eastern Europe, and Latin America, as well as my own research in Central Asia, have found that people consider it repugnant to offer bribes, use personal connections, and promise political support for necessities, even when they perceive the practices to be pervasive in their societies.[2] Thus, the idea that people's first preference is to avoid corruption is a sound assumption.

This book's arguments, however, do not require a particular judgment as to whether corruption to meet basic needs is good or bad. As noted in the first chapter, petty corruption can have both benefits and drawbacks. It can enable people to survive difficult economic circumstances, but it also undermines regime legitimacy, fuels economic and political inequality, and increases economic inefficiencies.[3] The arguments hold whether or not one finds corruption useful, harmful, or a mix of the two.

---

2. Javier Auyero, *Poor People's Politics: Peronist Survival Networks and the Legacy of Evita* (Durham, NC: Duke University Press, 2000); William Lockley Miller, Åse B. Grødeland, and Tatyana Y. Koshechkina, *A Culture of Corruption? Coping with Government in Post-Communist Europe* (Budapest: CEU Press, 2001); Daniel Jordan Smith, *A Culture of Corruption: Everyday Deception and Popular Discontent in Nigeria* (Princeton, NJ: Princeton University Press, 2007).

3. Miller, Grødeland, and Koshechkina, *A Culture of Corruption?* 11–13; Luis Roniger, "Political Clientelism, Democracy, and Market Economy," *Comparative Politics* 36, no. 3 (2004): 353–75, here 354; Susan Rose-Ackerman, *Corruption and Government: Causes, Consequences, and Reform*

In what ways can people meet their basic needs besides by engaging in illicit exchanges with government officials? Possible alternative sources of goods and services include formal government programs, markets, groups in society, and family members. Formal state assistance programs provide help to individuals based not on their particularistic characteristics, such as bureaucrat's relatives, but based on their fit within a category, such as veterans. The programs may provide employment, credit, money, food, clothing, or shelter. Specific examples include public employment, subsidies to enterprises to help increase hiring, and welfare benefits to individuals. Market actors, including private banks and owners of private companies, are most likely to provide credit or employment, although some perform charitable acts that help meet the other needs. Societal groups and family members may assist people with employment, credit, money, food, clothing, or shelter. Societal groups include places of worship, religious organizations, and secular charities, and family members include kin both inside and outside of a household.

Differences among Countries: Market Reform, Legacies, and Institutions

Under certain conditions, market reform can limit these alternatives and thus account for why corruption is more common in some countries. *Market reform* refers to efforts in the late twentieth and early twenty-first centuries to decrease state economic intervention through policies, such as privatization of state property, deregulation of industries, liberalization of trade, reduction of welfare expenditures, and increases in labor market flexibility. Market reform's promotion of corruption is ironic because the set of policies is designed to reduce the resources government officials have and expand opportunities for individuals to obtain assistance from private actors. For example, farmers should be able to secure credit from private banks instead of government programs. Moreover, individuals should obtain those limited goods and services that remain available from the state based on their membership in certain categories, such as "farmers eligible for credit," not based on their particularistic traits, such as their ability to exploit personal connections. In practice, however, people do take part in illicit exchanges in order to obtain assistance from government officials. And the

---

(Cambridge: Cambridge University Press, 1999), 2, 3, 12, 14, 16, 26; Eric M. Uslaner, *Corruption, Inequality, and the Rule of Law: The Bulging Pocket Makes the Easy Life* (Cambridge: Cambridge University Press, 2008), 17.

greater the number of people who lack substitute resources in a country, the more common corruption is.

Of the different market reform policies, the reduction of welfare expenditures has the greatest influence on citizens' abilities to meet their basic needs. A reduction in welfare expenditures can include a cutback in public employment and diminution of some benefit payments and an end to others. As a result, individuals have fewer formal government programs that they can turn to for assistance. Those government programs that do exist formally restrict the distribution of resources to individuals who meet narrow requirements in order to manage their scarcity. As a result, competition for these resources increases. At the same time, price liberalization can reduce the relative size of citizens' incomes, and privatization and reforms to increase labor market flexibility can result in layoffs and thus loss of income. Consequently, people's needs grow as government assistance shrinks.

Market reform can further undercut citizens' welfare by limiting resources from markets, societal groups, and extended family. This occurs when two conditions hold: (1) state involvement in the economy has been historically significant, and (2) market-enhancing institutions are weak or absent.

The first condition, *a legacy of significant state economic intervention*, historically created a scarcity of resources provided by nonstate individuals and organizations. The resources included employment, credit, and welfare assistance, for example. The scarcity existed because the government granted monopoly or near-monopoly rights to businesses, allowing only one or a few to provide each good or service. This limited the production of goods and services because few entrepreneurs had the rights and other entrepreneurs expended time and capital on lobbying for the rights instead of on production.[4] Some governments also outright prohibited anyone other than the state from providing particular goods and services. Even in the absence of a formal ban, entrepreneurs had little incentive to produce goods and services that the government was already providing.

States' attempts to control their countries' economies also limited the resources that societal groups could provide to individuals. State economic intervention resulted in a crowding out or banning of societal groups. In particular, governments that provided extensive welfare benefits reduced the need for secular and religious groups to provide charitable assistance. When states actually prohibited the creation of societal groups or severely limited their activities, these groups were even less likely to offer substitute resources.

---

4. James M. Buchanan, "Rent-Seeking and Profit-Seeking," in *Toward a Theory of the Rent-Seeking Society*, ed. James M. Buchanan, Robert D. Tollison, and Gordon Tullock (College Station: Texas A&M University, 1980), 3–15.

The breadth, length, and immediacy of state economic intervention vary across countries. The more goods and services that the state controls for a longer time closer to the onset of market reform, the more the legacy of the intervention will limit nonstate resources once market policies are adopted.

By reducing state economic intervention, market reform spurs the emergence of private businesses and societal groups; however, these new entities have difficulty immediately meeting people's basic needs. Market reform ends prohibitions on private market and charitable activities, and economic and social entrepreneurs have incentives to create private businesses and charitable organizations now that the state no longer provides extensive goods and services. These new businesses and charities, however, face obstacles in meeting people's needs for employment, credit, money, and other goods and services. The businesses and charities are beginning from scratch with few resources to distribute and little knowledge of how to distribute them. The broader, longer, and more recent the state economic intervention of the past, the fewer resources and less experience businesses and charities have when market reform is introduced.

Market-enhancing institutions are critical to helping these new businesses and charities to thrive, yet they have rarely been part of market reforms. *Market-enhancing institutions* are "[r]ules, enforcement mechanisms, and organizations . . . [that] help transmit information, enforce property rights and contracts, and manage competition in markets."[5] Credit registries, accounting firms, constitutions, judicial systems, and antimonopoly policies are some of the many rules, organizations, and enforcement mechanisms that count as market-enhancing institutions. By providing information about potential partners and by defining and enforcing property rights, market-enhancing institutions encourage market transactions and investment. By stimulating competition, they give new businesses the opportunity to prove their mettle and they help to ensure reasonable prices for inputs.

States must create, or at least encourage, the development of market-enhancing institutions. These institutions are public goods and, in some cases, represent constraints on market actors. Market competitors have little or no incentive to overcome the collective action problem in order to establish these public goods or to constrain their own profit-seeking behavior.

Consider in greater detail two market-enhancing institutions, credit registries and antimonopoly policies, that can be especially important to citizens' welfare. Credit registries, as well as credit bureaus, are databases that have information about the creditworthiness of individuals. Without this information, banks must

---

5. World Bank, *World Development Report 2002: Building Institutions for Markets* (New York: Oxford University Press, 2002), 4.

demand significant collateral to reduce the likelihood that clients will default and to reduce the losses to the banks if the clients do fail to repay their loans. In rural areas throughout much of the world, it is difficult for banks to collect this information on their own. Population density is low, so it is not profitable for banks to establish branches, which could collect the necessary information.[6] Banks could share credit information with one another, but they have little incentive to do this because they are competitors. Governments or entrepreneurs responding to government incentives typically create public credit registries or private credit bureaus, respectively. Credit registries or credit bureaus that cover much of the population enable banks to acquire credit information about potential borrowers without the cost of building branches in less populated areas. With this information, private banks can better determine which potential borrowers pose a sufficiently low risk that it would be profitable to lend to them. Improved coverage does not mean that all people become eligible to obtain credit—some individuals may be too risky—but it typically expands the pool of eligible borrowers.[7]

Governments also play an important role in encouraging market competition by developing and enforcing antimonopoly policies. When businesspeople are forced to buy from a monopoly provider, it is difficult for them to expand their businesses. Money paid for inflated electricity or agricultural processing prices cannot be reinvested to hire additional employees, for example.

Despite the importance of market-enhancing institutions, they were generally not part of market reforms for twenty years. Only in the early twenty-first century did market reform advocates, such as the World Bank, acknowledge that state withdrawal from the economy did not guarantee strong markets. Instead, along with liberalization, privatization, and deregulation, governments must actively develop market-enhancing institutions.

As a result of this oversight, market and societal actors, particularly in countries with a legacy of significant state economic intervention, cannot meet individuals' needs for employment, income, and credit. Fewer private businesses exist and those that do are less likely to expand and employ more people. As a result fewer people can earn income in private business. Similarly, fewer private banks

---

6. Daniel Verdier, *Moving Money: Banking and Finance in the Industrialized World* (Cambridge: Cambridge University Press, 2002).

7. As formal models of credit rationing indicate, banks may consider certain groups of individuals too risky to lend to even when the individuals are willing to pay higher rates and provide more valuable collateral. Most likely, these individuals would have no or poor credit histories. Joseph E. Stiglitz and Andrew Weiss, "Credit Rationing in Markets with Imperfect Information," *American Economic Review* 71, no. 3 (1981), 393–410.

exist and their credit-lending is more limited. When private firms are less profitable they engage in less charitable giving as well.

The lack of market-enhancing institutions as well as the legacy of significant state economic intervention limit the resources of groups in society too. The effect is both indirect and direct. Charitable organizations rely on membership dues and donations. To the extent that market actors are not prospering, individuals give less to places of worship, religious organizations, secular charities, and other societal groups. Furthermore, societal groups may also have the legal right to obtain credit or engage in business ventures in order to earn revenue to use toward their missions. So, societal groups can also be directly harmed by weak credit markets.

In sum, market reform in countries that have a legacy of significant state economic intervention and no or weak market-enhancing institutions not only reduces assistance from formal government programs but also limits help from markets, charities, and kin. The more extensive, lengthy, and recent the state economic intervention and the weaker the market-enhancing institutions, the more limited the assistance.

Individuals' Decisions: Market Reform's Differential Effect on Families

When resources citizens need are no longer available through formal state programs and are also not obtainable from outside the government, individuals engage in corruption.[8] However, because market reform has a differential effect on families, some individuals have kin who can help them and some do not.[9] This differential effect accounts for why some individuals, even in countries

---

8. The order in which citizens approach formal government programs, market actors, societal groups, and kin depends on ease of access and cultural characteristics, such as strength of family ties. Yet, eventually, they will either secure assistance from one of these individuals or groups and thus not need to engage in corruption or they will not secure assistance and thus need to engage in corruption.

9. Market reform has increased income inequality in wages. Julien Gourdon, Nicolas Maystre, and Jaime de Melo, "Openness, Inequality, and Poverty: Endowments Matter," *World Bank Policy Research Working Paper* 3981 (2006): 1–51, here 24, http://elibrary.worldbank.org/doi/book/10.1596/1813-9450-3981 (accessed December 19, 2013); Xubei Luo and Nong Zhu, "Rising Income Inequality in China: A Race to the Top," *World Bank Policy Research Working Paper* 4700 (2008): 1–23, here 20, http://go.worldbank.org/ZFIMAX6400 (accessed December 19, 2013); Lance Taylor and Rob Vos, "Balance of Payments Liberalization in Latin America: Effects on Growth, Distribution and Poverty," in *Economic Liberalization, Distribution, and Poverty: Latin America in the 1990s*, ed. Rob Vos, Lance Taylor, and Ricardo Paes de Barros (Northampton, MA: Edward Elgar, 2002), 1–53.

where corruption is pervasive, avoid engaging in corruption to meet their everyday needs.

Scholars have largely ignored these differences among individuals.[10] Institutional theories, such as explanations based on the overbearing state and weak state capacity, focus on national government institutions, and cultural explanations assume that everyone shares the same norms and habits. The only factor identified that can even address this variation is citizens' wealth.[11] However, studies have found that both the poor and nonpoor engage in corruption, so wealth cannot be the explanation.[12] Also, wealth cannot account for why some poor people nevertheless manage to avoid corruption.

This book's arguments explain that those individuals whose relatives have not prospered in the new market economy use bribes, personal connections, and promises of political support to try to obtain state resources. Those individuals whose relatives have prospered can avoid corruption. Initially, under market reform the economic situation of many families worsens; family members may lose state jobs and welfare benefits; however, some families also manage to enrich themselves.[13] In countries with a legacy of significant state economic intervention and lack of market-enhancing institutions, the long-term prospects for

---

10. Scholars have examined variation in corruption across regions within a country, but not across individuals. See, for example: J. David Brown, John S. Earle, and Scott Gehlbach, "Helping Hand or Grabbing Hand? State Bureaucracy and Privatization Effectiveness," *American Political Science Review* 103, no. 2 (2009), 264–83; Phyllis Dininio and Robert Orttung, "Explaining Patterns of Corruption in the Russian Regions," *World Politics* 57, no. 4 (2005), 500–529; Yan Sun, *Corruption and Market in Contemporary China* (Ithaca, NY: Cornell University Press, 2004), 121–57.

11. Herbert Kitschelt, "Linkages between Citizens and Politicians in Democratic Politics," *Comparative Political Studies* 33, no. 6 (2000): 845–79, here 857; Herbert Kitschelt and Steven Wilkinson, "Citizen-Politician Linkages: An Introduction," in *Patrons, Clients, and Policies: Patterns of Democratic Accountability and Political Competition*, ed. Kitschelt and Wilkinson (Cambridge: Cambridge University Press, 2007), 1–49, here 25; Claus Offe, "Political Corruption: Conceptual and Practical Issues," in *Building a Trustworthy State in Post-Socialist Transition*, ed. János Kornai and Susan Rose-Ackerman (New York: Palgrave Macmillan, 2004), 77–99, here 86; Simona Piattoni, "Clientelism in Historical and Comparative Perspective," in *Clientelism, Interests, and Democratic Representation: The European Experience in Historical and Comparative Perspective*, ed. Piattoni (Cambridge: Cambridge University Press, 2001), 1–30, here 17; James C. Scott, "Corruption, Machine Politics, and Political Change," *American Political Science Review* 63, no. 4 (1969): 1142–58; Alice Sindzingre, "A Comparative Analysis of African and East Asian Corruption," in *Political Corruption: Concepts and Contexts*, ed. Arnold J. Heidenheimer and Michael Johnston (New Brunswick, NJ: Transaction Publishers, 2002), 441–60, here 452; Susan C. Stokes, "Perverse Accountability: A Formal Model of Machine Politics with Evidence from Argentina," *American Political Science Review* 99, no. 3 (2005): 312–25, here 321–22.

12. See, for example, Judith Chubb, *Patronage, Power, and Poverty in Southern Italy: A Tale of Two Cities* (Cambridge: Cambridge University Press, 1982), 6–7.

13. The differential effect of market reform has been well documented in terms of increased inequality. Gourdon, Maystre, and de Melo, "Openness, Inequality, and Poverty," 24; Luo and Zhu, "Rising Income Inequality in China," 20; Taylor and Vos, "Balance of Payments Liberalization in Latin America."

initially impoverished families are gloomy because market and societal actors cannot provide money, employment, and credit for families to escape the dire economic circumstances. To meet their basic needs, members of these families turn to government officials.

Turning to a downsized state for material assistance is not the paradox that it might seem to be at first glance. How do government officials have resources to give in illicit exchanges if the state has been downsized by market reform? First of all, the state is still resource-rich relative to other institutions and groups. This is especially true in cases where the state historically had significant control of the economy, and reform did not establish effective market-enhancing institutions. Second, the resources individuals are seeking to meet basic needs are comparatively insignificant for the state to provide. Even in a downsized state, government officials can find some money, jobs, or credit for illicit exchanges.

In sum, citizens use bribes, personal connections, and promises of political support to try to obtain state resources when formal state assistance programs, market actors, societal groups, and family members do not have the means to meet their basic needs. The more extensive state economic intervention has been historically and the weaker the market enhancing-institutions in a country, the more individuals market reform causes to engage in petty corruption and the more corruption in the country.

A Parsimonious, Causal, Generalizable Explanation

This explanation for corruption is parsimonious, causal, and generalizable. Earlier corruption studies have provided valuable insights, but their explanations tend to take the form of a long list of possible causal factors, correlative statements, or conclusions limited to a particular location. Studies of a small number of countries have often resulted in long lists of causes of corruption. For example, Leslie Holmes identifies eighteen factors that have contributed to corruption in just one region of the world—the former Eastern bloc.[14] Statistical studies of many countries, or large-n analyses, have provided useful clues, but no causal explanations with compelling empirical support.[15] Field experiments avoid these

---

14. Leslie Holmes, *Rotten States? Corruption, Post-Communism, and Neoliberalism* (Durham, NC: Duke University Press, 2006).

15. A key problem is that these studies often rely on data that measure the perception of corruption, instead of corruption itself. See, for example: Uslaner, *Corruption, Inequality, and the Rule of Law*; Jong-Sung You and Sanjeev Khagram, "A Comparative Study of Inequality and Corruption," *American Sociological Review* 70, no. 1 (2005), 136–57. For a review of large-n analyses, see Daniel

problems, but their findings are less generalizable than those from this book, which combines comparative case study and large-n designs.[16]

The absence-of-alternatives approach provides a general, causal framework for understanding and combating corruption. An absence of alternatives to illicit exchanges with government officials is a necessary and sufficient condition for petty corruption. When can an absence of alternatives occur? Together the two conditions—a legacy of significant state economic involvement and poor or absent market-enhancing institutions—are sufficient for the causal factor, market reform, to result in an absence of alternatives and, subsequently, citizens' use of illicit means. Market reform is not the only factor that promotes petty corruption, and research has shown that market reform can decrease grand corruption by reducing government officials' responsibilities. However, considering its spread in the 1980s and 1990s, and the frequency of the conditions under which it encourages petty corruption, market reform is worthy of focus.

The direction of the causal relationship between market reform under the two conditions and corruption is clear. Logic and evidence indicate that corruption to meet everyday needs is unlikely to have caused market reform, weak or absent market-enhancing institutions, or a legacy of significant state economic intervention. Studies have suggested that grand corruption can result in market reform with weak or absent market-enhancing institutions, as government officials avoid creating market-enhancing institutions that would limit their ability to reap personal benefits from policies such as privatization. How ordinary citizens' illicit efforts to obtain basic goods and services would lead to market reform under the two conditions is neither evident nor supported by prior studies. Ordinary citizens are not likely to have such influence, nor would it be in their interest to support policies that ultimately limit their means of obtaining essential goods and services.[17]

Evidence from Central Asia supports the idea that market reform under the two conditions has resulted in petty corruption, not the reverse. Corruption to obtain basic goods and services developed after market reform began and after the period of significant state economic intervention, as described in chapter four. Corruption did exist in the Soviet era, prior to market reform; however, evidence in chapter four shows that the individuals who engage in illicit practices, the targets of their requests, and the goods and services sought have changed since

---

Treisman, "What Have We Learned about the Causes of Corruption from Ten Years of Cross-National Empirical Research," *Annual Review of Political Science* 19 (2007), 211–44.

16. For a review of field experiments, see Benjamin A. Olken and Rohini Pande, "Corruption in Developing Countries," *Annual Review of Economics* 4 (2012), 479–509.

17. Why market-enhancing institutions are weak and how corruption may play a role are important issues, but not the puzzles this book aims to solve.

the Soviet era. So today's petty corruption did not cause market reform, the weakness or absence of market-enhancing institutions, or the significant state economic intervention historically. Evidence in chapter four also demonstrates that the needs citizens seek to meet through corrupt practices developed in large part directly from market reform under the two conditions. This further supports the proposed causal relationship.

These same pieces of evidence about timing and needs and the analysis of the ninety-two countries suggest that the causal factor, conditions, and corruption are not all caused by something else. We know that market reform, not economic reform in general, is influential because the evidence shows that market reform under the two conditions created the needs that prompted the illicit behavior. The statistical analysis demonstrates that leading alternative explanations cannot account for market reform, the two conditions, and corruption. The fact that corruption to meet everyday needs has been less common in Uzbekistan further casts doubt on another factor causing all components of the argument. Uzbekistan shares many characteristics with Kazakhstan and Kyrgyzstan, including economic upheaval, which, in theory, could cause market reform, the conditions, and the corruption. Yet, even though it, too, experienced the economic chaos of the collapse of the Soviet Union, Uzbekistan has neither undertaken market reform nor exhibited the corruption for basic goods and services that Kazakhstan and Kyrgyzstan do.

The contrast with Uzbekistan also challenges the alternative explanation that a legacy of significant state economic intervention causes market reform and corruption. Uzbekistan experienced significant state economic intervention but neither market reform nor significant corruption to meet essential needs. Chapter four presents evidence from Central Asia that challenges all of these alternative explanations as well as a host of others and supports the causal argument proposed by this book.

The causal argument is parsimonious in the sense that this single idea that people engage in corruption when alternatives are not available is a framework that can explain multiple types of corruption in different settings. It is useful to identify varied proximate causes of different forms of corruption, but it is also helpful to have a framework with which to understand corruption generally. Earlier frameworks have considered only government officials' roles in corruption, and neglected citizens' roles. The absence-of-alternatives framework rectifies this problem.

Moreover, the absence-of-alternatives approach expands the study of corruption by examining nonstate and nonmarket resources. Most studies of corruption, especially those in the overbearing state school of thought, are based on the idea of a state monopoly of resources. A few others consider the influence of scarce market resources as well, contending that the state's monopoly on resources creates scarcity in the market, which encourages corruption.[18] However, their focus overlooks the possibility that nonmarket actors, such as kin, may be able to offer substitute resources. This insight has two important implications. Most broadly, resource scarcity in a territory affects individuals differently. Equally important, those individuals with resource-rich kin can avoid engaging in corruption by obtaining needed goods from family members. By examining the availability of resources from not only government officials and markets but also family members, this study acknowledges that resource scarcity has varied effects on individuals and that some individuals can avoid engaging in corruption even in countries where it is pervasive.

While expanding the focus to citizens and family and societal resources, the absence-of-alternatives approach remains parsimonious. With the basic idea that individuals consider alternatives before engaging in corruption, this framework can likely illuminate not only petty but also grand corruption. Petty and grand corruption are distinct phenomena, but the underlying dynamics may be similar enough for the framework to apply. In grand corruption, instead of average citizens meeting basic needs, the focus is on owners of large businesses seeking additional profit. If no alternatives other than illicit exchanges with government officials exist for earning additional profit, we would expect the business owners to offer bribes, use connections, and promise political support. While average citizens consider the availability of resources from market actors, societal groups, and family, large-scale business owners would be most affected by the resources of market actors. For example, if private banks did not provide credit, corrupt practices could be more appealing as a means to expand one's business. The applicability of this framework to grand corruption relies on the assumption that large-scale business owners, like average citizens, prefer not to engage in corruption. This is an empirical question that requires investigation.

The framework also allows for other possible causes of limited alternatives. Most boldly, a reversal of market reform, or the introduction of socialism, could limit alternatives and encourage corruption to meet everyday needs. Hypothetically, a state could circumscribe market activities, for example, through nation-

---

18. Chubb, *Patronage, Power, and Poverty in Southern Italy*; Rose-Ackerman, *Corruption and Government*; Andrew Hall Wedeman, *Double Paradox: Rapid Growth and Rising Corruption in China* (Ithaca, NY: Cornell University Press, 2012). In his work on political parties in Russia, Henry Hale reveals a situation somewhat contradictory to this thinking. He discovers that state control of resources, although not monopolies, and strong market actors coexist in the form of gubernatorial political machines and financial-industrial groups. He demonstrates that this combination serves as a substitute for programmatic political parties and encourages clientelism in their place. Henry E. Hale, "Correlates of Clientelism: Political Economy, Politicized Ethnicity, and Postcommunist Transition," in Kitschelt and Wilkinson, *Patrons, Clients, and Policies*, 227–50.

alization and price controls, while also abandoning government assistance programs and banning or severely restricting the activities of societal groups. In practice, these two measures have not typically accompanied the introduction of socialism—rather socialist policies tend to include an expansion of government assistance, and contemporary socialist governments, even if not all of their historical counterparts, have allowed societal groups to continue to assist citizens. Research on other eras, including the future, is likely to reveal other factors that limit alternatives and thus promote corruption. Although it is a simple framework, the absence-of-alternatives approach has the potential to explain a lot.

An Absence of Alternatives versus Economic Development and Poverty

At first glance, the absence-of-alternatives approach may resemble economic development or poverty theories, but it is, in fact, distinct from them in crucial ways and offers advantages over them. An absence of alternatives to illicit means to obtain essential goods and services does not necessarily result from economic underdevelopment or poverty. This is evident in the Central Asian cases; seeking assistance illicitly from the state to meet basic needs has not been common in Uzbekistan even though it exhibits levels of economic development and poverty similar to those in Kyrgyzstan. Instead, market reform under the two conditions is the cause. Unlike economic development studies, the absence-of-alternatives theory offers a causal account and an explanation for individual variation; unlike poverty theories, this approach takes into account not only individuals but also societal actors who may help them, and thus more accurately depicts individuals' decisions about engaging in corruption.

Economic development explanations are based on large-n analyses. Many of these studies have found correlations between economic development and perceived or "experienced" corruption.[19] They have found that higher levels of economic development coincide with lower levels of perceived or experienced corruption. The studies typically use per capita gross domestic product at purchasing power parity as a measure of economic development and one or more existing corruption data sets, such as Transparency International's Corruption Perception Index and Global Corruption Barometer or the World Bank's World Business Environment Survey and World Governance indicators. These data sets collect information about petty corruption and, in some cases, also grand

---

19. Surveys claiming to measure corruption that people have experienced are often instead only measuring corruption that people perceive.

corruption.[20] The relationship between economic development and corruption is robust; the relationship cannot be explained by influences such as inequality, trade, inflation, religion, ethnic heterogeneity, and region, as measured by a variety of control variables in these studies.[21]

The first weakness of these studies, however, is that, although they propose a causal explanation, they demonstrate only a correlation between economic development and corruption.[22] In fact, one review of these studies found that two common components of economic development—urbanization and greater average educational attainment—did not affect corruption levels,[23] suggesting that the relationship is at least poorly understood, if not spurious. Furthermore, these studies cannot explain variation among people in a country. They use country-level measures of corruption and economic development, overlooking the fact that within a country some individuals engage in corruption more than others do.

Explanations of corruption that focus on poverty avoid these two weaknesses; however, the absence-of-alternatives approach offers advantages. Poverty studies do provide helpful causal explanations, which clearly link poverty to corrupt actions: as James Scott wrote in 1969, "Poverty shortens a man's time horizons and maximizes the effectiveness of short-run material inducements. Quite rationally he is willing to accept a job, cash, or simply the promise of assistance when he needs it, in return for his vote and that of his family."[24] Compared to my approach, these theories are rather limited in scope because they focus on one type

---

20. The Corruption Perceptions Index and the World Bank's Worldwide Governance indicators use surveys of average citizens and domestic and international businesspeople and also business experts' ratings. The Global Corruption Barometer asks average citizens whether the respondent or anyone in the respondent's household has paid a bribe. The World Business Environment Survey surveys firms. For more information, see Transparency International, "Corruption Perceptions Index," http://www.transparency.org/ (accessed December 19, 2013); Transparency International, "Global Corruption Barometer," http://www.transparency.org/ (accessed December 19, 2013); Daniel Kaufman and Andrew H. W. Stone, "World Business Environment Survey," World Bank, 1999–2000, http://go.worldbank.org/RV060VBJU0 (accessed December 19, 2013); Daniel Kaufmann, Aart Kraay, and Massimo Mastruzzi, "The Worldwide Governance Indicators: Methodology and Analytical Issues" (Washington, DC: World Bank, 2010).

21. Treisman finds that the inclusion of variables for democratic institutions and free media does affect the relationship, suggesting that it may, in fact, be these aspects of highly economically developed countries that explain their lower levels of perceived and experienced corruption. However, this is only a preliminary finding. Treisman, "What Have We Learned About the Causes of Corruption," 225.

22. See the Alternative Explanations section of chapter four for a description of these theories and tests of them with the Central Asian cases.

23. Treisman, "What Have We Learned About the Causes of Corruption," 225.

24. Scott, "Corruption, Machine Politics, and Political Change," 1150. Others have reiterated this idea, for example, Kitschelt and Wilkinson, "Citizen-Politician Linkages," 25; Offe, "Political Corruption"; Sindzingre, "A Comparative Analysis of African and East Asian Corruption," 452–53.

of corruption—vote-selling or exchanging one's vote for a material good. More critically, they assume that only authorities, in this case party machines, are resource-rich. They overlook the possibility that there may be societal actors or kin who can help poor individuals meet their basic needs.

The absence-of-alternatives approach offers advantages over other corruption explanations. It accounts for differences in corruption among countries and among individuals, and it offers a parsimonious, generalizable, causal explanation for why people engage in corruption. These theoretical contributions translate into concrete policy recommendations, which are the focus of the concluding chapter of the book. The next chapter begins the process of illustrating the applicability of the theory to Central Asia and other regions of the world by describing corruption to meet basic needs in Kazakhstan and Kyrgyzstan.

BRIBERY, FAVORITISM, AND CLIENTELISM

Evidence from Kazakhstan and Kyrgyzstan

"I would need to have an acquaintance or pay a bribe," Marzhan, the villager from Kazakhstan, said, explaining the standard approach for obtaining credit from the local government in her district.[1] Marzhan had decided to apply for credit through the *raion akimat* (district administrative office) and establish a business because her family has been in dire straits. Both she and her husband, Temir, have been unemployed for several years, except for a few weeks in the summer when Temir finds work driving a combine. They have four children to support, and they bring in only 23 USD per month when it costs about 50 USD to run a six-person household. Despite these difficult economic circumstances, Marzhan abandoned her efforts to obtain credit when neighbors informed her that it was standard to offer a bribe or use a personal connection in the district office. As noted in the first chapter, she does not like to give bribes, and she did not have a personal connection in the *raion akimat*.

Marzhan's story about the route to obtaining credit highlights that in Kazakhstan citizens engage in corrupt practices in order to secure state resources that will help them to cope with economic challenges. This is true in Kyrgyzstan as well, and these practices are what this book seeks to explain. In this chapter the details of the corruption unfold. The interviews I conducted offer direct evidence that citizens use bribes, personal connections, and promises of political support to try to obtain money, credit, and employment from government officials. Whereas the interview data reveal the illicit nature of citizens' efforts to

---

1. Author's interview (#161), Kazakhstan, July 22, 2001.

secure resources from government officials, the survey data demonstrate how citizens are competing among themselves for state resources, and thus a bribe, connection, or promise of political support can provide an individual with an edge. The survey data also show how relatively common the practice of seeking help from government officials is. Citizens' most pressing needs are money, credit, and employment, and they try to obtain these resources from village leaders and *raion* and oblast (provincial) bureaucrats and to a lesser extent oblast and national deputies. The money, credit, and employment that officials can distribute for bribes and favors come from different sources. Village leaders can direct government welfare benefits and resources from state banks and societal organizations to supplicants; *raion* and oblast bureaucrats can distribute credit from state programs; oblast and national deputies can provide resources from other state positions they hold or, if they are personally wealthy, their own largesse.

Bribes, Personal Connections, and Promises of Political Support

Citizens use an array of informal techniques, including bribes, personal connections, and promises of political support. Individuals' decisions about which technique to try are influenced by a near universal preference for using connections, their own economic positions, and the identities, locations, and positions of the targeted officials. Using a connection is typically preferred to paying a bribe, which requires giving up one's money or, in some cases, a portion of the resource obtained. The most impoverished citizens are the least able to use bribes because they do not have the necessary funds, although they can share some of the goods and services they obtain with the officials. Those who are more affluent, yet still need employment, credit, or money, will sometimes choose to pay a bribe instead of owing a favor to a connection. For all citizens, the official's identity also matters. Is the official a personal connection or not? Even the poorest citizens tend to have useful connections because the officials targeted are low-ranking. One might not know a government minister, but one is likely to know a town bureaucrat. The large size of families, particularly in rural areas, and the legacy of mass education and promotion of rural cadres mean that even the poorest have kinship and school ties. Individuals also consider the location of the official and whether meeting face-to-face with the person would be prohibitively costly. Whether the official is elected is important too. A promise of electoral support is feasible only if the targeted official is elected. Those who can promise not only their own votes but also the votes of others can most effectively use this technique. For example, the promise of a respected elder to ensure numerous votes carries more weight than the promise of an ordinary citizen to provide his or her vote. The use of these three techniques to try to secure credit, employment, and money is evident from the 203 in-depth interviews I conducted with average citizens, government officials, and background informants.[2]

Bribery is prevalent in the government credit process, as Marzhan described and as government officials and local representatives of international financial institutions in Kazakhstan and Kyrgyzstan corroborated. An employee of a city government office for the support of small- and medium-size businesses in southern Kazakhstan volunteered that taking bribes from individuals seeking assistance was common in her line of work. In Kyrgyzstan a local employee of an international organization recounted, "I have heard that at the branches [of a government bank] they hold out their hat" to credit applicants, meaning that bribes are regularly given to bank officials.[3] Reacting to the prevalence of bribery in the credit process, a European Bank for Reconstruction and Development office in central Kazakhstan provides its clients with a letter to reduce the likelihood that they will need to pay a bribe in order to register their collateral with state officials.

Individuals who have personal connections with officials in government credit institutions will use those contacts instead of offering bribes. For example, despite high fuel prices, farmers in a southern district of Kazakhstan travel an hour and a half to another district to seek credit because they have personal ties with officials there, according to the head of a *raion* agency to support small- and medium-size business. The benefit of saving money makes personal connections common in credit transactions. "'I know your director,'" is a frequent refrain from potential clients, according to an employee of a bank with a state credit-lending program in southern Kazakhstan.[4] Farmers in northern Kyrgyzstan offered similar accounts. A farmer who grows fruits, vegetables, and animal feed and has twice obtained credit explained, "Connections have played a role. Without connections people would not receive credit."[5] Likewise, a farmer who grows wheat, clover, and corn; raises sheep; and has borrowed three times said,

---

2. The background informants included unsuccessful electoral candidates and representatives of electoral commissions, local media, and international financial institutions. I conducted an additional sixty-three interviews with societal actors, such as religious leaders and representatives of charities. Material from these interviews appears in chapter five.

3. Author's interview (#124), Kyrgyzstan, May 25, 2009.

4. Author's interview (#142), Kazakhstan, July 3, 2001.

5. Author's interview (#128), Kyrgyzstan, May 30, 2009.

"To receive credit you need connections."[6] Also in Kyrgyzstan a man now working as a driver explained that his auto mechanic business failed because he did not have the connections needed to obtain the credit to make his venture profitable.

Personal connections that citizens use include their acquaintances from post-secondary school and military service as well as people in their families, clans, ethnic groups, and regions. The employee of a bank with a state credit-lending program in southern Kazakhstan described how many potential clients would say, "'My uncle works here,' to try to influence the decisions."[7] Citizens use these personal connections not only to obtain credit but also to secure a job. In one oblast of Kyrgyzstan, the oblast prosecutor, head of the oblast office of a federal agency, and a *raion akim* (district leader) all have the same mother-in-law. A local journalist with independent media outlets indicated that the officials obtained their prominent positions through this family connection. I witnessed the use of personal connections to attempt to obtain employment firsthand in a Kyrgyz household in northern Kyrgyzstan. A distant acquaintance contacted the middle-aged parents in the household about meeting with them to discuss the possible marriage of his son to their daughter. At the meeting, the potential groom's father offered his son and then asked that the potential bride's parents have their son, the deputy head of a national government agency, provide the potential groom with a job. The potential bride's mother also received a request from her sister-in-law that the same son alter her niece's civil service exam results so that she could obtain a government job.

Personal connections can also be useful in maintaining one's job. A journalist in central Kyrgyzstan described how he required protection from government harassment because he worked for independent media outlets and therefore criticized authorities. His protection comes in the form of the district prosecutor, who is a friend from school, and the head of the district court, who is a former classmate of his wife, he explained.

Besides school and family connections, regional and clan affiliations are also commonly activated in exchanges between citizens and government officials. An editor at an oblast newspaper in southern Kyrgyzstan recounted how as part of the selection process for the position, staff members asked, "'Where are you from? What are your origins? Who was your mother?'"[8] Using the term *clan* in a professional setting is rare in Kazakhstan and Kyrgyzstan, but asking questions such as these can be considered appropriate.

---

6. Author's interview (#131), Kyrgyzstan, May 30, 2009.

7. Author's interview (#142), Kazakhstan, July 3, 2001.

8. Author's interview (#56), Kyrgyzstan, April 29, 1998.

Clan ties play a role in the credit process too. Government "bureaucrats try to get credit for their 'brothers,'" meaning those with whom they share clan or family ties, according to the manager of an agricultural consulting service in northern Kyrgyzstan.[9] An editor with a provincial government newspaper in central Kyrgyzstan gave a more specific example, explaining that state agricultural credit had been distributed in his region recently based on clan ties.

Ethnic ties have also been influential in obtaining and maintaining employment in government institutions. Posts in the customs, tax, and passport control agencies reportedly have tended to go to members of the titular ethnic groups because opportunities for extracting bribes when working in these positions make them some of the more lucrative government jobs. A staff member of an ethnic Russian organization that monitors the status of the Russian minority in Kyrgyzstan explained that officials often discriminate in favor of members of their own ethnic groups when distributing jobs with these agencies. Similarly, a young woman recounted to me how her father, an ethnic Russian, felt forced to retire from his position as an officer in the Kyrgyzstani military as hiring and promotion have increasingly favored ethnic Kyrgyz since the country became independent.

The use of ethnic ties in competition for state resources is also reflected in the mass surveys I conducted in the countries. Whereas 20 percent of Kazakh respondents have sought assistance from government officials in Kazakhstan in the past year, only 12 percent of non-Kazakh respondents have sought assistance. In Kyrgyzstan, 30 percent of Kyrgyz respondents have sought assistance from government officials, but only 13 percent of non-Kyrgyz have done so.[10]

Besides bribes and connections, promises of political support are exchanged in return for elected officials' help. For meeting everyday needs this form of corruption is least common because citizens are most likely to turn to more accessible lower-level officials, such as village leaders, but since independence they have been less likely to be elected than oblast and national deputies.[11] While citizens can promise political support other than votes, votes are most tangible. The evidence of clientelism thus comes mostly from higher levels of government and

---

9. Author's interview (#125), Kyrgyzstan, May 26, 2009.

10. These percentages come from the second question in a series of two. First, respondents answered the question "What are the three most serious problems you face in your daily life? Please call the first the most serious problem, then the second and third." Second, they responded to the question, "Which people and organizations have you relied on for help with these problems? Choose as many as apply." Respondents received a card with twenty-one actors and institutions listed, including "no one" and the option to list others. Interviewers read the card aloud.

11. Only since 2001 in Kyrgyzstan and 2006 in Kazakhstan has it been possible to elect village leaders, whereas deputies to representative bodies, *maslikhats* in Kazakhstan and *keneshes* in Kyrgyzstan, and to the national parliamentary bodies, Majlis in Kazakhstan and the Zhogorku Kenesh in Kyrgyzstan, have been elected since independence.

during electoral campaigns. For example, national deputies from different regions of Kyrgyzstan described how they received requests for material assistance from individual constituents and often distributed student stipends to grateful voters in response. One deputy explained that he also gives out gifts of 1,000 som, or 55 USD at the time, a sufficient amount to start some small businesses.

During electoral campaigns material assistance is too modest to help people solve the problem of insufficient money. Citizens demand small gifts, such as medicine, flour, sugar, tea, vodka, and little sums of money. Citizens also expect that national parliamentary candidates will host parties where they can get a free meal. This modest material assistance is not even available in all races. Few oblast candidates provide material assistance because, as a journalist in southern Kyrgyzstan explained, "There was no reason because what do they [oblast deputies] decide?"[12] In other words, oblast deputies have few responsibilities and little influence, so candidates typically do not put much effort into these races. Instead, material assistance is typically only available from candidates in higher-level races.

Another election-time clientelist exchange, though, does have an effect on long-term material stability: individuals exchanging political loyalty for job security. Although job loss for political activity is possible at any time, it is more likely during elections when people are more politically engaged.[13] A common occurrence is that government employees support an incumbent's electoral bid in order not to lose their jobs. For example, in the presidential election in Kyrgyzstan in the summer of 2008, state university staff collected signatures on petitions nominating incumbent Kurmanbek Bakiyev so as to keep their jobs. Whereas these individuals exchanged political assistance for continued employment, others use bribes, personal connections, and other forms of political support to try to obtain employment, credit, or money.

The State as an Arena for Competition

Individuals in Kazakhstan and Kyrgyzstan use these informal techniques because they believe that such methods will provide them with an advantage in the competition for state resources. People in these countries describe their states primarily as arenas where they compete for goods and services for themselves and their families. In the surveys, respondents were asked to agree or disagree

---

12. Author's interview (#54), Kyrgyzstan, April 28, 1998.

13. Kelly M. McMann, *Economic Autonomy and Democracy: Hybrid Regimes in Russia and Kyrgyzstan* (Cambridge: Cambridge University Press, 2006).

with a series of statements representing different relationships between individuals and their states. In Kazakhstan 70 percent of respondents and in Kyrgyzstan 61 percent strongly agreed or agreed with the statement "Citizens compete to possess state resources, such as jobs."

By contrast, other descriptions of individual–state relations—the state as a guarantor of resources and the Western social contract—did not resonate with most survey respondents. Only about 30 percent of respondents in each country affirmed the statement "Citizens use state resources, such as medical services and education." The idea that people "use" state resources was a particularly common way to describe the Soviet welfare state. The Soviet state provided extensive social services to the population. Many consumer products and some services were of poor quality and there were shortages of some goods by the 1980s. Nonetheless, for decades Soviet citizens had received basic cradle-to-grave support.[14] With the birth of a child, a family received supplemental income. Free or highly subsidized day care, education, and recreation for the child followed. Upon graduation the child, now an adult, received a job assignment from the state. Through the workplace, the individual acquired subsidized housing and utilities, received health care and vacations, and had access to credit for consumer purchases. In addition, the individual earned income to use toward the purchase of highly subsidized basic goods. Union dues and money to support a poverty fund were taken directly from citizens' pay; however, these deductions were not comparable to the payment of taxes. The distribution of these resources was not linked to a citizen's obligation to pay taxes; the state was the guarantor of goods and services regardless. According to Kazakhstanis and Kyrgyzstanis their states are no longer guarantors of goods and services.

The governments of Kazakhstan and Kyrgyzstan have promoted the idea of the Western social contract through both their economic reforms and their rhetoric; however, most citizens do not find that this accurately describes individual–state relations either. Only about 30 percent of respondents in each country affirmed the statement "Citizens expect that the state will provide services if they pay their taxes," as Table 3.1 shows. An even smaller number of people found relevant paradigms of individual–state relations drawn from studies of other regions of the world. Less than 20 percent of respondents described citizens as incorporated in the state, the state as highly involved in citizens' lives, or the state as embedded in, yet autonomous from society.[15]

---

14. Linda J. Cook, *The Soviet Social Contract and Why It Failed: Welfare Policy and Workers' Politics from Brezhnev to Yeltsin* (Cambridge, MA: Harvard University Press, 1993), 25–53.

15. The other models are incorporation, the overdeveloped state, and embedded autonomy. For definitions of these, see: Victor Azarya, "Reordering State-Society Relations: Incorporation and Dis-

TABLE 3.1. Citizens' relationships with states in Kazakhstan and Kyrgyzstan: Arena of competition, guarantor, social contract (percentage of respondents, rounded)

	CITIZENS COMPETE TO POSSESS STATE RESOURCES, SUCH AS JOBS	CITIZENS USE STATE RESOURCES, SUCH AS MEDICAL SERVICES AND EDUCATION	CITIZENS EXPECT THAT THE STATE WILL PROVIDE SERVICES IF THEY PAY THEIR TAXES
KAZAKHSTAN			
Strongly agree or agree	70	28	28
Somewhat agree/ disagree	13	36	29
Disagree or strongly disagree	11	35	35
Difficult to answer	6	2	8
Decline to answer	1	1	1
TOTAL (rounded)	100	100	100
KYRGYZSTAN			
Strongly agree or agree	61	34	36
Somewhat agree/ disagree	20	35	24
Disagree or strongly disagree	12	29	32
Difficult to answer	7	3	8
Decline to answer	<1	<1	<1
TOTAL (rounded)	100	100	100

Note: $n = 1,500$ for each country. Percentages for each country do not necessarily total to 100 because they are rounded.

For each country the difference in percentages between the most popular statement and each of the less popular statements is statistically significant at the .001 level, meaning that such a difference would be observed due to random chance approximately .1 percent of the time.

Most citizens in Kazakhstan and Kyrgyzstan consider the state primarily an arena for competition; however, only a portion of citizens compete for state resources themselves. In Kazakhstan 19 percent of survey respondents and in Kyrgyzstan 24 percent turned to a state institution or official for assistance in the previous year. Nonetheless, more people sought help from the state than from any other societal or market actor. At most, 4 percent of respondents in Kazakhstan and 4 percent in Kyrgyzstan sought help from a particular societal

engagement," in *The Precarious Balance: State and Society in Africa*, ed. Donald S. Rothchild and Naomi Chazan (Boulder, CO: Westview Press, 1988), 3–21, here 6; Peter B. Evans, "The State as Problem and Solution: Predation, Embedded Autonomy, and Structural Change," in *The Politics of Economic Adjustment: International Constraints, Distributive Conflicts, and the State*, ed. Stephan Haggard and Robert R. Kaufman (Princeton: Princeton University Press, 1992), 139–81, here 165–66; Atul Kohli, *Democracy and Discontent: India's Growing Crisis of Governability* (Cambridge: Cambridge University Press, 1990); Joel S. Migdal, Atul Kohli, and Vivienne Shue, *State Power and Social Forces: Domination and Transformation in the Third World* (Cambridge: Cambridge University Press, 1994), 25.

TABLE 3.2. Individuals and institutions from whom citizens have sought assistance in the past year in Kazakhstan and Kyrgyzstan (percentage of respondents, rounded)

	KAZAKHSTAN	KYRGYZSTAN
STATE ACTORS		
Any state actor[a]	*19*	*24*
Government official	16	23
MARKET AND SOCIETAL ACTORS[b]		
Any market or societal actor	*16*	*14*
Bank[c]	3	1
Current employer[c]	4	3
Former employer[c]	4	2
Local company where you don't work[c]	3	<1
Foreign company where you don't work	<1	0
Religious institution/leader	1	2
Foreign charitable organization	<1	1
Local, private charitable organization	1	2
Labor union[c]	1	1
Respected male elder	1	4
Educational institution[c]	<1	2
PERSONAL CONTACT		
Any family or friend[d]	*39*	*47*
Family[e]	35	42

Note: *n* = 1,200 for Kazakhstan and 1,199 for Kyrgyzstan. A portion of the 1,500 respondents in each country claimed that they had no problems or that describing their problems was too difficult and thus some respondents were not asked this question about seeking assistance.

[a] The broader state category includes the replies of a small number of respondents who specified law enforcement, social security, and government employment offices as separate from "government officials."

[b] Another societal institution is the *mahalla*, a subdivision of urban neighborhoods, particularly Uzbek ones, and a favorite topic among Central Asian observers. I did not include it in the survey because the concept is relevant primarily to urban, ethnic Uzbek communities. However, there is overlap with the category of neighbors in Kazakhstan and Kyrgyzstan, and the survey question did allow respondents to list other institutions. No one in Kazakhstan or Kyrgyzstan listed the *mahalla* as a place to turn for help.

[c] Some employers, local companies, banks, labor unions, and educational institutions remain state institutions in these countries as a result of the communist period; however, market reforms have ensured that most are now nonstate entities. Including all these actors and institutions in the "market and societal actors" category increases the difficulty of arguing that the reliance on the state is greater than reliance on nonstate actors.

[d] Included in this category were members of households, relatives living in one's own country, relatives living in another country, neighbors, friends who are not neighbors, acquaintances, and coworkers.

[e] Included in this category were members of households, relatives living in one's own country, and relatives living in another country.

or market actor, as indicated in Table 3.2. Individuals seeking state assistance typically turn to government officials once, twice, or four times a year, as Table 3.3 shows. More popular than any of the state, societal, or market sources of assistance, however, is family; reliance on family is the focus of chapter six. Although not ubiquitous, the pursuit of state resources instead of societal or market ones is a significant practice because it violates the intent of market reform to reduce state reliance. Because this contact with the state often involves

TABLE 3.3. Frequency of seeking assistance from state actors in Kazakhstan and Kyrgyzstan (percentage of respondents, rounded)

	KAZAKHSTAN	KYRGYZSTAN
Once in the past year	31	26
Twice in the past year	25	27
Four times in the past year	20	24
Each month in the past year	12	11
Twice monthly in the past year	4	4
Weekly in the past year	1	2
Every day in the past year	0	1
Not the past year, but the previous year	7	4
TOTAL (rounded)	100	100

Note: $n = 229$ for Kazakhstan and 293 for Kyrgyzstan for the number of respondents who sought assistance from state actors. State actors includes the category "government officials" as well as the replies of a small number of respondents who specified law enforcement, social security, and government employment offices as separate from "government officials." When a respondent offered more than one of these categories, the response of greatest frequency was used. Percentages for each country do not necessarily total to 100 because they are rounded.

bribery, personal connections, and promises of political support, these interactions also introduce the negative implications of petty corruption.

Those who seek assistance from state officials come from many different demographic backgrounds. Men and women and people of all ages have sought help from the state, as indicated in Table 3.4. Females are slightly more represented among those who have sought assistance in Kazakhstan and less represented in Kyrgyzstan. These small differences in percentages of men and women seeking state aid challenge the stereotype, often propagated by casual observers of Central Asia, of women in the region as passive. The absence of significant age differences is interesting because we might expect individuals who were adults in the Soviet era to be more likely to seek state assistance because of the extensive state benefits and the absence of nonstate alternatives in that period. Instead, the minimal differences in age suggest that as a group older people have adapted to new welfare circumstances, adopting coping strategies similar to their younger counterparts.

What does distinguish those who seek and do not seek help are ethnicity, place of residence, and economic circumstances. These differences are evidence in support of the argument that market reform promotes corrupt practices, as described later in this chapter and chapter four. Later sections of this chapter describe how differences in ethnicity and place of residence relate to forms and targets of corruption, respectively; chapter four marshals the evidence about all three types of differences in support of the argument.

TABLE 3.4. Demographic similarities of those who seek and do not seek help from state officials in Kazakhstan and Kyrgyzstan (percentage of respondents, rounded)

	KAZAKHSTAN		KYRGYZSTAN	
	SEEK HELP	**DO NOT SEEK HELP**	**SEEK HELP**	**DO NOT SEEK HELP**
GENDER				
Male	43	46	51	43
Female	57	54	49	57
TOTAL	100	100	100	100
AGE				
75 or older	8	4	3	4
65–74	11	10	6	8
55–64	16	11	10	10
45–54	15	18	14	14
35–44	24	24	25	22
25–34	18	18	26	24
18–24	7	15	17	20
TOTAL	100	100	100	100

Note: $n = 229$ for those who seek help and 1,271 for those who do not seek help in Kazakhstan and 293 for those who seek help and 1,207 for those who do not seek help in Kyrgyzstan. Percentages for each column do not necessarily total 100 because they are rounded.

Resources Sought from Government Officials

People in Kazakhstan and Kyrgyzstan seek money, credit, and employment from state officials because a common problem in both countries is lack of funds. Eighty-three percent and 52 percent of respondents who had sought help from state officials in Kazakhstan and Kyrgyzstan, respectively, identified lack of money as one of their top three problems in daily life, as indicated in Table 3.5. Unemployment was the source of money problems for 40 percent and 23 percent of respondents who sought state help, respectively. Other root causes were inability to obtain credit, low salaries, and high prices, as well as unpaid wages, pensions, and children's benefits. Respondents reported that lack of money made it difficult to afford housing, utilities, medical services and medications, public transportation, education, livestock, fodder, and fuel.

Government officials in Kazakhstan and Kyrgyzstan also described how people lack funds and subsequently request money, credit, and employment.[16] For example, a deputy in an *oblast maslikhat* (regional representative body) in central Kazakhstan explained that his constituents request money to pay for utilities, and

---

16. This paragraph presents representative evidence from interviews with seventy-two government officials in Kazakhstan and Kyrgyzstan.

TABLE 3.5. Types of problems for which respondents sought assistance from state officials in Kazakhstan and Kyrgyzstan (percentage of respondents, rounded)

	KAZAKHSTAN	KYRGYZSTAN
Lack of money	83	52
Poor public infrastructure	31	61
Personal crises[a]	14	8
Bureaucratic challenges[b]	12	5
Societal crises[c]	10	2
Economic difficulties[d]	6	17

Note: $n = 229$ for Kazakhstan and 293 for Kyrgyzstan for the number of people who turned to state officials for assistance in the past year. The percentages for each country exceed 100 because respondents could list up to three problems.

[a] Personal crises include poor health, death or imprisonment of a loved one, caring for old or ill parents, raising one's children, completing one's education, and dealing with an unreasonable boss.
[b] Examples of bureaucratic challenges include "red tape," officials' abuse of power, and unfair tax and nationalities policies.
[c] Societal crises include crime, environmental degradation, HIV/AIDS, alcoholism, drug addiction, homelessness of children, dishonest people, and distrust among people.
[d] Economic difficulties include insufficient arable land, decline of agriculture, limited economic opportunities for nontitular language speakers, poor quality goods, and foot and mouth disease among livestock.

assistance in finding jobs. A deputy in an oblast *kenesh* (regional representative body) in southern Kyrgyzstan recounted that people request money for utility payments as well as medical services, home repairs, and, when pension payments are delayed, daily expenses. He also regularly receives requests for credit and for assistance in finding a job. A deputy governor in central Kyrgyzstan said that residents of his region approach him about finding jobs for members of their households, especially when every adult member is without work. At public meetings with the governor, individual constituents frequently demand funds to resolve personal problems, according to a local journalist who covers these events. A deputy to the national parliament, the Zhogorku Kenesh, from southern Kyrgyzstan described how credit and employment requests are also made of him. Besides lack of money, the poor quality of public infrastructure is a common challenge.[17] Less common problems include personal crises, bureaucratic challenges, societal crises, and other economic difficulties, as the data in Table 3.5 show.

---

17. Because of the relative poverty of Kyrgyzstan compared to Kazakhstan, poor public infrastructure poses a greater challenge to residents of Kyrgyzstan. Sixty-seven percent of the population in Kyrgyzstan was living on less than 2 USD per day in 2002 versus 22 percent in Kazakhstan. In Kyrgyzstan and Kazakhstan, respectively, 47 percent and 16 percent of respondents who sought state help identified the difficulty of obtaining water for drinking and irrigation as a main problem. Some locations have never had access to reliable, safe sources of water, whereas others have witnessed the deterioration of canals that used to provide water. Respondents in Kyrgyzstan and Kazakhstan also identified the absence and poor quality of other utilities, including electricity, cooking gas, and sew-

Targets of Citizens' Demands

While citizens do request help from oblast and national officials, their most common targets in their search for assistance are village and *raion* officials. Text-box 3.1 depicts the different levels of government. Of the survey respondents who had sought assistance from government officials in the previous year, 80 percent in Kazakhstan and 54 percent in Kyrgyzstan requested help from village or city officials, as indicated in Table 3.6. However, village officials are really the main players: twenty-two percent of rural residents in Kazakhstan and 31 percent in Kyrgyzstan have sought government assistance compared to only 9 percent and 6 percent of urban dwellers, respectively. The next most popular officials to turn to are *raion* ones. In Kazakhstan 29 percent and in Kyrgyzstan 39 percent of respondents had turned to *raion* officials for assistance. The figures were only 6 percent and 13 percent for oblast officials and 3 percent and 5 percent for national officials in Kazakhstan and Kyrgyzstan, respectively.[18] A higher percentage of survey respondents turn to local officials in Kazakhstan relative to Kyrgyzstan, likely reflecting the larger size of Kazakhstan. In Kazakhstan the average oblast size is 167,000 square kilometers, whereas in Kyrgyzstan it is only 28,000 square kilometers.[19]

Box 3.1 Levels of Government

National

Oblast

Raion

Local (village and city)

Individuals in both countries are most likely to seek assistance from local officials because they are most accessible. Particularly for rural residents, it is dif-

---

age systems, as problems. The lack of paved roads and public transportation as well as the poor quality of those that do exist pose challenges. Respondents also complained about the availability and quality of medical facilities and educational institutions.

18. Respondents could select more than one type of official.

19. These figures are calculated from data available from "Regions of Kazakhstan, 2005–2009" (Astana: Agency of Statistics of the Republic of Kazakhstan, 2010), 4; National Statistics Committee of the Kyrgyz Republic, "Itogi pervoi natsional'noi perepisi naseleniia Kyrgyzskoi Respubliki 1999 goda" [First Results of the National Population Census of the Kyrgyz Republic in 1999] (National Statistics Committee of the Kyrgyz Republic), http://www.stat.kg/stat.files/census.pdf. (accessed December 19, 2013).

TABLE 3.6. State officials from whom people sought assistance in Kazakhstan and Kyrgyzstan (percentage of respondents, rounded)

	KAZAKHSTAN	KYRGYZSTAN
Village or city	80	54
Raion	29	39
Oblast	6	13
National	3	5

Note: $n = 229$ for Kazakhstan and 293 for Kyrgyzstan for the number of people who turned to state officials for assistance in the previous year.

ficult to reach oblast and national officials. Much of the countries' transportation infrastructures are of low quality, thus inflating travel times, and the cost of gasoline can make travel prohibitive. Furthermore, the public transportation systems have eroded. National parliamentarians and sometimes oblast *kenesh* officials have constituent offices in towns, but even those can be difficult and expensive for rural residents to reach. Moreover, mail service is slow and unreliable, and phone calls can be prohibitively expensive.

To better understand the practice of citizens turning to local officials, particularly village officials, consider the village in southern Kazakhstan where Marzhan resides and where I lived, observed, and conducted interviews for nearly two months. In this village more than 20 people visit the deputy *akim* each day throughout the year with requests for work, social assistance, and credit.[20] The village comprises 650 homes with a total of approximately 3,300 people. The village formed in 1935 around the sovkhoz, where Marzhan and her husband used to work. Employment at the sovkhoz dropped from 780 to 11 individuals, none of whom receive a salary now. Half the able people in the village are unemployed. After the village leader, *raion* officials are the most common targets of those requesting help; seeking assistance from oblast officials is rare because of distance and transportation. By car the village is twenty minutes from the *raion* center and one and a half hours from the oblast capital. A bus travels three times a day from the village to the *raion* center, but not to the oblast capital. Some villagers with access to cars ferry neighbors back and forth to the *raion* center for a fee. Travel in a car to the oblast capital was prohibitively expensive for all. As in all rural areas, the village leader was most accessible. Reliance on *raion*, but not oblast, officials is common in villages because the *raion* center is typically closer.

---

20. The deputy *akim* is the de facto, day-to-day leader of this village because the *akim* is based in the district capital and oversees multiple villages.

Government Officials' Sources of Money, Credit, and Employment

What resources do officials at different levels have to respond to citizens' requests for assistance and potentially to distribute in return for bribes and other favors? Village officials—the most likely individuals to receive requests—direct national benefit payments and international charitable donations to residents of their villages and seek additional resources from better-off residents and businesses. *Raion* and oblast bureaucrats channel credit from formal programs under their auspices. Members of oblast representative bodies and national parliamentary deputies typically hold a second state job that gives them access to resources, and both sets of officials can share their personal wealth.

Village Leaders' Resources

Village governments have little money to spend, but they can acquire funds informally. The national governments in Kazakhstan and Kyrgyzstan have undertaken decentralization campaigns that have devolved responsibilities, but not adequate funding, to local governments. As a result, local leaders, particularly in villages where economies tend to be poor, are short of funds. Only by acting as gatekeepers to benefits, credit, and charity from outside their villages and by seeking donations from wealthy residents do village leaders have access to some resources.

Village governments are short on funds because tax revenue goes to higher authorities, who tend to redistribute it in an arbitrary fashion. As the deputy *akim* of the village in southern Kazakhstan, explained, "The tax proceeds all go to the *raion*. There is nothing left. There is not enough left to buy a pen."[21] During much of the independence period, all local tax revenue in Kazakhstan and 80 percent in Kyrgyzstan has gone to higher levels of government, and with the exception of land taxes in Kazakhstan, local officials cannot create new taxes.[22] The higher levels of government then redistribute the local tax revenue in a rather

---

21. Author's interview (#172), Kazakhstan, July 26, 2001.

22. Meruert Makhmutova, "Local Government in Kazakhstan," in *Developing New Rules in the Old Environment: Local Governments in Eastern Europe, in the Caucasus and Central Asia*, vol. 3, ed. Igor Munteanu and Victor Popa (Budapest: Central European University Press, 2003), 403–68, here 439; Nuruipa Mukanova, "Assessing 'New Public Management' Reforms in Kyrgyzstan," in *Mixes, Matches, and Mistakes: New Public Management in Russia and the Former Soviet Republics*, ed. B. Guy Peters (Budapest: Open Society Institute/Local Government and Public Sector Reform Initiative, 2008), 197–296, here 209.

A change in Kazakhstan allowed village governments to keep more tax revenue; however, the rates were simultaneously reduced so that village governments will not have significantly more funds. World Bank, "Republic of Kazakhstan: Tax Strategy Paper, Volume 1: A Strategic Plan for Increasing the Neutrality of the Tax System in Non-Extractive Sectors," 36494-KZ (2008), here 19.

arbitrary manner, meaning that some villages receive more resources than others but none can be sure of how much they will receive at any given time.[23]

Restricted taxation abilities and arbitrary redistribution are especially problematic because village governments have been given greater welfare responsibilities as a part of the decentralization campaigns that the national governments have mounted. The funds that village governments have are simply too scant to cover the welfare responsibilities they have been delegated.[24] By one estimate, 70 percent of local government functions in Kyrgyzstan have been delegated from above without funding. Consequently, local governments are able to perform at most four of the eleven functions that are their responsibility. Unperformed functions include road repair and maintenance of schools, medical facilities, and communal transport, among other responsibilities.[25]

Although village leaders do not have money to spare, they can direct resources to individuals because they serve as gatekeepers. Village leaders are formal gatekeepers in the sense that the national governments have made them responsible for identifying who should receive benefits in their villages. Identification of who is financially needy has become particularly important with the reform of the welfare systems. Each country has moved from the Soviet system of privileges for all members of particular groups to monetary assistance based on need.[26] For example, children under age sixteen, students up to age twenty-one, people unable to work, and pensioners qualify for a monthly payment in Kyrgyzstan if their average per capita family income falls below the guaranteed minimum consumer level of 200 som (about 5 USD) per person per month. In Kazakhstan, people who receive similar assistance include children whose family income is less than 1,550 tenge (about 11 USD) per month per person and people who pay more than 30 percent of their income to utilities and have less than eighteen square meters of living space per person.

----

23. A. N. Deryugin, "The Challenges of Decentralization in the Kyrgyz Republic: The Kyrgyz Republic: Government Structure and Reform of the Budgetary System" (Budapest: Open Society Institute/Local Government and Public Sector Reform Initiative: Fiscal Decentralization Initiative for Central and Eastern Europe, 2007), here 7; S. Slukhai and O. Honcharenko, "The Challenges of Decentralization in the Kyrgyz Republic: Financial Equalization at the Sub-National Level in the Ukraine, the Republic of Belarus, and the Kyrgyz Republic" (Budapest: Open Society Institute/Local Government and Public Sector Reform Initiative: Fiscal Decentralization Initiative for Central and Eastern Europe, 2007), here 8.

24. Makhmutova, "Local Government in Kazakhstan," 432.

25. Mukanova, "Assessing 'New Public Management' Reforms in Kyrgyzstan," 216–17.

26. A small portion of people receive assistance regardless of need. In Kyrgyzstan these individuals include children who have lost a breadwinner or both parents, mothers of many children, and people with certain disabilities. In Kazakhstan unemployed individuals who were two years shy of pension age, have many or invalid children, or who are ethnic Kazakhs who returned to the country, among others, are eligible for unemployment benefits regardless of need.

Villager leaders evaluate who is eligible for assistance and thus have significant control over the resources. In Kazakhstan each village *akim*, working with a team he forms, develops a list of those in his village who meet the financial requirements to receive monetary assistance. The *akim* is also responsible for issuing certificates to establish that an individual has characteristics, such as being a mother of a disabled child, that make him or her eligible for a government benefit. Those who receive benefits must then regularly demonstrate to the *akim* that they are still eligible for them. For example, a mother of a disabled child must prove to the *akim* that her child remains disabled. In Kyrgyzstan the heads of the *aiyl okmota* (village council) play a similar role in determining who should receive benefits. Each country's ministry of social protection relies on the certificates and lists generated by village leaders to determine who receives help.

These responsibilities give the village leaders considerable influence in the distribution of state benefits. For example, in Kazakhstan Marzhan recounted how the leader of her village rejected her request to be eligible for state monetary assistance, "He said, 'You are rich. You have a tractor and a cow.'" I asked if she then traveled to the *raion* capital to ask those officials for help. "Where would I go in [the *raion* capital]? If the village *akim* would not help, why would they? They would ask, 'From where did you appear?'" she replied.[27] The head of a *raion* office of the department of labor, employment, and social protection corroborated that the question of whether a person has a right to receive a benefit rarely reaches him. One of his superiors at the oblast level confirmed that to receive benefits an individual must have his or her village *akim*'s support and only then can the individual continue with the process.

Village leaders are gatekeepers not only to state benefits, but also to state and nonstate credit and charitable assistance. State banks, state credit programs, professional associations, and charitable organizations rely on *akims*' authority to issue documents and knowledge of villagers' needs. For example, the head of the credit department for a state bank in Kyrgyzstan described how the bank works closely with village leaders to lend microcredit to the needy. In Kazakhstan an oblast credit program requires applicants first to submit their materials to their local *akims* for review. In Kyrgyzstan village leaders also use their influence in the credit process to encourage repayment of loans. A manager at a state bank explained, "*Aksakals* and the *aiyl okmota* leaders go [to the clients] and say, 'Kids, you need to pay.'"[28] *Aksakals* have some influence because of the respect for elders in these countries.

---

27. Author's interview (#161), Kazakhstan, July 22, 2001.
28. Author's interview (#126), Kyrgyzstan, May 27, 2009.

Village leaders also play a role in directing the resources of charitable associations. The head of a *raion* branch of the Red Cross/Red Crescent in southern Kazakhstan explained that she distributes donations, such as children's clothing, using the lists of the needy that the village leaders create. "The village authorities do research into who needs assistance because people do not tell the truth or they are ashamed," she explained.[29]

Village leaders are also informal gatekeepers in the sense that they are a vital source of information about resources beyond the village. They receive information about employment and credit opportunities because they are contact people for entities operating outside the village. For example, the head of a nongovernmental agricultural association in Kazakhstan explained that he shared information about acquiring credit with the village *akims* in the *raion* where he works and they disseminated it to residents of their villages. Village officials also know to refer their residents to *raion* or oblast government employment centers, which then provide the *akims* with a small number of people funded by the government to do public works, such as cleaning canals and streets, removing snow, and fighting steppe fires, for two to three months.

In addition to serving as formal and informal gatekeepers to credit and assistance from outside the village, village leaders obtain funds from comparatively wealthy residents in their village. As the deputy *akim* of the village in southern Kazakhstan put it, "The only money comes from the population." Using donations from local families, he employs villagers for public works projects. He explained, "I asked the uncles and kids to go down their streets and ask each family for 30 tenge to use to clean the water canals."[30] The wealthier families contributed and the money went toward the wages of those the deputy *akim* employed. The deputy *akim* also created a program where thirty better-off families in the village provide assistance, usually food, to another poor family a few times a year. The phenomenon of contributions from better-off community members is not limited to this village. In fact, the deputy *akim* borrowed the idea from another village. Wealthier villagers play the same role in Kyrgyzstan. The generosity of these individuals is limited, of course, by their own resources and by their own evaluation of what makes a worthy cause. Marzhan's uncle, Kanat, the well-off private farmer, described how the deputy *akim* had asked him to donate money so that the village could host a concert. Kanat declined to contribute and responded, "I would rather sing myself."[31]

---

29. Author's interview (#160), Kazakhstan, July 20, 2001.
30. Author's interview (#172), Kazakhstan, July 26, 2001.
31. Author's interview (#153), Kazakhstan, multiple dates in July and August 2001.

City leaders do not play the roles of formal and informal gatekeepers as village leaders do for a number of reasons. Kazakhstan and Kyrgyzstan have departments of social protection staffed with bureaucrats and based in cities. These departments establish whether urban residents are eligible for benefits, so city *akims* in Kazakhstan and *shaar bashchylar* (mayors) in Kyrgyzstan do not carry out these tasks. Population densities are high enough in urban areas to locate these departments there, but this is not the case in rural areas. Because urban residents readily have access to these specialized bureaucrats, they do not rely on city *akims* and *shaar bashchylar* for information about resources outside the city. In addition, urban dwellers have access to more media and nonstate organizations, such as banks and charities, than rural residents, and thus can obtain information without the help of local officials. Organizations also rely less on city *akims* and *shaar bashchylar* than village leaders for information about their residents because the specialized bureaucracies exist and because city leaders do not know their residents as well. City leaders are not directly involved in the collection of information about residents' needs and there are simply too many people in urban areas for city leaders to personally know or regularly interact with. Instead, urban residents seek assistance from *raion* and oblast bureaucrats, as some rural residents do as well.

Raion and Oblast Bureaucrats' Resources

Raion and oblast bureaucrats manage credit programs from which they can redirect funds to those who seek assistance.[32] Urban residents and villagers living near *raion* and oblast capitals have easy access to *raion* and oblast bureaucrats who administer these programs. Residents of villages far from capitals travel to seek assistance from *raion* and oblast bureaucrats only if they can secure free or inexpensive transportation with a family member, friend, or stranger who has a car.

Government business-credit programs, administered by oblast or *raion* bureaucrats and funded by oblast and national governments, were created because credit from private banks and microcredit companies has been in limited supply for much of the independence period, as described in chapter four. The objectives of most government programs are to shift the economy from subsistence farming and small trade to commercial agriculture, manufacturing, and

---

32. The *raion* and oblast levels also have government-run employment centers; however, I found no evidence of citizens' use of informal practices to obtain jobs through these centers, most likely because only the least appealing jobs are advertised through centers. Lucrative jobs have already been snatched up through bribes and connections, and never reach the employment center.

services.[33] To meet their objectives, the government programs lend to start-ups, agricultural ventures, and borrowers with minimal collateral and no other source of income, and demand repayment in relatively fewer intervals over a longer period of time. This is in contrast to most private banks and reputable microcredit programs. As a result, this credit is a valuable resource for government officials to dispense.

Many of the government credit programs lend to agricultural ventures, helping to address the problem of lack of credit in rural areas. Some programs provide start-up funds, enabling those who have lost their jobs or no longer receive their salaries, but have not yet developed businesses, to potentially earn income. For example, throughout Kazakhstan the national government funds a microcredit program run by oblast *akimats*. The program provides 400 USD interest-free to unemployed individuals to begin a business. The director of one of the oblast programs stressed the minimal requirements: "If a person has hands and skills, they get microcredit."[34] Projects include purchasing seeds to grow and sell potatoes and buying materials to start a shoe repair business.

Government programs have also mitigated the problem of steep collateral requirements. In Kyrgyzstan a program run through a government bank to provide assistance in rural areas accepts rural homes, farm equipment and buildings, and livestock as collateral. This program also offers the option of community collateral, where other residents provide collateral on a borrower's behalf. An oblast *akimat* in southern Kazakhstan has established a communal collateral fund, where the borrower contributes 30 percent of the collateral and the *akimat* contributes 70 percent using oblast buildings, such as hospitals, offices, theaters, and hotels. Businesspeople have borrowed through this program to develop businesses in the livestock and wheat industries and to build a water park.

Longer loan and repayment periods are also available through government credit programs. An oblast government in southern Kazakhstan offers longer periods through its own credit program and one through a bank, which the national government partially owns. In both cases, the programs aim to address farmers' difficulties in repaying loans during growing seasons. The *akimat* program offers loans for two-year periods, and farmers have borrowed in order to secure seeds, animals, fertilizer, land, and equipment. The program through the bank lends for eighteen months with a grace period for repayment if necessary. Farmers have purchased seed and fuel through this program. The agricultural

---

33. These government credit programs are not market-enhancing institutions themselves but instead are examples of government provision of a service that a market actor cannot provide because of the absence of market-enhancing institutions. Market-enhancing institutions enable market actors to engage in their activities; they are not government substitutes for those activities.

34. Author's interview (#204), Kazakhstan, June 11, 2001.

credit program that operates through the government bank in Kyrgyzstan has extended the payment periods beyond one month to reduce risk for farmers there.

Government programs also offer loans at zero percent or a low percent. A national fund provided credit interest-free to poor families in agricultural regions. In a rural *raion* in southern Kazakhstan some farmers benefited from *raion* and oblast programs that lent at zero percent. The two-year program and eighteen-month program described above lend money for 7 percent and 8 percent, respectively, instead of the typical 22–33 percent for one year. However, few farmers, traders, and other businesspeople in Kazakhstan and Kyrgyzstan indicated to me that loan rates were a problem: most of the entrepreneurs I interviewed had not even been able to obtain credit or had such difficulty securing it because of these restrictions that the rate was of less concern. Only those who borrow from the newest microcredit companies have encountered problems with high rates. The next chapter describes how these companies have proliferated in recent years and typically charge exorbitant rates.

The less stringent requirements of government credit programs make them a valuable resource that *raion* and oblast officials can distribute. Because these programs are relatively small, as chapter four describes, competition to obtain these resources is intense.

Oblast and National Deputies' Resources

In their oblasts citizens seek assistance not only from bureaucrats who manage credit programs but also from deputies to the oblast *maslikhat* or *kenesh*. National deputies who represent their oblasts in the country's parliament are also possible targets, although they are the least accessible of all the officials to whom citizens turn for help. The resources that oblast and national deputies can provide to citizens depend less on their authority as representatives than on their second jobs or personal wealth. Many oblast and national deputies hold another state job from which they can take resources to use in clientelist exchanges.[35] For example, oblast deputies who are doctors at state hospitals in Kyrgyzstan report that they provide free medicine and secure hospital admissions for constituents. An oblast deputy who works in the state coal industry in Kazakhstan is able to provide heat to people in his district. An oblast deputy in southern Kyrgyzstan used capital from his private advertising and information agency to open an

---

35. For example, in the mid-1990s more than two-thirds of the deputies in the Assembly of People's Representatives in the Zhogorku Kenesh also had another position in the state administration. Eric McGlinchey, *Chaos, Violence, Dynasty: Politics and Islam in Central Asia* (Pittsburgh, PA: University of Pittsburgh Press, 2011), 91.

auto service shop, a photography laboratory, and a press to provide jobs to constituents.[36] Through their second jobs or from their personal largesse oblast and national deputies secure resources that they can provide to constituents.

In Kazakhstan and Kyrgyzstan individuals compete for state resources from village leaders, *raion* and oblast bureaucrats, and, to a lesser extent, oblast and national deputies in order to meet their everyday needs; extensive welfare goods and services from the state are no longer guaranteed to each person as they were in the Soviet era. In the competition for resources from these officials, citizens use bribes, personal connections, and promises of political support. The next chapter shows how market reform, in the context of a legacy of significant state economic intervention and absent or weak market-enhancing institutions, accounts for these practices. Specifically, it explains why citizens turn to government officials instead of market actors and why citizens use corruption in their interactions with leaders.

---

36. For additional accounts of clientelism in Kyrgyzstan, see Scott Radnitz, *Weapons of the Wealthy: Predatory Regimes and Elite-Led Protests in Central Asia* (Ithaca, NY: Cornell University Press, 2010), 85–86.

MARKET ACTORS AS AN UNREALIZED ALTERNATIVE

The Effect of Market Reforms

"Everybody lives on their own," Marzhan said to explain how people cope now without the Soviet welfare state.[1] The idea of "living on one's own," in other words, being accountable for one's own survival, is a frequent refrain among people in both Kazakhstan and Kyrgyzstan. It is also the governments' stance and thus a partial explanation for why individuals use corrupt practices when trying to obtain state resources. Through the media and their conversations with citizens, government officials tell individuals that they are responsible for their own economic success or failure because Kazakhstan and Kyrgyzstan are now market reformers. Faced with this message, individuals without alternative sources of assistance offer government officials personal incentives, such as bribes, to make an exception to the mantra and provide them with state resources.

While government rhetoric about market reform encourages the use of corrupt practices, the economic effect of market reform drives individuals to seek state assistance in the first place. By limiting alternative resources from market and societal actors, market reform has promoted corruption. In theory, this reform policy creates market goods and services to replace state ones. However, under the two conditions, a legacy of significant state economic intervention and weak or absent market-enhancing institutions, this has not occurred. Instead, market actors, such as private banks and entrepreneurs, have not been able to provide sufficient credit and employment for people to earn adequate income

---

1. Author's interview (#161), Kazakhstan, July 22, 2001.

and avoid engaging in corruption. Market reform under these circumstances has also hindered societal actors' ability to provide substitutes for state welfare, as described in the next chapter. In an environment where market and societal actors cannot assist with economic survival, individuals turn to government officials for assistance. Yet market reform has also limited the resources of government officials, increasing the competition among citizens for state goods and services and thus encouraging them to engage in corrupt practices to gain an edge.

How do we know market reform has limited market actors' ability to provide goods and services and thus has encouraged citizens to seek them illicitly from government officials—the claim of this chapter? Numerous pieces of evidence build the case. Reports of international financial institutions and economic histories show that market reform, a legacy of significant state economic intervention, and absent or weak market-enhancing institutions—the causal factor and two conditions—exist in Kazakhstan and Kyrgyzstan. Market actors and government officials from the countries describe how markets are not an alternative to corruption because of the absent or weak institutions. Consistent with this, my survey data show that individuals tend not to turn to market actors to try to solve their everyday problems. Moreover, the demands individuals make of the state match challenges brought about by market reform under these conditions. Interviews with ordinary citizens and officials reveal that market reform has reduced the availability of government resources and discouraged reliance on the state, thus providing incentives for individuals to use corruption in the competition to secure state goods and services. The survey data indicate that, in contrast, competition for basic state resources is not as common in Uzbekistan, a country that has not undertaken market reform but otherwise resembles Kazakhstan and Kyrgyzstan on many factors thought to cause corruption. Finally, analysis of global data suggests that this effect of market reform extends beyond Central Asia.

From Economic Intervention to Market Reform without Market-Enhancing Institutions

In Kazakhstan and Kyrgyzstan the significant state economic intervention of the Soviet era has been replaced with market economies, albeit ones lacking market-enhancing institutions. In the Soviet era, state economic intervention was substantial. The state owned the means of production in all spheres, and state employees produced the goods and services. The state allocated resources, including

TABLE 4.1.　Market reforms in Kazakhstan and Kyrgyzstan

	KAZAKHSTAN	KYRGYZSTAN
LIBERALIZATION		
Current account convertibility	full	full
Interest rate liberalization	full	full
Trade liberalization	almost full	full
Price liberalization	almost full	almost full
PRIVATIZATION		
Small firms	full	full
Land	full[a]	full[b]
Private pensions	yes	yes
DEREGULATION		
Wages deregulated	yes	yes

Source: European Bank for Reconstruction and Development "Transition indicators by country," at "Forecasts, Macro Data, Transition Indicators," http://www.ebrd.com/pages/research/economics/data/macro.shtml#t. The data are from 2003, the year of my survey research.

[a] Land is fully tradable except by foreigners.
[b] Land is fully tradable; however, there have been difficulties implementing this policy.

capital and labor, according to a national economic plan. It also set prices.[2] Market activity was officially banned and as a result was nearly nonexistent. A second economy compensated for the weaknesses of Soviet socialism. The Soviet party-state put little emphasis on consumer services and goods, so their quality tended to be poor, and, periodically they, as well as productive goods, were in short supply. As a result, individuals traded these outside of the official economy. For example, haircuts, appliance repair, better cuts of meat, contraband Western literature, high-quality shoes, and scarce industrial and agricultural inputs were available in the second economy.[3] Even with the second economy, however, the Soviet Union was characterized by significant state economic intervention.

Since becoming independent countries in 1991, Kazakhstan and Kyrgyzstan have undertaken numerous market reforms, in the areas of liberalization, privatization, and deregulation. The reforms have included the establishment of current account convertibility; liberalization of interest rates, trade, and prices; deregulation of wages; and privatization of small firms, land, and pensions, as indicated in Table 4.1.

Although Kazakhstan and Kyrgyzstan have undertaken market reforms, these reforms have not included the development of market-enhancing institutions. Credit bureaus and registries and effective competition policies would be par-

---

2. V. Bunce, "Elementy neopredelennosti v perekhodnyi period" [Elements of uncertainty in the transition period], *Polis* 1 (1993), 44–51.

3. Paul R. Gregory and Robert C. Stuart, *Soviet Economic Structure and Performance*, 4th ed. (New York: Harper and Row, 1990), 274–76.

TABLE 4.2.   Private credit bureau coverage in Kazakhstan and Kyrgyzstan (percentage of adults)

	KAZAKHSTAN	KYRGYZSTAN
2004	0	0
2005	0	0.2
2006	5.5	0.4
2007	13.7	1.6
2008	25.6	3.7
2009	29.5	5.9
2010	29.9	11.9
2011	37.6	18.7
2012	39.3	24.6
2013	45.6	32.1

Source: International Finance Corporation and World Bank, "Doing Business: Measuring Business Regulations," http://www.doingbusiness.org/custom-query.

ticularly helpful in these economies. Yet, the countries have not had private credit bureaus, public credit registries, or effective competition policies throughout most of their independence periods. The World Bank and International Finance Corporation reported that neither country had a private or public credit bureau at the time of my surveys. Beginning in 2005 in Kyrgyzstan and 2006 in Kazakhstan, private credit bureaus slowly began to develop, and by 2013, they covered approximately 46 percent of the adult population in Kazakhstan and 32 percent in Kyrgyzstan—far from the 100 percent found in most developed economies.[4] This trend is visible in Table 4.2. The governments of Kazakhstan and Kyrgyzstan still have not created public credit registries nor have they established effective competition policies. The European Bank for Reconstruction and Development (EBRD) describes the countries as having only limited competition policies from the time of the surveys to 2013.[5]

Inadequate Market Goods and Services

In this economic context, market actors have not been able to offer goods and services to meet everyone's basic needs, so citizens use illicit means to obtain

---

4. International Finance Corporation and World Bank, "Doing Business: Measuring Business Regulations," http://www.doingbusiness.org/custom-query (accessed December 19, 2013).

5. See EBRD, "Transition Indicators by Country," at "Forecasts, Macro Data, Transition Indicators," http://www.ebrd.com/pages/research/economics/data/macro.shtml#t (accessed December 19, 2013). EBRD, "Transition Report 2009: Transition in Crisis" (London, 2009); EBRD, "Transition Report 2013: Stuck in Transition?" (London, 2013).

them. The private businesses that exist today in Kazakhstan and Kyrgyzstan began from scratch immediately prior to the collapse of the Soviet Union and in the independence era. With the end of the ban on private enterprise in the late Soviet era, private banks, microcredit companies, and other private ventures began to emerge. The absence of some market-enhancing institutions and the weakness of others have limited the market goods and services provided by these businesses. The absence of credit registries and bureaus has prevented private banks and most microcredit companies from lending in rural areas, in particular. The lack of government regulation of the microfinance industry has hindered the emergence of sound credit, encouraging predatory lending instead. The dearth of effective government antimonopoly policies has stifled business expansion by enabling suppliers to charge inflated prices. As a result, credit, employment, and charitable donations from private ventures have not been adequate to meet people's needs.

Private banks and responsible microcredit companies have adopted stringent lending requirements in response to the absence of credit registries and bureaus. The requirements reduce the risks of lending and minimize the losses from borrowers who default on their loans. These restrictions, in turn, have prevented much of the populations, particularly rural residents, from obtaining credit except from predatory lenders. Private banks' business credit programs typically require that borrowers have an existing business, seek funds for nonagricultural ventures, possess valuable collateral, and repay the funds in frequent intervals within a short period.[6] Responsible microcredit companies demand some other source of income and repayment in frequent intervals.

People who need assistance do not have the existing business that private lenders require or the other source of income that responsible microcredit companies prefer. Typically these individuals have lost their jobs and do not already have a business on the side or some other source of income. Approximately half of the people who inquire about small-business credit request start-up funds and are turned away, according to a specialist who directs a credit program that operates through many private banks in a city of central Kazakhstan. The general manager of a microcredit company in Kyrgyzstan explained that all the company's first-time borrowers have another source of income.

Many private banks will not lend money to farmers. This practice excludes much of the population in each country from obtaining credit because 46 percent and 65 percent of the population is rural in Kazakhstan and Kyrgyzstan,

---

6. The 2007–9 global economic crisis increased banks' aversion to risk, albeit temporarily. International Monetary Fund, "Republic of Kazakhstan 2012 Article IV Consultation" (Washington, DC, 2012).

respectively. Banks' refusals to lend to farmers stem, in part, from the lack of valuable collateral in rural areas. Private banks generally accept only homes and cars as collateral. In rural areas, homes are worth little, which makes them ineligible to serve as collateral. Car ownership was not common in the Soviet era, and today, particularly in rural areas, personal cars are not ubiquitous. Farm equipment, future harvests, livestock, and land would be difficult for banks to realize when clients default, so this property is typically not accepted for collateral. Farm equipment is mostly Soviet-made and has little value, and banks have not developed the networks to sell farm products and livestock. Furthermore, the value of harvests and livestock can unexpectedly drop. Drought and disease can destroy crops, and theft and illness can reduce herds. Land has been difficult for banks to convert into cash for numerous reasons: some areas have an excess of land; farmers tend to have long-term leases instead of ownership of land; most farmers do not have the capital to rent or purchase additional land; and foreigners cannot buy it. Private banks typically do not accept smaller household objects, such as televisions, because they can be difficult to locate. Lack of collateral is not a problem exclusively in rural areas. In towns and even in some cities, apartments are of so little value that collateral can be difficult to obtain. An auto parts distributor, Sulushash, explained how she looked for two years for credit to begin her business but repeatedly found that her city apartment was not worth enough to serve as collateral.

Private banks tend to offer only short-loan periods, and both private banks and responsible microcredit companies typically require the repayment of loans in installments. These requirements are prohibitive for farmers; as the head of a *raion* association of independent farmers in southern Kazakhstan explained, "If we had long-term credit we could all get on our feet."[7] During the crop-growing season, which lasts from approximately April to October, farmers do not have funds to make loan payments. They do not have available funds until they harvest their crops in the fall. For this reason, those few private programs that lend to farmers typically require them to have a nonagricultural business in addition to their farming venture; however, few farmers are in such a position. Farmers explained to me that they need longer loan periods, three years for example, to be able to repay loans for the purchase of seed or fertilizer, even if they suffered a bad harvest. Private banks' credit programs are even less conducive to livestock ventures, as most animals need to mature approximately five years for farmers to recoup their investments. These programs also do not meet the needs of farmers or urban entrepreneurs who want to invest in equipment. Many farmers need to replace Soviet-era farm equipment. Some farmers are also interested in

---

7. Author's interview (#169), Kazakhstan, July 25, 2001.

selling processed goods in order to obtain a greater profit. In order to process their crops and livestock into flour, macaroni, or juice, for example, they have to purchase equipment. Similarly, urban entrepreneurs, most of whom buy goods in one location and sell them in another, have to invest in equipment, for manufacturing or higher-end service industries, in order to further develop their businesses. For these types of purchases farmers and urban entrepreneurs need a five- to ten-year loan period.

Credit is more readily available from microcredit companies engaged in predatory lending, but the risk of default and greater impoverishment is high. These companies offer larger loans at exorbitant rates of 50–70 percent per annum and typically obfuscate the terms and risks from the borrowers. The growth of predatory lending has been enabled by the absence of another market-enhancing institution—government regulations. For example, in Kyrgyzstan an individual with only 2,175 USD and no microfinance or banking expertise can establish a microfinance institution. Today 100 are in operation and another 350 have been created in Kyrgyzstan.[8] In Kazakhstan about half of the 1,800 microcredit organizations created are in operation.[9]

Islamic banks and financial institutions represent another new, but not very promising market alternative to state assistance. In Kazakhstan the government passed a law allowing Islamic banks and financing organizations to operate in the country, and Kyrgyzstan has embarked on a pilot Islamic banking project.[10] These institutions invest directly in business ventures, instead of granting interest-bearing loans. Advocates claim that this approach is more transparent and creates a relationship between the institutions and their clients, suggesting that predatory behaviors are less likely. Unfortunately, investment from Islamic banks and financing institutions has not significantly expanded opportunities for business capital in its first few years. One report points to the reluctance of secular elites to embrace Islamic institutions,[11] although enthusiasm has grown for learning about Islam. Nonetheless, Islamic banks and financing institutions do not currently provide a significant alternative to state assistance.

---

8. Myles G. Smith, "Kyrgyzstan: Could Microfinance Bubble Burst?" EurasiaNet, June 11, 2012, http://www.eurasianet.org/node/65527 (accessed December 19, 2013).

9. "Regulation of Microcredit Organisation Becomes Tougher," CaspioNet, June 28, 2012, http://caspionet.kz/eng/general/Regulation_of_microcredit_organisation_becomes_tougher _1340857351.html (accessed November 28, 2012).

10. "Central Asia: Governments, Banks Gradually Open up to Islamic Banking," EurasiaNet, July 12, 2007, http://www.eurasianet.org/departments/insight/articles/pp071307f.shtml (accessed December 19, 2013); Agency of the Republic of Kazakhstan on Regulation of Activities of the Regional Financial Centre of Almaty City, "Islamic Financing," http://www.rfca.gov.kz/6196 (accessed November 28, 2012).

11. Justin Vela, "Kyrgyzstan: Islamic Banking Offers Alternative to the 'European System,'" EurasiaNet, June 14, 2011, http://www.eurasianet.org/node/63675 (accessed December 19, 2013).

Accounts of those in the banking and government sectors confirm that the absence, and more recently, the limited coverage, of credit registries and bureaus restricts the ability of private secular banks and responsible microfinance firms to provide credit. The manager of a microcredit company set the scene, explaining, "There is still high demand for credit. The market is not saturated."[12] An official with the Agency of the Republic of Kazakhstan for the Regulation of Natural Monopolies, Protection of Competitiveness, and Support of Small Business attributed the lack of legitimate small business capital available in the country to the lack of information about current and potential entrepreneurs' creditworthiness. The general manager of the head office of a private bank in Kyrgyzstan elaborated on how government officials verbally encouraged the expansion of private credit into rural areas but did not provide the institutions essential to making it possible. "The government has requested that we issue agricultural credit,"[13] he began. And, then he proceeded to explain that his bank would need a network of branches in rural areas in order to collect information about potential clients. He added that fifteen banks have formed the nascent credit bureau, but none has data on rural residents, so the collective has not made lending in rural areas possible. Moreover, a representative of the World Bank in Kyrgyzstan explained to me that the banks hold back much of their information from the collective effort because they are competing with one another.

Private banks' limited collective efforts to pool creditworthiness databases could be successful with incentives from the governments of Kazakhstan and Kyrgyzstan. Ironically, however, in Kyrgyzstan the government has the most information about the creditworthiness of rural residents but it has refused to provide it to private banks. The head of the credit department of a government bank with an agricultural lending program explained that the bank has data on creditworthiness of some rural residents because they have specialists based in *raions*. Of all the banks, this one has the largest number of credit histories, the department head revealed, but it opted not to join the collective effort. "It would not have been an even exchange of information" because the private banks had so little information, he explained.[14]

Microcredit companies view this absence of credit histories and the weak regulatory environment as a profit-making opportunity. The head of one of the largest microcredit firms in Kyrgyzstan, Babur Tolbaev of Mol Bulak Finance, stated: "Every month we have new customers without credit histories. I believe there is room for growth, maybe not like the last two years, but there is."[15] While these

---

12. Author's interview (#134), Kyrgyzstan, June 4, 2009.
13. Author's interview (#122), Kyrgyzstan, May 25, 2009.
14. Author's interview (#127), Kyrgyzstan, May 28, 2009.
15. Smith, "Kyrgyzstan: Could Microfinance Bubble Burst?"

firms' pursuit of profit has expanded credit, the expectation by industry watchers is that a microfinance bubble has formed and will soon pop, with the consequence that borrowers will default and have even greater difficulties meeting their basic needs. In response, Kyrgyzstan's national bank closed ninety-four microcredit lenders in 2012, and the parliament of Kazakhstan has considered legislation to regulate the industry. Microcredit institutions themselves have not been able to agree to self-regulate to address the problem. Guidelines proposed by the Foundation for International Community Assistance (FINCA), an American microcredit nonprofit, were rejected by other microcredit institutions.[16]

The weakness of another market-enhancing institution, government antimonopoly policies, has made it difficult for individuals to obtain income and employment in Kazakhstan and Kyrgyzstan. Although both countries have government antimonopoly committees, neither has been effective in reducing monopolies, particularly in rural areas. Because rural residents face monopolies in energy, processing, and purchasing, they cannot readily obtain these goods and services as they once did from the state.

Energy monopolies have inflated prices, so it is difficult for farmers to purchase inputs and to make a profit. In Kyrgyzstan the government broke the state energy concern, Kyrgyzenergo, into eight companies but continues to protect them from competition.[17] The head of the credit department in the government bank in Kyrgyzstan lamented, "The antimonopoly committee does not help. For example, oil prices fell but the committee kept prices high locally. Not until the president made a request did the committee help."[18] The deputy director of the Agency for the Regulation of Natural Monopolies in Kazakhstan acknowledged to me that the government has not addressed the problem of middlemen who are inflating the cost of electricity to rural areas. Farmers in the village in southern Kazakhstan where I lived confirmed the high costs of electricity resulting from middlemen. In Kyrgyzstan, a monopoly on diesel fuel has forced farmers to pay 38 som per liter; they earn only 12 som for a kilo of wheat. At these prices, a farmer growing wheat on forty-two hectares, one of the larger plots available through privatization, pays 3.32 USD per gallon of gas and earns 5,800 USD, before expenses, from a good harvest. With the 5,800 USD he could purchase thirty-six gallons of gas each week for a year for planting, harvesting, and marketing but have nothing left over.

---

16. "Regulation of Microcredit Organisation Becomes Tougher"; Smith, "Kyrgyzstan: Could Microfinance Bubble Burst?"

17. Cholpon Orozobekova, "Kyrgyzstan: Bishkek Food Prices Soaring, Discontent Brews," EurasiaNet, March 3, 2011, http://www.eurasianet.org/node/62999 (accessed December 19, 2013).

18. Author's interview (#127), Kyrgyzstan, May 28, 2009.

In addition to energy monopolies, national and local processing monopolies are obstacles to profitable farming. A processing facility can monopolize business in a locale because farmers cannot afford to transport their products great distances to another processing facility. Kyrgyzstan has had only two sugar-processing plants and two cotton-washing facilities, one of which is now closed, so these facilities can demand a high percentage of farmers' output. In the southern part of Kyrgyzstan, farmers have struggled to have their cotton ginned at a reasonable price. The south has multiple cotton gins, but they have colluded on price. The manager of a nonprofit rural consulting association for Talas and Issik-Kul' Oblasts explained that he had encountered regional processing monopolies in these two oblasts as well as in Osh Oblast. Marzhan's uncle in southern Kazakhstan described a similar situation in his region. "It is a monopoly," Kanat complained, when he recounted how the miller, the only one in the vicinity, requires 40 percent of his grain as payment.[19]

As for purchasing monopolies, the manager of the agricultural consulting service in Kyrgyzstan explained, "The government has control over the buyers and officials profit personally."[20] A single foreign firm buys all the tobacco from southern Kyrgyzstan and therefore can unilaterally set the price. On a smaller scale, another foreign firm buys all the beans from Talas Oblast. The Kyrgyz Bakers' Union has lodged a complaint with the government antimonopoly agency over the agency's inattention to the problem of purchasing monopolies for baked goods. To the extent that the antimonopoly committees in Kazakhstan and Kyrgyzstan have been active, they have focused on prices consumers pay instead of energy, processing, and purchasing monopolies that affect farmers and other small business owners.[21] The lack of government antimonopoly policies to support business and data on citizens' creditworthiness has stifled business in Kazakhstan and Kyrgyzstan.

Consequently, the weakness or absence of market-enhancing institutions has made it difficult for market actors to meet people's demands. Most directly, private banks and responsible microcredit companies cannot lend to many who need credit.[22] "There are many good hands and heads, but people do not have

---

19. Author's interview (#153), Kazakhstan, multiple dates in July and August 2001.

20. Author's interview (#125), Kyrgyzstan, May 26, 2009.

21. Antimonopoly committees are not the sole remedy for processing and purchasing monopolies. Governments could also invest in public transportation, ensuring that roads are of decent quality and passable year-round, for example. This would enable farmers to more easily buy, process, and sell outside of their locales.

22. As formal models of credit rationing indicate, some individuals will be too risky to lend to. Most likely, their credit histories would indicate this, or they would have no credit histories. Joseph E. Stiglitz and Andrew Weiss, "Credit Rationing in Markets with Imperfect Information." *American Economic Review* 71, no. 3 (1981), 393–410.

capital today," the head of a *raion* committee for the support of small and medium business in southern Kazakhstan explained.[23] Lack of credit has been the main problem in agriculture and has stymied its growth. "If this question had been resolved, agriculture would have improved long ago,"[24] a director of an oblast committee for the support of small and medium-size business in southern Kazakhstan clarified. With limited credit and with the inflated prices resulting from monopolies, entrepreneurs cannot boost their own incomes. As market actors themselves, entrepreneurs also cannot expand their businesses to employ more people and thus provide others with the employment and income they need. Consider, for example, Marzhan's uncle Kanat, the successful private farmer. He would like to earn more income and employ more people by purchasing equipment, at a cost of 12,000 USD, to mill the wheat he grows himself instead of relying on the single miller in the area. He would also like to build a factory to produce macaroni from his flour. He cannot do either, however, because of the difficulty of obtaining credit and the milling monopoly. Credit would enable him to purchase the necessary equipment and build a facility. More competitive milling prices would allow him to save money to fund the expansion of his business. Similarly, Nikolai, a successful store owner in a small town in central Kazakhstan explained, "I would prefer to be engaged in industry instead of trade . . . but I do not have the capital to do it."[25] He cannot obtain the credit needed to purchase or establish a plant. Were these businesspeople able to execute their plans they would be able to offer jobs to more people and potentially have enough income to make generous charitable donations, thus helping others meet their needs for employment and money.

The inability of businesspeople to make generous charitable donations alludes to another effect of weak or absent market-enhancing institutions. The weaknesses or absence of these institutions has had direct and indirect effects on societal actors. They have had difficulty obtaining credit. Limited market opportunities also have meant that most individuals, particularly in rural areas, have not had sufficient income to make generous donations to societal groups, such as mosques and charities. The case of Marzhan's uncle is one example of this.

The evidence given in this section about the effect of weak or absent market-enhancing institutions also explains the greater corruption in rural areas and it challenges an alternative explanation. The more significant effect of weak or absent market-enhancing institutions in rural areas helps to explain why informal

---

23. Author's interview (#170), Kazakhstan July 25, 2001.
24. Author's interview (#148), Kazakhstan, July 9, 2001.
25. Author's interview (#191), Kazakhstan, June 5, 2001.

competition for state goods and services is greater there. This evidence about why effective market-enhancing institutions are weak or absent and how this limits markets actors' ability to meet everyday needs also casts doubt on the idea that some other factor accounts for both the institutions' weakness or absence and corruption.

Minimal Reliance on Market Actors

Market actors' difficulty in providing necessary goods and services is also evident from how little citizens rely on them. At most, 4 percent of survey respondents had sought assistance from a particular market actor in the preceding year (see Table 4.3). Only 3 percent of survey respondents in Kazakhstan and 1 percent in Kyrgyzstan had turned to a private bank for help. The figures for one's current employer and former employers were, respectively, 4 percent and 4 percent in Kazakhstan and 3 percent and 2 percent in Kyrgyzstan. The numbers for local companies where one does not work and foreign companies where one does not work were even lower. For Kazakhstan the proportions were 3 percent and less than 1 percent, and for Kyrgyzstan they were less than 1 percent and zero, respectively. Respondents also did not use the services of private employment agencies even though unemployment was one of the most common problems.[26] These employment agencies typically offer job hunters leads for a range of positions: manual labor jobs, such as construction worker; service jobs, including bartender, security guard, and waiter; and positions requiring education, such as a senior accountant or computer programmer. The job hunter pays for the service; one employment agency in central Kazakhstan charges individuals 300 tenge, approximately 2 USD, for each lead and an additional 1000 tenge or 7 USD once a position is accepted. The reason these agencies are used rarely is that the unemployed do not have funds to pay for the services because price liberalization wiped out people's savings. As a result, most of these private employment agencies last only six months before going under. Those that have operated longer typically have another business that subsidizes the employment agency.[27]

---

26. "Private employment agency" was not an option on the survey, but respondents were able to list additional places to which they turned for assistance. No one listed private employment agencies and my interviews indicate why few people turn to them.

27. Local and foreign companies are also examined in the next chapter because they have the potential to provide charitable assistance, as societal groups do.

TABLE 4.3. Market actors from whom citizens have sought assistance in the past year in Kazakhstan and Kyrgyzstan (percentage of respondents, rounded)

	KAZAKHSTAN	KYRGYZSTAN
Bank[a]	3	1
Current employer[a]	4	3
Former employer[a]	4	2
Local company where you don't work[a]	3	<1
Foreign company where you don't work	<1	0

Note: $n = 1,200$ for Kazakhstan and 1,199 for Kyrgyzstan. A portion of the 1,500 respondents in each country claimed that they had no problems or that describing their problems was too difficult and thus some respondents were not asked this question about seeking assistance.

[a] Some banks, employers, and local companies remain state institutions in these countries as a result of the communist period; however, market reforms have ensured that most are now nonstate entities. Counting all of them as market actors increases the difficulty of arguing that the reliance on the state is greater than reliance on market actors.

Challenges and Demands

Without assistance available from market actors or societal groups, individuals turn to government officials for help. The fact that the demands made of government officials by individuals in Kazakhstan and Kyrgyzstan match the challenges brought about by market reforms and absent or weak market-enhancing institutions further increases our confidence that these are a causal factor and an important condition, respectively. Market reforms without market-enhancing institutions resulted in unemployment, insufficient income, and limited credit—the very problems for which citizens seek government officials' help. Specifically, privatization led to job loss, price liberalization and ineffective antimonopoly efforts made incomes insufficient, and the absence of credit registries and bureaus hampered borrowing. The demise of the Soviet economy also contributed to these problems; however, it was market reform under these conditions that made them dire.

The collapse of the Soviet Union disrupted the economies of the former republics so that the governments and state enterprises of the newly independent countries, including Kazakhstan and Kyrgyzstan, faced significant crises. The economies of the Soviet republics had been highly specialized, so, as a result, many individual goods were available from only one location. With the disintegration of the Union it became difficult for state enterprises—including factories, farms, and natural resource concerns—to obtain inputs from other former republics. Moscow no longer guided the flow of inputs, and new borders and currencies further hampered the movement of inputs.

To respond to the structural problems of the Soviet economy and obtain foreign financial assistance for the immediate crisis, Kazakhstan and Kyrgyzstan began to implement the market reforms advocated by the World Bank and International Monetary Fund. Both state enterprises and the governments took a financial hit as a result of these reforms. The reforms meant that state enterprises lost their guarantees of government purchases. Price liberalization further burdened state enterprises as energy costs skyrocketed. State enterprises as well as the government institutions of the former republics also lost subsidies from Moscow because of the collapse of the Soviet Union. Having adopted a market reform approach and lacking substantial revenue from enterprises and subsidies from Moscow, the governments of Kazakhstan and Kyrgyzstan could not prop up every state concern. Many were privatized; others, in industries such as construction, mining, energy production, and public transportation, were maintained by the governments.

These economic shocks to state industrial and agricultural enterprises further reduced funds in government coffers. As a result, nearly all Kazakhstanis and Kyrgyzstanis suffered as everyone was an employee of either a state enterprise or, in the case of teachers, medical personnel, and bureaucrats, the government. Employees of state enterprises, whether privatized or not, lost income. Privatization offered little in the way of job security. Some enterprise managers wrested shares from employees and then stripped the enterprises of assets, putting employees out of work. Some investors, entrepreneurial managers, and employee collectives downsized enterprises in order to make them more internationally competitive. As a result a portion of the employees lost their jobs. For example, Marzhan was laid off from her job in the accounting office of the sovkhoz (state farm) in the village in 1998 as it struggled financially. Of the survey respondents, 19 percent in Kazakhstan and 26 percent in Kyrgyzstan were unemployed,[28] and this was in 2003, after the worst of the economic crisis had passed.

In other cases, workers did not lose their jobs but did not receive their salaries because the enterprises faced the challenges of obtaining inputs and finding buyers. As an employee remaining at the bankrupt sovkhoz in southern Kazakhstan put it, "We receive no pay. We work for free. For a 'thank you.'"[29] Marzhan's husband Temir, an electrician at the sovkhoz, left his job in 1999 because the

---

28. These respondents selected "I am temporarily without a job, am looking for work" to describe why they were unemployed. Others without a job, but not included in this statistic, were students, pensioners, the physically disabled, those caring for a child, or individuals who chose not to work. These figures are preferable to official statistics, which are typically based on those who have registered as unemployed. Unemployment benefits are not widely available in Kazakhstan and Kyrgyzstan, so people have little incentive to register and thus official statistics underreport unemployment. For example, the World Bank reports unemployment figures of 10 percent and 9 percent in Kazakhstan and Kyrgyzstan, respectively, for the same time period. Data are from World Bank, "World Databank," http://databank.worldbank.org/ddp/home.do (accessed December 19, 2013).

29. Author's interview (#159), Kazakhstan, July 19, 2001.

sovkhoz was unable to pay him. In some workplaces in Kazakhstan and Kyrgyzstan, employees were paid with the goods they produced. While employees could use some of the goods they received, in many cases they needed to sell most of them. This was difficult, particularly when an enterprise dominated the labor force in a locale and thus many individuals received the same good. Even employees of the government and state enterprises that were not privatized faced hardship; as government coffers shrunk, the state also delayed payment of salaries or paid workers in goods.

Compared to those working at state enterprises at the time of the collapse, pensioners were no better off. Some people retired early thinking that earning a pension during the economic crisis would be preferable. But the value of pensions fell dramatically because of price liberalization and the resulting inflation in Kyrgyzstan, where pensions were not simultaneously increased. Furthermore, delayed and unpaid pensions have been common in both countries. New and newly privatized companies concerned with their bottom lines failed to contribute to the pension system, and local officials used pension funds to pay other social benefits. Pension reform in the mid-1990s in Kazakhstan and in the late 1990s in Kyrgyzstan mitigated delayed pay and nonpayment problems in the new century, but the size of pensions for many retired people remains too small.[30]

Any money people do earn does not go far, as inflation, fueled by price liberalization, has been steep and many goods and services are no longer free or subsidized. While inflation has tapered off, it saw highs of 1,880 percent in Kazakhstan and 885 percent in Kyrgyzstan in the early 1990s, as noted in Table 4.4. In reaction to the economic crisis and new market reform approach, workplaces—the provider of most benefits in the Soviet era—and local governments curbed goods and services. Or in the case of dissolved enterprises, the enterprises no longer existed to provide benefits. Medical care, medications, utilities, home repairs, day care, and vacations—once highly subsidized—are now expensive. Most people in Kazakhstan and Kyrgyzstan now have to pay for textbooks, heat,

---

30. Kazakhstan's system underwent a transition from pay-as-you-go, where current workers pay from their salaries the pensions of current retirees, to individual retirement accounts into which workers pay from their salaries for their future pensions. Pension reform in Kyrgyzstan involved increasing the retirement age and ending additional pension payments to some categories of people. William Baldridge, "Pension Reform in Kazakhstan," in *Central Asia 2010: Prospects for Human Development*, ed. United Nations Development Programme Regional Bureau for Europe and the CIS (1999), 176–81, here 177; Edward Palmer, "Pension Reform and the Development of Pension Systems: An Evaluation of Work Bank Assistance, Kazakhstan Country Study" (Washington, DC: World Bank, 2007); Edward Palmer, "Pension Reform and the Development of Pension Systems: An Evaluation of Work Bank Assistance, Kyrgyzstan Country Study" (Washington, DC: World Bank, 2007).

TABLE 4.4. Inflation statistics from Kazakhstan and Kyrgyzstan

	KAZAKHSTAN	KYRGYZSTAN
1991	91	85
1992	1,516	855
1993	1,662	772
1994	1,880	229
1995	176	53
1996	39	32
1997	17	23
1998	7	10
1999	8	37
2000	13	19
2001	8	7
2002	6	2
2003	6	3
2004	7	4
2005	8	4
2006	9	6
2007	11	10
2008	17	25
2009	7	7
2010	7	8
2011	8	16
2012	5	3

Source: Years 1991–95 are from International Monetary Fund, "The World Economic Outlook (WEO) Database April 1999," http://www.imf.org/external/pubs/ft/weo/1999/01/data/index.htm. Years 1996–2012 are from World Bank, "World Databank," http://databank.worldbank.org/ddp/home.do.

Note: Neither data set covers the entire time period. Each data set gives the annual percent change in the cost to the average consumer of purchasing a selection of goods and services. The World Economic Outlook information notes that for some transition countries for earlier years a retail price index, instead of a consumer price index, is used; however, further details are not given. The latest data are presented.

and repairs for their children's schools and higher education, whereas these were free in the Soviet era.[31]

With the introduction of market reforms, most people lost their source of income or experienced a precipitous drop in income while also having to pay for more goods and services, of which there is a much broader selection. A resident of a city in central Kazakhstan summarized the change from the Soviet era: "Everything is in stores. Now the problem is money."[32] These challenges match the demands of those who try to obtain government help. Of those who sought as-

---

31. In rural areas the problem is compounded by shortages of goods and services. Many day-care centers, village clubs, stores, schools, and medical clinics have closed in rural areas. Some villages no longer have access to certain utilities because some villagers are unable to pay and the private firms have cut off services to villages rather than provide utilities to a smaller number of people unprofitably.

32. Author's interview (#186), Kazakhstan, June 3, 2001.

sistance from state officials in Kazakhstan and Kyrgyzstan, 83 percent and 52 percent, respectively, identified lack of money as one of their top problems. It is also clear from government officials' accounts in the previous chapter that assistance sought matches outcomes from market reform. These officials described how people request money, credit, and employment because they lack funds.

The characteristics of those who seek help from government officials also support the argument that market reform promotes these interactions. Those who have been most adversely affected by market reform in Kazakhstan and Kyrgyzstan are the individuals most likely to approach government officials. Specifically, those who are unemployed in Kazakhstan and Kyrgyzstan are more likely to seek help from officials. Among individuals who have sought assistance from government officials, 29 percent in Kazakhstan and 40 percent in Kyrgyzstan are unemployed, compared to the adult population unemployment averages of 19 percent and 26 percent, respectively. As a result of market reform without market-enhancing institutions, citizens have economic needs that they hope government officials can meet.

Scarcity of Government Goods and Services

Market reform has also made government resources scarce, so citizens seeking government assistance try to gain an advantage in the competition for state resources by using corrupt practices. The reforms have ended or shrunk formal government programs so fewer resources are available to *raion* and oblast bureaucrats, village leaders, and deputies. Those programs that do exist formally restrict the distribution of resources to individuals who meet narrow requirements in order to manage their scarcity.

Raion and oblast credit programs, as described in the previous chapter, are the governments' response to the new challenges posed by the market economy and the loss of extensive welfare assistance under the Soviet economy. However, there is not enough credit to meet demand, so individuals use illicit means to try to obtain it. The comments from the head of a large government agricultural credit program in Kyrgyzstan illustrate the relationship among these factors well: "We do not have enough money and we have more demand. . . . Some people are offended if they are denied credit and they say 'give me credit because I have this acquaintance.' "[33]

---

33. Author's interview (#127), Kyrgyzstan, 2009.

The number of loans made also indicates that demand has not been met. In Kazakhstan, a country of about fifteen million, and Kyrgyzstan, a country of about five million people, approximately three million people in each were poor at the time I conducted the surveys. The numbers of rural residents in the countries were approximately six million and three million, respectively.[34] The most productive credit program has been the government bank program targeted at rural areas in Kyrgyzstan, yet it has not helped the three million rural residents in the area. This bank has made approximately ninety thousand loans in five years, and many of the loans are to repeat customers. Other programs in Kyrgyzstan fall far short of these numbers. In Kazakhstan the Agriculture Financial Support Fund established to help low-income residents and small businesses in rural areas met only 2 percent of demand for microcredit.[35] The national microcredit program in Kazakhstan has assisted 890 people in a southern oblast where I worked and 150 people each year for a few years in a central, more urbanized oblast where I worked. Yet these oblasts each have approximately one million residents.[36] Other programs, described in the preceding chapter, have lent to considerably fewer people. In the southern oblast in Kazakhstan only six people in three years have borrowed through the communal collateral fund. In the same oblast, approximately two hundred people applied for the eighteen-month loans, but only twenty people received them. Steep competition is typical; one hundred applications for fourteen loans is not uncommon, according to an official with an oblast committee for the support of small and medium-size business also in the south.

Besides having the resources to offer only small numbers of loans, government credit programs tend to have liberal requirements in some respects and restrictive requirements in others, thus effectively excluding much of the populations from borrowing. For example, the program through the national bank in Kyrgyzstan offers more options for collateral and thus is less restrictive in this respect, but it prefers that its borrowers have another business as a further protection. Similarly, the oblast agricultural credit program in southern Kazakhstan that lends for eighteen months has a longer period but requires another business, such as a store, on the side. The microcredit provided through the oblasts nationwide and the national fund in Kazakhstan have the benefit of being inter-

---

34. I calculated these figures using the World Bank's population numbers, rural residence data, and statistics on the percentage of the population living on less than 2 USD per day. The rural residence figures are for 2003 and the poverty statistics are for 2002 because none was available for 2003. World Bank, "World Databank."

35. Shoplan Gaisina, "Credit Policies for Kazakhstani Agriculture," *Central Asian Survey* 30, no. 2 (2011): 257–74, here 265.

36. "Regions of Kazakhstan, 2005–2009" (Astana: Agency of Statistics of the Republic of Kazakhstan, 2010), 1–24, here 5.

est free, but the money must be returned in one year. Numerous government credit programs in Kazakhstan are targeted only at large-scale agricultural concerns, instead of medium and small ones.[37] Restrictions are a way for the governments to manage scarce credit, but these restrictions as well as the scarcity encourage people to engage in corruption to try to obtain credit.

Government officials at other levels also do not have abundant resources. Village leaders have little national money and tax revenue at their disposal, but they can direct state benefits, state and nonstate credit, and charitable assistance and they can obtain donations. For these reasons, villagers have incentives to propose a corrupt exchange to village leaders.

Money, credit, and employment from deputies to representative bodies are also scarce. Deputies can secure state resources if they have another government job and they can distribute their personal wealth if they have a successful business. Yet many deputies do not have access to such resources, and those that do have insufficient resources to support all of their constituents. This scarcity encourages citizens to promise their political support to deputies in exchange for goods from either the state or deputies' own property.

Government Message

Besides scarcity, the governments' message about market reform also gives individuals an incentive to engage in corruption. Through the media the governments of Kazakhstan and Kyrgyzstan emphasize that they are market reformers. In their direct interactions with individuals, government officials in both countries convey the message that because of these market reforms individuals can no longer turn to them for assistance. Individuals, thus, have an incentive to offer bribes, use personal connections, and promise political support to try to circumvent this new philosophy.

A content analysis of state newspapers highlights the governments' market reform message. Approximately one-third of the thirty issues of *Kazakhstanskaia pravda* and *Slovo Kyrgyzstana* published immediately prior to the surveys included at least one article about market reform.[38] Deregulation was a popular topic, with articles on the importance of the market determining wages, the decreased role of the government, and the state's responsibility only to ensure safety in the production process. Articles also emphasized that work in the private sector and

---

37. Gaisina, "Credit Policies for Kazakhstani Agriculture."

38. This calculation does not include laws published in the newspapers.

assistance from local and foreign nongovernmental organizations were solutions to poverty.[39]

Government officials' and citizens' accounts of their interactions with each other make it clear that individuals are, in fact, responsible for their own economic well-being. Consider, for example, the remark of a minister of labor and social protection in Kazakhstan, Alikhan Baimenov: "People should become less accustomed to state paternalism."[40] He elaborated that the government has given more responsibility to the private sector and people should be more independent. This message comes not only from officials in the capital but also from those at lower levels. The head of a *raion*-level social assistance office in Kazakhstan explained that "In the USSR everyone relied on the state. Recently people have begun to understand that without action you cannot do anything, and they have begun to work. You cannot count on anyone. You cannot count on some uncle to help you. . . . You can work a piece of land, take care of a herd, trade, but you cannot sit around. You are on your own."[41] The message that the governments are now market reformers reaches down to the village *akims* and is central in their discussions with villagers. The leader of the village in southern Kazakhstan remarked, "We tell them each person needs to earn money on his own. . . . Earlier the state fed and clothed them, but now they are on their own."[42] Even the head of a government unemployment center in a central city of Kazakhstan conveyed the new philosophy: "During the transition to a market economy, we need to wake up people who are accustomed to receiving benefits."[43] The message is the same in Kyrgyzstan.

In both countries average citizens have, in many cases grudgingly, accepted this message. A farmer in Kyrgyzstan said, "The government cannot help us. We rely on ourselves. We feed the government. . . . You can only survive on your own with your own family."[44] However, a Russian woman in the village in Kazakhstan, Irina, noted that the government's strategy of devolving responsibility

---

39. Gul'banu Aimanbetova, "Bol'she ekonomicheskoi svobody" [Greater Economic Freedom], *Kazakhstanskaia pravda*, October 21, 2003; "Kakoi byt' oplate truda?" [What Is to Become of Wages?], *Kazakhstanskaia pravda*, October 25, 2003; T. Karateeva, "Vyvesti biznes iz-pod pressa" [To Take Business out from under the Press], *Slovo Kyrgyzstana*, October 14, 2003; L. Pavlovich, "Shag k svobode. Ekonomicheskoi" [Step toward Freedom. Economic], *Slovo Kyrgyzstana*, October 31, 2003; Natal'ia Todorova, "Glavnoe sredstvo bor'by s nishchetoi" [The Main Way of Fighting Poverty], *Kazakhstanskaia pravda*, October 4, 2003; "Za strokoi poslaniia Prezidenta Kyrgyzskoi Respubliki. Rynochnoi ekonomike-sotsial'noe litso" [Beyond the Lines of the Kyrgyz Republic President's Message. To Market Reform: A Social Face], *Slovo Kyrgyzstana*, October 28, 2003.

40. Author's interview (#261), Kazakhstan, May 21, 2001.

41. Author's interview (#164), Kazakhstan, July 24, 2001.

42. Author's interview (#172), Kazakhstan, July 26, 2001.

43. Author's interview (#185), Kazakhstan, June 1, 2001.

44. Author's interview (#128), Kyrgyzstan, May 30, 2009.

for welfare sometimes fails: "The state has distanced itself . . . we live on our own strengths, no one else's. . . . The government cannot be counted on for assistance but now not everyone can help a neighbor."[45] Because the governments are market reformers they are not receptive to requests for help. "We need the state to provide subsidies, but officials do not want to do this because they say this would be biased against the market," a deputy director of an oblast agricultural department in Kazakhstan said, explaining the farming community's need for state assistance.[46] Through the media and their conversations with government officials, citizens in Kazakhstan and Kyrgyzstan learn that market reform has brought an end to extensive state welfare guarantees and conclude that they have to compete for the remaining state resources.

The Nonmarket Reformer Uzbekistan

A comparison between Uzbekistan and Kazakhstan and Kyrgyzstan bolsters the claim that the presence or absence of market reform accounts for different levels of corruption. In Uzbekistan individuals have been less likely than their counterparts in Kazakhstan and Kyrgyzstan to engage in corruption for basic state goods and services. Individuals' relationship with the state in Uzbekistan has been characterized chiefly by a guarantee of state goods and services, whereas in Kazakhstan and Kyrgyzstan the relationship has been a competition for resources often involving corrupt practices. At first glance the lower level of corruption in Uzbekistan is surprising, considering the many ways in which Uzbekistan resembles Kazakhstan and Kyrgyzstan. However, Uzbekistan has not undertaken market reform.

From the survey data it is evident that individuals in Uzbekistan typically receive basic state provisions without competing. People in Uzbekistan do seek assistance from government officials. In fact, the proportions across the three countries—16 percent, 23 percent, and 19 percent—for Kazakhstan, Kyrgyzstan, and Uzbekistan, respectively, are similar.[47] However, survey respondents in Uzbekistan described their state as a guarantor of goods and services more than as an

---

45. Author's interview (#158), Kazakhstan, July 19, 2001.

46. Author's interview (#145), Kazakhstan, July 4, 2001.

47. These findings are consistent with those of Scott Radnitz. He found that for a loan people in Uzbekistan were hypothetically more likely to turn to a state, rather than a nonstate, entity than were people in Kyrgyzstan. Because Uzbekistan has not undertaken market reform but Kyrgyzstan has, Uzbekistan has many more state institutions. The statistic I present here includes only government officials, not other state institutions, such as state banks and state agricultural and industrial enterprises. Scott Radnitz, *Weapons of the Wealthy: Predatory Regimes and Elite-Led Protests in Central Asia* (Ithaca, NY: Cornell University Press, 2010).

arena for competition. By contrast, respondents in Kazakhstan and Kyrgyzstan described the state as foremost an arena of competition. The survey finding that competition for state resources is less common in Uzbekistan than in Kazakhstan and Kyrgyzstan suggests that corruption for basic goods and services is also less common in Uzbekistan. In other words, not competing for state resources precludes the possibility that one is using illicit techniques to gain limited goods and services from government officials. This logic is further substantiated by the in-depth interviews and observational studies in Kazakhstan and Kyrgyzstan. These direct measures of corruption demonstrate that bribes, personal connections, and promises of political support are the techniques used in this competition in Kazakhstan and Kyrgyzstan.

In Uzbekistan the main characterization of the state is as a guarantor of goods and services, not as an arena for competition as is the case in Kazakhstan and Kyrgyzstan. Whereas 51 percent of survey respondents in Uzbekistan characterized citizens as using state resources, the figures were only 28 percent and 34 percent for Kazakhstan and Kyrgyzstan, respectively (see Table 4.5). Only 46 percent of respondents in Uzbekistan strongly agreed or agreed with the description of their state as an arena for competition. By contrast, 70 percent of respondents in Kazakhstan and 61 percent in Kyrgyzstan did. The social contract characterization, where citizens pay taxes in return for state services, also resonated more in Uzbekistan. Forty-three percent of respondents in Uzbekistan but only 28 percent in Kazakhstan and, more similarly, 36 percent in Kyrgyzstan, selected this option.

The greater resonance of the state-as-a-guarantor description in Uzbekistan reflects the more extensive array of state goods and services that Uzbekistanis have received from their government in the independence period. Throughout much of the independence period, the government of Uzbekistan has maintained state enterprises, provided guaranteed inputs and orders, and subsidized consumer goods, such as energy.[48] These goods and services have been guaranteed; citizens did not have to compete for them. Moreover, individuals who seek assistance from state officials more commonly approach them about access to medical specialists in local hospitals and family turmoil, as in the Soviet era, rather than about a lack of money.[49] Only 36 percent of respondents who sought

---

48. It is important to note that since the survey was conducted in Uzbekistan in 2003, the state has increasingly failed to provide guaranteed goods and services. Uzbekistanis have experienced growing wage arrears, delayed pensions, and energy shortages in recent years. On the government's earlier provision of necessities, see EBRD, "Transition Report 2003: Integration and Regional Cooperation" (London, 2003); Gregory Gleason, *Markets and Politics in Central Asia: Structural Reform and Political Change* (New York: Routledge, 2003).

49. At the time of the survey respondents were also concerned about an outbreak of foot-and-mouth disease in livestock.

TABLE 4.5. Citizens' relationships with states: Guarantor, arena of competition, social contract (percentage of respondents, rounded)

	CITIZENS USE STATE RESOURCES, SUCH AS MEDICAL SERVICES AND EDUCATION	CITIZENS COMPETE TO POSSESS STATE RESOURCES, SUCH AS JOBS	CITIZENS EXPECT THAT THE STATE WILL PROVIDE SERVICES IF THEY PAY THEIR TAXES
UZBEKISTAN			
Strongly agree or agree	51	46	43
Somewhat agree/disagree	28	21	23
Disagree or strongly disagree	16	14	20
Difficult to answer	4	19	14
Decline to answer	1	1	1
TOTAL (rounded)	100	100	100
KAZAKHSTAN			
Strongly agree or agree	28	70	28
Somewhat agree/disagree	36	13	29
Disagree or strongly disagree	35	11	35
Difficult to answer	2	6	8
Decline to answer	1	1	1
TOTAL (rounded)	100	100	100
KYRGYZSTAN			
Strongly agree or agree	34	61	36
Somewhat agree/disagree	35	20	24
Disagree or strongly disagree	29	12	32
Difficult to answer	3	7	8
Decline to answer	<1	<1	<1
TOTAL (rounded)	100	100	100

Note: $n = 1{,}500$ for each country. Percentages for each country do not necessarily total to 100 because they are rounded. For each country the difference in percentages between the most popular statement and each of the less popular statements is statistically significant at the .001 level, meaning that such a difference would be observed due to random chance approximately .1 percent of the time.

assistance from state officials in Uzbekistan identified lack of money as one of their main problems, whereas the proportions were 83 percent for Kazakhstan and 52 percent for Kyrgyzstan. Similarly, in Uzbekistan 20 percent of those who sought assistance from government officials are unemployed, and this figure is close to the unemployed proportion of the population (17 percent). As noted previously the proportions of those who sought assistance who are unemployed were 10 percent and 14 percent higher than the overall unemployment figures in Kazakhstan and Kyrgyzstan, respectively. Uzbekistan's continued provision of state goods and services and its citizens' less severe problems with money and unemployment underscore that market reform, more than the Soviet economic collapse, reduced government assistance and exacerbated economic challenges in Kazakhstan and Kyrgyzstan. After all, Uzbekistan, like Kazakhstan and Kyrgyzstan, also suffered from the collapse of the Soviet economy but did not undertake market reform.

TABLE 4.6. Market reforms and their absence

	NONREFORMER	REFORMERS	
	UZBEKISTAN	**KAZAKHSTAN**	**KYRGYZSTAN**
LIBERALIZATION			
Current account convertibility	limited	full	full
Interest rate liberalization	limited	full	full
Trade liberalization	limited	almost full	almost full
Price liberalization	limited	almost full	almost full
PRIVATIZATION			
Small firms	limited	full	full
Land	limited	full[a]	full[b]
Private pensions	no	yes	yes
DEREGULATION			
Wages deregulated	no	yes	yes

Source: European Bank for Reconstruction and Development, "Transition indicators by country," at "Forecasts, Macro Data, Transition Indicators," http://www.ebrd.com/pages/research/economics/data/macro.shtml#t. The data are from 2003, the year of my survey research.

[a] Land is fully tradable except by foreigners.
[b] Land is fully tradable; however, there have been difficulties implementing this policy.

According to standard measures of market reform, the government of Uzbekistan has done nothing or only very little. As Table 4.6 shows, current account convertibility is limited. The government has done little to liberalize interest rates, trade, and prices. Privatization of small firms and land has occurred on only a limited scale. Private pensions do not exist and wages remain regulated. In the past few years the government slightly expanded small-scale privatization and liberalized foreign exchange and trade, but not enough to merit a different characterization.[50]

Uzbekistan has not undertaken market reform, but the two conditions of the argument—a legacy of significant state economic intervention and an absence or weakness of market-enhancing institutions—are present. As a former republic of the Soviet Union, Uzbekistan was also subject to the Soviet party-state's control of the economy. In this respect, it was not different from Kazakhstan and Kyrgyzstan. Also like its neighbors, Uzbekistan has not actively developed market-enhancing institutions. The World Bank and International Finance Corporation reported that Uzbekistan has not had a private credit registry or public credit bureau for most of its independence period. From 2008 to 2011 less than 10 percent of the population was covered by either type of institution with the number jumping to approximately 17 percent in 2013.[51] The EBRD describes

50. The latest data available for interest rate liberalization are from 2010. See "Transition indicators by country," in EBRD, "Transition Report 2009: Transition in Crisis."
51. International Finance Corporation and Bank, "Doing Business: Measuring Business Regulations," http://www.doingbusiness.org/custom-query (accessed December 19, 2013).

TABLE 4.7. Market and societal actors and institutions from whom citizens have sought assistance in the past year

	UZBEKISTAN	KAZAKHSTAN	KYRGYZSTAN
MARKET ACTORS			
Bank	1	3	1
Current employer	5	4	3
Former employer	2	4	2
Local company where you don't work	<1	3	<1
Foreign company where you don't work	<1	<1	0
SOCIETAL ACTORS			
Religious institution or leader	<1	1	2
Local, private charitable organization	1	1	2
Foreign charity	<1	<1	1
Labor union	1	1	1
Respected male elder	13	1	4
Educational establishment	<1	<1	2

Note: $n = 1,200$ for Kazakhstan, 1,199 for Kyrgyzstan, and 1,170 for Uzbekistan. A portion of the 1,500 respondents in each country claimed that they had no problems or that describing their problems was too difficult and thus some respondents were not asked this question about seeking assistance.

Uzbekistan as having almost no competition policy from the time of the surveys to 2013.[52]

The absence of market reform and the presence of the two conditions in Uzbekistan, as well as the lower level of competition for basic state goods and services in the country, support the argument that market reform in the context of the two conditions promotes corruption. Evidence of Uzbekistanis' weak reliance on market and societal actors further corroborates this account. The lower level of competition for state resources in Uzbekistan is, in fact, because the government continued to guarantee goods and services, rather than because market and societal actors in Uzbekistan offer an alternative to the state. The percentages of Uzbekistanis who have sought assistance from market and societal actors are comparable to the percentages of Kazakhstanis and Kyrgyzstanis who have done so (see Table 4.7). The legacy of state economic intervention and the absence of market-enhancing institutions has hindered the development of market and societal alternatives in Kazakhstan and Kyrgyzstan. In Uzbekistan, where market reform has not taken place, the continuing state economic intervention likely reduces the resources available to market and social actors as the legacy of intervention in Kazakhstan and Kyrgyzstan has.

The only exception in terms of reliance on market and societal actors is that more Uzbekistanis turn to respected male elders than people in Kazakhstan and

---

52. See "Transition Indicators by Country," in EBRD, "Transition Report 2009"; EBRD, "Transition Report 2013: Stuck in Transition?"

Kyrgyzstan do. This is explained by a few villages and small cities in Uzbekistan where many people have turned to respected male elders. Excluding these locations brings the results in line with Kyrgyzstan's. People in these locations in Uzbekistan also turned to government officials at rates consistent with or higher than the country average, indicating that elders were not an alternative to the state. Unlike these few pockets of likely resource-rich male elders, the state guarantee of goods and services can explain lower levels of corruption for everyday needs throughout Uzbekistan. In sum, the contrast between Uzbekistan and Kazakhstan and Kyrgyzstan demonstrates that the outcome of interest— corruption to meet everyday needs—is weak where the causal factor—market reform—is absent.

Alternative Explanations

Other theories of corruption offer valuable insights into illicit behavior, but they cannot account for why corruption to meet everyday needs is more common in Kazakhstan and Kyrgyzstan than Uzbekistan. The other explanations examined below are drawn from the limited number of studies of petty corruption as well as investigations of grand corruption. They include institutional, economic, and cultural theories.

Institutional Explanations

Returning to the discussion of the overbearing state and weak state capacity theories,[53] we find that these explanations do not shed light on the difference in Central Asia. As republics in the former Soviet Union, Kazakhstan, Kyrgyzstan, and Uzbekistan were all part of an "overbearing state." Today standard measures of state regulation, the amount of time and the number of procedures needed to establish a business, cannot account for the difference.[54] The time required to complete the procedures to operate a business is lower in Uzbekistan than in Kazakhstan, but is similar to Kyrgyzstan in 2013. In 2003 Uzbekistan was higher on this measure than both of the other countries. Uzbekistan fell between Kazakhstan and Kyrgyzstan in terms of the number of procedures to register a business in 2013. In 2003 Uzbekistan was lower than Kazakhstan but similar to

---

53. See footnotes four and five in chapter one.

54. Simeon Djankov et al., "The Regulation of Entry," *Quarterly Journal of Economics* 117, no. 1 (2002), 1–37.

Kyrgyzstan on this measure (see Table 4.8). Thus, state regulation does not seem to be a plausible explanation. Moreover, designating state regulation as a cause of corruption is questionable as it could just as easily be a symptom. Government officials already engaged in corruption could create additional state regulations to enable illicit exchanges. Weak state capacity is also an unsatisfying explanation. With independence, each country lost state capacity as resources from Moscow declined, trade with other former republics diminished, and chaos ensued in the unexpected shift from provinces to sovereign states.[55]

A second group of institutional theories of corruption focuses on the importance of democratic institutions, but these also fail to explain the greater corruption in Kazakhstan and Kyrgyzstan. Political parties are one democratic institution that has garnered significant attention, beginning with Martin Shefter's work in the 1970s. Shefter argued that clientelist parties were more likely to develop when the introduction of democratic institutions preceded the professionalization of the bureaucracy.[56] However, Kazakhstan, Kyrgyzstan, and Uzbekistan were all subject to the same sequencing of bureaucratization and party-building. Each inherited the remnants of the Soviet bureaucracy while trying to develop a new bureaucracy for a sovereign state and witnessing the emergence of a multiparty system.

Since Shefter's work, scholars, including Herbert Kitschelt and Steven Wilkinson, Conor O'Dwyer, and Anna Grzymała-Busse have identified weak party competition as an explanation for party clientelism, patronage, and material gain from state assets, respectively.[57] Because party competition is weak, as defined by

---

55. Martha Brill Olcott, *Central Asia's New States: Independence, Foreign Policy, and Regional Security* (Washington, DC: United States Institute of Peace Press, 1996), 4–5, 9; Richard W. T. Pomfret, *The Economies of Central Asia* (Princeton, NJ: Princeton University Press, 1995), 5.

56. Martin Shefter, "Party and Patronage: Germany, England, and Italy," *Politics and Society* 7, no. 4 (1977), 403–51.

57. O'Dwyer's examination of patronage focuses on parties' distribution of state jobs. Grzymała-Busse investigates how parties enrich themselves by staffing state offices and thus controlling fiscal resources, by privatizing state entities and establishing new agencies, and by hindering the development of government oversight and control institutions. Other works, such as those by Heidenheimer, Holmes, and Scott, have mentioned the influence of electoral competition. Anna Grzymała-Busse, *Rebuilding Leviathan: Party Competition and State Exploitation in Post-Communist Democracies* (Cambridge: Cambridge University Press, 2007); Arnold J. Heidenheimer, "Parties, Campaign Finance and Political Corruption: Tracing Long-Term Comparative Dynamics," in *Political Corruption: Concepts and Contexts*, ed. Arnold J. Heidenheimer and Michael Johnston (New Brunswick, NJ: Transaction, 2002), 761–76; Leslie Holmes, *Rotten States? Corruption, Post-Communism, and Neoliberalism* (Durham, NC: Duke University Press, 2006), 188; Conor O'Dwyer, *Runaway State-Building: Patronage Politics and Democratic Development* (Baltimore, MD: Johns Hopkins University Press, 2006); James C. Scott, "Corruption, Machine Politics, and Political Change," *American Political Science Review* 63, no. 4 (1969): 1142–58, here 1143.

TABLE 4.8. State regulation

| | MARKET REFORMERS | | | | NONMARKET REFORMER | |
| | KAZAKHSTAN | | KYRGYZSTAN | | UZBEKISTAN | |
	2003	2013	2003	2013	2003	2013
Time required to complete procedures to operate a business (days)[a]	26	12	21	8	29	9
Procedures to register a business (number)[b]	10	6	9	2	8	4

Source: World Bank, "World Databank," http://databank.worldbank.org/ddp/home.do. The latest data are provided.

[a] According to the World Bank, "the [t]ime required to start a business is the number of calendar days needed to complete the procedures to legally operate a business. If a procedure can be speeded up at additional cost, the fastest procedure, independent of cost, is chosen."

[b] The World Bank Databank site states, "Start-up procedures are those required to start a business, including interactions to obtain necessary permits and licenses and to complete all inscriptions, verifications, and notifications to start operations. Data are for businesses with specific characteristics of ownership, size, and type of production."

these scholars,[58] in each of the Central Asian countries, these explanations are also not illuminating. For example, in each country, citizens and candidates have strong incentives to find supporters for their side in national elections, but generally not in local elections, where offices involve little responsibility and offer even fewer resources. Both the national and subnational candidates are typically "local notables" with a minimal or no platform, so they do not present clear preferences. In some cases they are simply fake candidates running at the behest of incumbents to make elections appear democratic. True opposition candidates encounter significant obstacles to winning: incumbents, in some cases backed by a "party of power," wield administrative resources, such as state funds, media control, sanctions by inspectors, and threats of job loss. In none of the countries has there been a "clear, plausible, and critical governing alternative,"[59] to use Grzymała-Busse's terms, and thus party competition cannot explain the variation in corruption.

---

58. Herbert Kitschelt and Steven Wilkinson define party systems as competitive "when citizens and politicians have strong incentives to try hard to win supporters at the margin for one or the other partisan camp." Herbert Kitschelt and Steven Wilkinson, "Citizen-Politician Linkages: An Introduction," in *Patrons, Clients, and Policies: Patterns of Democratic Accountability and Political Competition*, ed. Kitschelt and Wilkinson (Cambridge: Cambridge University Press, 2007), 1–49, here 29. O'Dwyer considers there to be party competition when there is no dominant party and there is a "manageable number of stable parties with familiar coalition-building preferences." O'Dwyer, *Runaway State-Building*, 7. For Grzymała-Busse what matters is "opposition parties that offer a clear, plausible, and critical governing alternative that threatens the governing coalition with replacement." Grzymała-Busse, *Rebuilding Leviathan*, 1.

59. Grzymała-Busse, *Rebuilding Leviathan*, 1.

TABLE 4.9. Political rights and civil liberties ratings

	KAZAKHSTAN		KYRGYZSTAN		UZBEKISTAN	
	POLITICAL RIGHTS	**CIVIL LIBERTIES**	**POLITICAL RIGHTS**	**CIVIL LIBERTIES**	**POLITICAL RIGHTS**	**CIVIL LIBERTIES**
1991	5	4	5	4	6	5
1992	5	5	4	2	6	6
1993	6	4	5	3	7	7
1994	6	5	4	3	7	7
1995	6	5	4	4	7	7
1996	6	5	4	4	7	6
1997	6	5	4	4	7	6
1998	6	5	5	5	7	6
1999	6	5	5	5	7	6
2000	6	5	6	5	7	6
2001	6	5	6	5	7	6
2002	6	5	6	5	7	6
2003	6	5	6	5	7	6
2004	6	5	6	5	7	6
2005	6	5	6	5	7	6
2006	6	5	5	4	7	7
2007	6	5	5	4	7	7
2008	6	5	5	4	7	7
2009	6	5	5	4	7	7
2010	6	5	6	5	7	7
2011	6	5	5	5	7	7
2012	6	5	5	5	7	7
2013	6	5	5	5	7	7

Source: "Country Ratings and Status, FIW 1973–2013" (Freedom House), available from http://www
.freedomhouse.org/.

Note: Ratings range from 1 to 7, with 7 being the least freedom.

Another line of reasoning about democratic institutions suggests that respect for civil liberties can reduce corruption by enabling independent media, watchdog groups, and opposition forces to check government officials.[60] However, Kazakhstan and Kyrgyzstan, the countries with more corruption to meet everyday needs, are also the countries where the governments have shown greater respect for civil liberties and political rights. From independence in 1991 to 2013, Kazakhstan and Kyrgyzstan have consistently scored better on Freedom House's rating of civil liberties, which include freedom of expression and association, and political liberties, which include the right to join a political party (see Table 4.9).

---

60. Alícia Adserá, Carles Boix, and Mark Payne, "Are You Being Served? Political Accountability and Quality of Government," *Journal of Law Economics and Organization* 19, no. 2 (2003), 445–90; Aymo Brunetti and Beatrice Weder, "A Free Press Is Bad News for Corruption," *Journal of Public Economics* 87, no. 7–8 (2003), 1801–24; Holmes, *Rotten States?* 186–87; Simona Piattoni, "Clientelism in Historical and Comparative Perspective," in *Clientelism, Interests, and Democratic Representation: The European Experience in Historical and Comparative Perspective*, ed. Piattoni (Cambridge: Cambridge University Press, 2001), 1–30, here 17.

Others have suggested that the introduction of democratic institutions can encourage corruption. One idea is that the establishment of an electoral system leads politicians to engage in illicit practices to fund their campaigns.[61] Another idea is that the political liberalization process itself is to blame. Much of the logic about political liberalization mirrors the logic regarding economic liberalization: confusion over new procedures facilitates corruption because citizens do not know their rights; officials may use corrupt means to ensure their own survival; and officials may block new reforms if they benefit from the status quo.[62] Kazakhstan, Kyrgyzstan, and Uzbekistan all experienced political liberalization in the late Soviet and early independence periods. Social and political organizations and media unaffiliated with the Communist Party were allowed, multicandidate elections were held, and restrictions on personal freedoms including speech and travel were reduced. So, this explanation does not account for the difference in corruption. Scholars have also argued that certain institutions, namely, presidential systems instead of parliamentary ones, are more conducive to corruption,[63] but all three Central Asian states have had presidential systems for all or nearly all of their independence periods.[64]

Theories about democratic institutions as well as a host of other institutional theories point to decentralization as a cause of corruption. The idea that decentralization contributes to corruption is not universally accepted,[65] but one school

---

61. Gulnaz Sharafutdinova, *Political Consequences of Crony Capitalism inside Russia* (Notre Dame, IN: University of Notre Dame Press, 2010).

62. Alexandra Vacroux, "Regulation and Corruption in Transition: The Case of Russian Pharmaceutical Markets," in *Building a Trustworthy State in Post-Socialist Transition*, ed. János Kornai and Susan Rose-Ackerman (New York: Palgrave Macmillan, 2004), 135–50, here 146.

63. John Gerring and Strom C. Thacker, "Political Institutions and Corruption: The Role of Unitarism and Parliamentarism," *British Journal of Political Science* 34, no. 2 (2004), 233–54; Jana Kunicová and Susan Rose-Ackerman, "Electoral Rules and Constitutional Structures as Constraints on Corruption," *British Journal of Political Science* 35, no. 4 (2005), 573–606; Daniel Lederman, Norman V. Loayza, and Rodrigo R. Soares, "Accountability and Corruption: Political Institutions Matter," *Economics and Politics* 17, no. 1 (2005), 1–35.

64. Kyrgyzstan established a parliamentary system in the winter of 2011.

65. Pranab Bardhan provides a useful review of the literature on this question. Pranab Bardhan, "Corruption and Development: A Review of Issues," in *Political Corruption: Concepts and Contexts*, ed. Arnold J. Heidenheimer and Michael Johnston (New Brunswick, NJ: Transaction, 2002), 321–38. For a sampling of different findings on this topic, see: Ray Fisman and Roberta Gatti, "Decentralization and Corruption: Evidence across Countries," *Journal of Public Economics* 83 (2002), 325–45; Arthur A. Goldsmith, "Slapping the Grasping Hand: Correlates of Political Corruption in Emerging Markets," *American Journal of Economics and Sociology* 58, no. 4 (1999), 865–83; Anwar Shah, "Corruption and Decentralized Public Governance," *World Bank Policy Research Working Paper* 3824 (2006), http://elibrary.worldbank.org/doi/book/10.1596/1813-9450-3824 (accessed December 19, 2013); Andrei Shleifer and Robert W. Vishny, "Corruption," *Quarterly Journal of Economics* 108, no. 3 (1993), 599–617; Daniel Treisman, "The Causes of Corruption: A Cross-National Study," *Journal of Public Economics* 76, no. 3 (2000), 399–457; Daniel Treisman, "Fiscal Decentralization, Governance, and Economic Performance: A Reconsideration," *Economics and Politics* 18, no. 2 (2006), 219–35.

of thought does suggest that by increasing the number of officials who make decisions and have access to public resources, decentralization creates more opportunities for corruption. Moreover, according to this school of thought, central governments have greater difficulty monitoring a larger number of officials, thus hindering corruption prevention and eradication efforts.[66] Decentralization is often a component of democratic reform, so scholars have also attributed corruption to the decentralizing tendencies of democratic transitions and institutions.[67] For example, local elections may provide central party leaders with information and incentives to distribute patronage more effectively to voters in order to ensure that local officials do not operate independently of the party.[68] All of these arguments, however, shed little light on the three Central Asian countries, which have been similar in terms of decentralization, according to the World Bank.[69]

Cultural Explanations

Because the Central Asian countries share many cultural characteristics, cultural theories of corruption offer little help. Of the different types of corruption theories, cultural explanations are the least popular. They are most common to account for corruption in less developed countries, and they are most often advocated by sociologists.[70] Their adherents attribute corruption to present-day culture derived from the precolonial and colonial periods. They view precolonial culture as "traditional" culture and emphasize how hierarchical relationships and the importance of family ties encourage corruption.[71] The pre-Soviet cultures of the territories of present-day Kazakhstan, Kyrgyzstan, and Uzbekistan were

---

66. Goldsmith, "Slapping the Grasping Hand," 878.

67. Christoph H. Stefes, *Understanding Post-Soviet Transitions: Corruption, Collusion and Clientelism* (New York: Palgrave Macmillan, 2006), 55.

68. Anoop Sadanandan, "Patronage and Decentralization: The Politics of Poverty in India," *Comparative Politics* 44, no. 2 (2012), 211–28.

69. World Bank, "Decentralization in the Transition Economies: Challenges and the Road Ahead," 25132 (Washington, DC: World Bank, 2001).

70. Political scientists and economists typically identify institutional and economic causes, and anthropologists historically have not studied corruption. Giorgio Blundo, "Corruption in Africa and the Social Sciences: A Review of the Literature," in *Everyday Corruption and the State: Citizens and Public Officials in Africa*, ed. Giorgio Blundo and Jean-Pierre Olivier de Sardan (New York: Zed, 2006), 15–68, here 25–26; Johann Graf Lambsdorff, "Causes and Consequences of Corruption: What Do We Know from a Cross-Section of Countries?" in Rose-Ackerman, *International Handbook on the Economics of Corruption*, 3–51, here 17.

71. Blundo and Olivier de Sardan, *Everyday Corruption and the State*, 97–98; Bryan W. Husted, "Wealth, Culture, and Corruption," *Journal of International Business Studies* 30, no. 2 (1999), 339–59.

similar in these respects. Although present-day Kazakhstan and Kyrgyzstan were inhabited by nomads and present-day Uzbekistan was home to oasis peoples, all shared hierarchical social structures, including respect for authority and elders, and strong family networks. Vestiges of this traditional culture exist today in each country.[72]

Regarding colonial culture, studies have found less corruption in countries that experienced British rule, perhaps because of British legal culture.[73] None of these Central Asian countries experienced British rule, so this cannot explain corruption. More generally, scholars have highlighted how the practice of ignoring rules imposed by the metropole and stealing from a state viewed as illegitimate encourage independence-era corruption.[74] In the Soviet context, numerous corrupting influences have been identified. These include the hierarchical nature of the communist system, atheist policies, leaders' ability to act with impunity, a focus on goals instead of procedures, a blurring of state and society, an absence of transparency, the primacy of informal institutions over formal ones, and the need to cut through bureaucratic "red tape."[75] Moreover, bribery and personal connections to obtain state goods and services were common in the Soviet Union.[76] Yet Uzbekistan, as well as Kazakhstan and Kyrgyzstan, experienced these Soviet institutions and practices, raising doubt about their explanatory powers in these cases. In Kazakhstan and Kyrgyzstan, the individuals who engage in illicit practices, the targets of their requests, and the goods and services sought have changed since the Soviet era. This indicates that these practices are not a continuation of Soviet-era habits but a new phenomenon that, like market reform, emerged after the Soviet collapse.

---

72. Lucy Earle, "Community Development, 'Tradition' and the Civil Society Strengthening Agenda in Central Asia," *Central Asian Survey* 24, no. 3 (2005): 245–60, here 249, 252; Gregory Gleason, *The Central Asian States: Discovering Independence* (Boulder, CO: Westview Press, 1997), 38; Alisher Ilkhamov, "The Thorny Path of Civil Society in Uzbekistan," *Central Asian Survey* 24, no. 3 (2005): 297–317, here 307; Martha Brill Olcott, "Central Asia: The Reformers Challenge a Traditional Society," in *The Nationalities Factor in Soviet Politics and Society*, ed. Lubomyr Hajda and Mark R. Beissinger (Boulder, CO: Westview Press, 1990), 253–80, here 254, 269.

73. Gerring and Thacker, "Political Institutions and Corruption"; Treisman, "The Causes of Corruption."

74. Blundo, "Corruption in Africa and the Social Sciences," 45–47.

75. Holmes, *Rotten States?* 183–86; Rasma Karklins, *The System Made Me Do It: Corruption in Post-Communist Societies* (Armonk, NY: M. E. Sharpe, 2005), 14–15, 81; Alena V. Ledeneva, *How Russia Really Works: The Informal Practices That Shaped Post-Soviet Politics and Business* (Ithaca, NY: Cornell University Press, 2006), 22.

76. Alena V. Ledeneva, *Russia's Economy of Favours: Blat, Networking, and Informal Exchange* (Cambridge: Cambridge University Press, 1998). Promises of political support in exchange for state goods and services were less evident in the Soviet Union because elections were not competitive and promises of political support are most visible in connection with elections.

The first piece of clarifying evidence shows that those who sought assistance from the Soviet state are not the same individuals who seek government help today. In Kazakhstan 83 percent of survey respondents and in Kyrgyzstan 89 percent who have turned to government officials in the independence period did not seek help from the Soviet state.[77] These percentages cannot be explained on the basis that the respondents were children during the Soviet era. On the contrary, 91 percent and 87 percent of respondents who seek government assistance today responded that they were adults in the Soviet era.

The fact that the targets of citizens' requests have changed also shows that these practices are not a continuation of Soviet era ones. In the Soviet period the most popular state entities to turn to for assistance were places of employment and labor unions. Through official workplaces and the party-controlled labor unions, individuals received state benefits, so it is understandable that they also turned to them for additional help. In Kazakhstan 19 percent and 18 percent of respondents sought help from places of employment and labor unions, respectively, in the Soviet era. The figures were 16 percent and 12 percent, respectively, for Kyrgyzstan. By contrast, in each country only 7 percent turned to Soviet party or government officials. Today, state enterprises and labor unions are rare and government officials instead are the common target of citizens' requests. In Kazakhstan and Kyrgyzstan 4 percent and 3 percent, respectively, had turned to their employer for help in the past year. In each country only 1 percent of survey respondents sought assistance from a labor union.

Finally, individuals today are not seeking the same goods and services from the state as they did in the Soviet era. In the Soviet period an individual was guaranteed a job and basic necessities such as food, so bribes and connections were useful primarily for obtaining higher quality goods and services, such as a better job or better cut of meat.[78] In contemporary Kazakhstan and Kyrgyzstan extensive welfare guarantees do not exist, so bribes, connections, and promises of political support are useful for meeting basic needs, such as a job, credit, and money, which can, in turn, allow one to secure food and clothes.

This evidence that corruption for basic state goods and services today is not a continuation of Soviet practices is particularly important to this argument because it challenges the reverse causal argument—corruption promotes market

---

77. Respondents were asked, "Before 1991 whom did you rely on for help with everyday problems? Choose as many as apply." Respondents received a card with twenty-one actors and institutions listed, including the options to list others and to note "I was a child during the Soviet era." Interviewers read the card aloud. Each country had 1,500 respondents.

78. In the Soviet era, isolated periods of shortages occurred and also certain regions experienced shortages. In these circumstances, bribes and connections were also useful in obtaining basic goods. Ledeneva, *Russia's Economy of Favours.*

reform without market-enhancing institutions. Instead by showing that market reform preceded this corruption for obtaining basic state goods and services, the evidence bolsters the claim of this book that market reform promotes corruption.

A final set of cultural explanations is linked to present-day ethnic composition,[79] low levels of generalized trust,[80] and absence of Protestantism.[81] These explanations also do not illuminate the difference in Central Asia. Theories about ethnicity suggest that corruption, especially clientelist networks, is more likely in multiethnic societies because ethnic divides facilitate their development and endurance. Patrons and clients can develop within an ethnic group and feel greater loyalty to each other than to the national community, including its laws. Each of the three countries examined here has a multiethnic population, as indicated in Table 4.10, so this explanation offers little insight in this instance.[82]

In none of the countries is generalized trust high. Approximately half of all respondents in my survey volunteered that they trusted no one when they were asked to rank a series of market and societal actors from most trusted to least trusted.[83] Protestantism is weak in all three countries as the populations are predominantly Muslim.

Economic Explanations

A final set of explanations focuses on economic causes of corruption. Scholars have attributed corruption to poverty, economic underdevelopment, inequality,

---

79. Elmer E. Cornwell Jr., "Bosses, Machines, and Ethnic Groups," *Annals of the American Academy of Political and Social Science* 353 (1964), 27–39; Samuel P. Huntington, "Modernization and Corruption," in Heidenheimer and Johnston, *Political Corruption*, 253–63, here 257; Kitschelt and Wilkinson, "Citizen-Politician Linkages." Kanchan Chandra's work, which examines the interaction between ethnicity and clientelism, focuses on a different relationship: how clientelism can encourage ethnic voting. Kanchan Chandra, *Why Ethnic Parties Succeed: Patronage and Ethnic Head Counts in India* (Cambridge: Cambridge University Press, 2004).

80. Christian Bjørnskov and Marin Paldam, "Corruption Trends," in *The New Institutional Economics of Corruption*, ed. Johann Lambsdorff, Markus Taube, and Matthias Schramm (New York: Routledge, 2005), 59–75; Stephen D. Morris and Joseph L. Klesner, "Corruption and Trust: Theoretical Considerations and Evidence from Mexico," *Comparative Political Studies* 43, no. 10 (2010), 1258–85.

81. Seymour Martin Lipset and Gabriel Salman Lenz, "Corruption, Culture, and Markets," in *Culture Matters: How Values Shape Human Progress*, ed. Samuel P. Huntington and Lawrence E. Harrison (New York: Basic Books, 2000), 112–24, here 120–22; Treisman, "The Causes of Corruption," 427–28.

82. None of the theories indicates that the greater share of the titular ethnic group in Uzbekistan versus the other countries should have an effect on corruption.

83. The actors were one's employer, a respected male elder, government organs, religious institution or leader, charitable organization, and a company where one does not work.

TABLE 4.10. Ethnic composition

	KAZAKHSTAN		KYRGYZSTAN		UZBEKISTAN[a]	
	1999	**2009**	**1999**	**2009**	**1996**	**2009**
Titular	53	63	65	71	80	NA
Uzbek	3	3	14	14	(see Titular)	NA
Russian	30	24	13	8	6	NA
Other	14	10	8	7	14	NA

Source: Figures for Kazakhstan and Kyrgyzstan for 2009 are based on national census results: Agency of Statistics of the Republic of Kazakhstan, "The Results of the National Population Census in 2009," 2010, http://www.eng.stat.kz/perepis_nasl; National Statistical Committee of the Kyrgyz Republic, "Population and Housing Census of the Kyrgyz Republic of 2009 Book I: Main social and demographic characteristics of population and number of housing units," 2009, http://unstats.un.org/unsd/demographic/sources/census /2010_phc/Kyrgyzstan/A5-2PopulationAndHousingCensusOfTheKyrgyzRepublicOf2009.pdf. The latest data are presented. The 1999 figures for Kazakhstan and Kyrgyzstan are based on the 1999 census. For Kazakhstan and Uzbekistan, they are from Central Intelligence Agency, "The World Factbook 2002," 2002, https://www.cia .gov/library/publications/download/download-2002. The figures for Kyrgyzstan are available from the National Statistical Committee publication cited above.

[a] Uzbekistan did not conduct a census in 2009. The 1996 figures are demographers' estimates based on the 1989 census results.

abundant natural resources, trade isolationism, and a large supply of international funds. None of these explains the difference in Central Asia.

Poor people, according to existing literature, use corruption to survive.[84] They must pay bribes for goods and services that the privileged can obtain for free,[85] and they tend to trade their votes for immediate concrete benefits instead of future intangible policy changes.[86] Economic underdevelopment promotes corruption by increasing poverty and also by increasing inequality.[87] One theory is that inequality facilitates corruption by reducing trust across groups and increasing trust within groups.[88] Another idea is that those who are well-off sell

---

84. Tatiana Kostadinova, *Political Corruption in Eastern Europe: Politics after Communism* (Boulder, CO: Lynne Rienner, 2012); Piattoni, "Clientelism in Historical and Comparative Perspective," 17; Alice Sindzingre, "A Comparative Analysis of African and East Asian Corruption," in Heidenheimer and Johnson, *Political Corruption: Concepts and Contexts*, 441–60, here 452.

85. Claus Offe, "Political Corruption: Conceptual and Practical Issues," in Kornai and Rose-Ackerman, *Building a Trustworthy State in Post-Socialist Transition*, 77–99, here 86.

86. Kitschelt, "Linkages between Citizens and Politicians in Democratic Politics," 857; Kitschelt and Wilkinson, "Citizen-Politician Linkages," 25; Scott, "Corruption, Machine Politics, and Political Change," 1150–51.

87. Treisman, "The Causes of Corruption." For a review of studies that have found correlations between economic underdevelopment and corruption, see Benjamin A. Olken and Rohini Pande, "Corruption in Developing Countries," *Annual Review of Economics* 4 (2012), 479–509. An economic underdevelopment argument about firms, instead of individuals, finds that firms engage in bribery instead of lobbying when their level of capital is low, a situation more common in poorer countries. Bärd Harstad and Jakob Svensson, "Bribes, Lobbying, and Development," *American Political Science Review* 105, no. 1 (2011), 46–63.

88. Eric M. Uslaner, *Corruption, Inequality, and the Rule of Law: The Bulging Pocket Makes the Easy Life* (Cambridge: Cambridge University Press, 2008).

access to privileges and goods to the lower classes, particularly in democracies where outright oppression to maximize one's wealth is not acceptable. The greater the inequality the more difficult it is for lower classes to monitor the wealthy and hold them accountable and thus to uncover and punish corruption.[89] Economic underdevelopment has also been linked to corruption through the idea of weak state capacity. A poorer state cannot prevent, investigate, and punish corruption as effectively as a wealthier state, according to the argument. Furthermore, studies have found that poorer governments pay their employees less, which increases bureaucrats' incentives to engage in illicit activities.[90]

The remaining economic explanations focus more on grand corruption, especially between government and big business, but they are worth considering briefly. From the resource curse literature and corruption studies, we know that resource wealth is correlated with corruption. Scholars have argued that abundant natural resources create opportunities for government officials to provide rents, meaning rights to produce or trade, such as drilling permits, in return for payment.[91] Countries less open to international trade further exacerbate this problem because they strengthen domestic monopolies, enabling government officials to grant more rents.[92] International capital whether in the form of investments in natural resource extraction or other industries, as well as foreign aid, may also increase corruption by providing additional opportunities for government officials to enrich themselves.[93]

These economic explanations do not, however, explain the differences in Central Asia. On measures of poverty and economic underdevelopment—gross domestic product (GDP), the percentage of the population living on less than 2 USD per day, and the percentage of urban population—Uzbekistan resembles Kyrgyzstan, and citizens of both countries are considerably worse off than those in Kazakhstan (see Table 4.11). Levels of inequality, as measured by the Gini index, are comparable across the three countries, thus also not an explanation.

---

89. Jong-Sung You and Sanjeev Khagram, "A Comparative Study of Inequality and Corruption," *American Sociological Review* 70, no. 1 (2005), 136–57.

90. Kostadinova, *Political Corruption in Eastern Europe: Politics after Communism.*

91. Alberto Ades and Rafael Di Tella, "Rents, Competition, and Corruption," *American Economic Review* 89, no. 4 (1999), 982–93; Carlos Leite and Jens Weidmann, "Does Mother Nature Corrupt? Natural Resources, Corruption, and Economic Growth," *IMF Working Paper* 99/85 (1999).

92. Ades and Di Tella, "Rents, Competition, and Corruption"; John Gerring and Strom C. Thacker, "Do Neoliberal Policies Deter Political Corruption?" *International Organization* 59, no. 1 (2005), 233–54; Wayne Sandholtz and Mark M. Gray, "International Integration and National Corruption," *International Organization* 57, no. 4 (2003), 761–800; Wayne Sandholtz and William Koetzle, "Accounting for Corruption: Economic Structure, Democracy, and Trade," *International Studies Quarterly* 44 (2000), 31–50.

93. Blundo, "Corruption in Africa and the Social Sciences," 57; William Reno, *Corruption and State Politics in Sierra Leone* (Cambridge: Cambridge University Press, 1995).

TABLE 4.11. Socioeconomic characteristics

| | MARKET REFORMERS | | | | NONMARKET REFORMER | |
| | KAZAKHSTAN | | KYRGYZSTAN | | UZBEKISTAN | |
	2003[a]	2012	2003[a]	2012	2003[a]	2012
GDP (nominal per capita, USD)	2,068	11,935	381	1,160	396	1,717
Percentage of the population living on less than 2 USD per day (in 2002)[b]	22	1	67	22	76	NA
Urban population (percentage of total population)	55	54	35	35	37	36
Gini index (in 2002)[c]	35	29	32	33	35	NA
Energy production (thousand metric tons of oil equivalent)[d]	101,918	160,148	1,290	1,620	56,416	57,268
Imports of goods and services (percentage of GDP)[e]	43	30	45	82	31	31
Foreign direct investment (millions, USD)[f]	2,092	13,227	46	693	83	1,403
Foreign direct investment (percentage of GDP)[f]	7	7	2	11	1	3
Foreign aid and development assistance (millions, USD)[g]	294	213	200	523	195	215
Foreign aid and development assistance (percentage of GDP)[g]	1	.11	10	8	2	.47

Source: World Bank, "World Databank," available from http://databank.worldbank.org/ddp/home.do. The latest data are presented.

[a] The data in these columns are for 2003 with the exception of the percentage of the population living on less than 2 USD per day and the Gini index. See notes (b) and (c) below.

[b] This statistic is called the "Poverty headcount ratio at $2 per day," and it is expressed in U.S. dollars at 2005 international prices. Poverty statistics are not available for Kyrgyzstan in 2003 and for Kazakhstan and Kyrgyzstan in 2010 or 2011, so instead I use 2002 and 2009 data. For comparability I use the 2002 data for Uzbekistan, which is only one percentage point lower than the 2003 number. The latest year for which this statistic is available for Uzbekistan is 2003. The statistic for Uzbekistan was accessed from the database in 2011. Poverty statistics no longer appear in the online Databank for Uzbekistan. A comparable statistic, 71.7 percent for 2000, appears in a spreadsheet titled "WDI Uzbekistan," provided by the World Bank and available from the author.

[c] The Gini index measures income inequality, with zero indicating perfect equality and 100 indicating perfect inequality. A description of the calculation can be found on the website. Statistics were not available for Uzbekistan after 2003. Statistics for Kazakhstan and Kyrgyzstan are from the most recent years available: 2009 and 2011, respectively.

[d] According to the World Bank, "Energy production refers to forms of primary energy—petroleum (crude oil, natural gas liquids, and oil from nonconventional sources), natural gas, solid fuels (coal, lignite, and other derived fuels), and combustible renewables and waste—and primary electricity, all converted into oil equivalents." Scholars who have made this argument use fuel, ore, and metal exports instead of energy production, but the former are not available for Uzbekistan. These statistics are from 2011, the most recent year available.

[e] These statistics are from the latest years available: 2012 for Kazakhstan, and 2011 for Kyrgyzstan and Uzbekistan.

[f] These statistics appear in the database as "Foreign direct investment, net inflows" and they are "the net inflows of investment to acquire a lasting management interest (10 percent or more of voting stock) in an enterprise operating in an economy other than that of the investor. It is the sum of equity capital, reinvestment of earnings, other long-term capital, and short-term capital as shown in the balance of payments. This series shows net inflows (new investment inflows less disinvestment) in the reporting economy from foreign investors." The statistics for Uzbekistan are from 2011, the latest year available.

[g] This statistic is called "Net official development assistance and official aid received" and is measured in current U.S. dollars. These figures include grants and loans that include grants of at least 25 percent from foreign countries and multilateral institutions for economic development and welfare. The percentages of GDP were calculated using the GDP figures from the website. These statistics are for 2011, the latest year available.

Energy production figures show that Kazakhstan and Uzbekistan, but not Kyrgyzstan, are more likely to suffer from the resource curse. Both Kazakhstan and Uzbekistan have an abundance of natural resources. Kazakhstan has large amounts of oil and natural gas, but I came across no evidence that resources used for petty corruption were from oil revenues in Kazakhstan or that individuals expected government money because of this revenue source. Moreover, Uzbekistan also has reserves, albeit smaller, while Kyrgyzstan has almost no natural resources, with the exception of a small amount of gold. A common measure of international trade openness, imports of goods and services as a percentage of GDP, predicts that Kyrgyzstan, but not Kazakhstan, would experience more corruption than Uzbekistan currently. In 2003 the percentages were similar across the three countries. Measures of foreign direct investment and foreign aid and development assistance suggest that international capital is also not the answer. Uzbekistan's numbers for foreign direct investment were between those of Kazakhstan and Kyrgyzstan each year. As a percentage of GDP, foreign direct investment in Uzbekistan was slightly lower than in Kazakhstan and Kyrgyzstan in 2011 but comparable to Kyrgyzstan in 2003. Measures of foreign aid and development assistance for Uzbekistan were comparable to either Kazakhstan or Kyrgyzstan each year.

In sum, alternative institutional, cultural, and economic explanations are not helpful in explaining the difference in Central Asia. Instead, the evidence points to market reform as promoting corruption when a legacy of significant state economic intervention is present and market-enhancing institutions are absent or weak. Analyzing the specific challenges of market reform, the absence of state substitutes, the scarcity of government goods and services, and official proscriptions on state reliance in Kazakhstan and Kyrgyzstan illustrated why individuals informally seek state resources in response to market reform. Comparing present-day Kazakhstan and Kyrgyzstan with contemporary Uzbekistan demonstrated that individuals are more likely to engage in corruption for basic state resources when market reforms have been undertaken.

The Rest of the World

The argument that market reform promotes corruption when a legacy of significant state economic intervention is present and market-enhancing institutions are absent or weak is not limited to Central Asia but appears generalizable and fundamentally important. This is evident from an analysis of a larger set of countries in the world, which vary on the causal factor and two conditions. This larger set of countries enables me to directly test the importance of state intervention legacies and market-enhancing institutions, conditions that are consistent across my three Central Asian cases. The statistical results unambiguously demonstrate the claim of my argument concerning the importance of market-enhancing institutions for reducing corruption. Most likely because corruption data sets measure perceptions of petty and grand corruption, support is weaker for my assertions about the influence of market reform and significant state intervention legacies on corruption.

This analysis of many countries also allows for an additional test of alternative explanations. The constellation of factors highlighted in this book is not the only cause of corruption. We would expect that expanding the investigation to countries outside of Central Asia would reveal that alternative explanations that were not helpful to understanding the three countries are useful in the broader context.

From the many alternative explanations, I selected three—state regulation, poverty, and natural resource endowment—to test. I chose these because they are the most likely to be able to account not only for corruption but also for the factors that I contend explain corruption. This approach allows me to examine the likelihood that the results of the analysis are spurious, whether one of these other factors accounts for market reform, legacies of significant state economic intervention, market-enhancing institutions, and corruption.

Conceivably state regulation could account for all of the factors. High state regulation historically would be part of a legacy of significant state economic intervention. Government officials would implement market reform because they would see it as offering additional opportunities to enrich themselves, and difficult economic circumstances may bring international pressure to undertake reforms in return for financial assistance. High state regulation would also promote corruption by affording bureaucrats many opportunities to engage in corruption.

Poverty can plausibly explain most of the factors. Government officials could undertake market reform to alleviate poverty, but with so little wealth in the country, no one may bother to create market-enhancing institutions such as credit registries. As others have argued, poor people engage in corruption to survive. Conceivably, poverty could account for all of my explanatory factors except for significant state economic intervention.

One can imagine that an abundance of natural resources could also explain significant state economic intervention, market reform, weak or absent market-enhancing institutions, and corruption. Natural resources are often state-controlled, so significant state economic intervention could exist historically. Government officials would implement market reform, especially privatization, because they see opportunities to enrich themselves or they need investment to extract more resources. The dominance of the natural resource industry would discourage the development of market-enhancing institutions, such as credit registries, that are useful to small businesses. The resources would also facilitate at least grand corruption, by allowing government officials to provide rents in return for payment.

Although these alternative explanations are logical, a statistical analysis shows that neither state regulation, poverty, or natural resource endowment can account for all of my explanatory factors. In other words, this suggests that my argument is not spurious. The results do show that state regulation and poverty are additional causes of corruption. This confirms that the factors highlighted in this book are sufficient but not necessary causes of corruption, as I have argued.

Measurement and Data

One challenge of conducting an analysis of many countries is that no excellent measures of corruption exist. Many corruption data sets measure perceived, instead of experienced, corruption, and they combine data on petty and grand corruption. Measuring the other components of my argument posed fewer challenges.

Even those data sets that claim to measure experience typically measure perception. Because corruption is a sensitive topic, these data sets ask survey respondents to comment on the experience of people like them, rather than their own experience. In other words, they measure perceived corruption instead of actual corruption.

An additional challenge for my analysis is that corruption data sets typically focus more on grand corruption than petty corruption. I use Transparency International's Corruption Perceptions Index (CPI) because it is the closest global proxy for petty corruption. The CPI is based on surveys of local and foreign business people's perceptions and experiences and country experts' assessments. It combines reports of different corrupt practices, such as bribery, to derive country scores ranging from zero to 10 with 10 indicating the least corruption.[94] The CPI is not an ideal measure of corruption, as numerous reviews of the index have highlighted.[95] For my purposes, it is a significant drawback that the CPI

---

94. In 2012 the scale switched to zero to 100. Johann Graf Lambsdorff, "Framework Document 2004: Background Paper to the 2004 Corruption Perceptions Index," Transparency International, 2004, http://www.transparency.org/content/download/1528/7959/file/framework_en.pdf (accessed December 19, 2013).

95. The studies have highlighted how the perception of corruption is not as valid a measure as actual corruption. Reviewers have also criticized the CPI for relying on surveys with high propor-

does not focus exclusively on petty corruption. The survey respondents, who are included in the CPI, likely draw on petty corruption experiences they and their acquaintances have had, but they are also influenced by media reports and investigations of grand corruption.[96] That said, the CPI is the best measure available for my analysis.[97] The CPI scores for the countries in my data set range from 1.9 to 9.4.

My study of Kazakhstan and Kyrgyzstan offers guidance about how to measure the other components of the argument. From that analysis it was evident that public credit registries, private credit bureaus, and government competition

---

tions of respondents who are not from the countries they are evaluating, in particular Western businesspeople. The concern is that the CPI presents only the perspective of Western businesspeople. From this concern follow criticisms about the CPI's focus on government corruption in business transactions, with an emphasis on bribes. The CPI's exclusion of private-sector corruption has raised additional concerns that developed countries might appear comparatively less corrupt than they actually are. Incidentally, the exclusion of private-sector corruption is an advantage to my study, which focuses on corruption involving government officials. Scholars have also challenged the CPI's methodology, highlighting difficulties comparing scores across years and across countries, and the varying definitions of corruption from the different surveys and assessments that the index aggregates. A final set of criticisms focus not on the index itself, but on how businesses might use it to make investment decisions and how governments and international organizations have used it to inform aid policies. As sample reviews, see Staffan Andersson and Paul M. Heywood, "The Politics of Perception: Use and Abuse of Transparency International's Approach to Measuring Corruption," *Political Studies* 57 (2009), 746–67; Stephen Knack, "Measuring Corruption: A Critique of Indicators in Eastern Europe and Central Asia," *Journal of Public Policy* 27, no. 3 (2007), 255–91; Mireille Razafindrakoto and Francois Roubard, "Are International Databases on Corruption Reliable? A Comparison of Expert Opinion Surveys and Household Surveys in Sub-Saharan Africa," *World Development* 38, no. 8 (2010), 1057–69; Danielle E. Warren and William S. Laufer, "Are Corruption Indices a Self-Fulfilling Prophecy? A Social Labeling Perspective of Corruption," *Journal of Business Ethics* 88, Supplement 4 (2009), 841–49.

96. The problems of the CPI data set for this project are starkest when the scores for the three Central Asian countries are considered. Kazakhstan and Kyrgyzstan receive scores of 2.7 and 2.1, respectively, and Uzbekistan receives a score of 1.6, indicating that by this measure Uzbekistan is slightly more corrupt. This suggests that the measure masks the use of corruption to meet everyday needs in Kazakhstan and Kyrgyzstan.

97. Other data sets posed more severe problems for my project. For example, Transparency International's Global Corruption Barometer provides data for only half the countries I examine, and the World Bank and EBRD's Business Environment and Enterprise Performance Survey (BEEPS) sought information only from firm managers and owners, whereas I am interested in the experiences of a broader group of people. BEEPS data and reports based on them do not explore individuals' experiences in seeking basic goods and services. For example, the report "Trends in Corruption and Regulatory Burden in Eastern Europe and Central Asia" describes firms' experiences in securing public contracts, importing goods, and using the courts to resolve commercial disputes. As my survey and field research show, most individuals seeking assistance from government officials are unemployed people, individuals hoping to start businesses, or small-scale traders, not firm managers and owners, so little to no overlap is likely in the survey respondents. For a review of different indices and surveys on corruption, see Treisman, "What Have We Learned About the Causes of Corruption from Ten Years of Cross-National Empirical Research," *Annual Review of Political Science* 19 (2007), 211–44; World Bank, "Trends in Corruption and Regulatory Burden in Eastern Europe and Central Asia" (Washington, DC, 2011).

policies are key market-enhancing institutions. The World Bank and the International Finance Corporation supply information about credit registries and credit bureaus, recording what percentage of adults each institution covers in a country. For each country in the data set I added the two values, between zero and 100, which created a scale from zero to 134.3 in practice. I use data from 2009 because that is the latest year for which data are available for all the variables. Comparable data on government competition policies are available only for postcommunist states from the EBRD, so I cannot include this variable in my data set. However, in an earlier study of postcommunist states I found that corruption is lower in countries with more effective government competition policies.[98]

The remaining two components of the argument, a legacy of state economic intervention and market reform, are related. Market reform reduced state economic intervention, so the underlying concept should be the same for these variables. Market reform, or a reduction in state economic intervention, includes many different policies, but the study of Kazakhstan and Kyrgyzstan highlights the importance of credit and thus the importance of the banking industry. Therefore, I use measures of bank ownership to capture a legacy of state economic intervention and market reform. For the legacy variable I use the percentage of bank deposits held in state-owned banks versus privately owned banks in 1975. This is the most recent year that data are available before countries of the world began to embark on market reform. The index ranges from zero to 10, with zero indicating the greatest state involvement. The data come from the World Bank.[99] The market reform variable is the 2009 value for this measure minus the 1975 value for each country. The possible range is from −10 to 10, with 10 representing the greatest reduction in state ownership of banks, zero indicating no change, and negative numbers signifying different degrees of increase in state ownership.

To test the alternative explanations—state regulation, poverty, and natural resource endowment—I include a measure for each. The measure of state regulation is the number of procedures required to start a business, as reported by

---

98. Kelly M. McMann, "Market Reform as a Stimulus to Particularistic Politics," *Comparative Political Studies* 42, no. 7 (2009), 971–94.

99. The data were compiled by the Fraser Institute from work by the World Bank's James R. Barth, Gerard Caprio Jr., and Ross Levine, "Bank Regulation and Supervision," World Bank, http://go.worldbank.org/SNUSW978P0; (accessed December 19, 2013); James R. Barth, Gerard Caprio, and Ross Levine, *Rethinking Bank Regulation: Till Angels Govern* (Cambridge: Cambridge University Press, 2006); James Gwartney and Robert Lawson, "Economic Freedom of the World: 2009 Annual Report," Fraser Institute, 2009, http://www.fraserinstitute.org/publicationdisplay.aspx?id=13006&terms=economic+freedom+of+the+world+2009 (accessed November 28, 2012).

the World Bank and International Finance Corporation.[100] This seemed to be a more valid measure of state regulation than the alternative, the time required to start a business. In this data set the number of required procedures ranges from 1 to 17. To measure poverty, I use GDP per capita in current U.S. dollars, which ranges in this group of countries from 175 USD to 104,354 USD. Natural resource endowment is captured by the World Bank's energy production data, measured in thousand metric tons of oil equivalent. As described by the World Bank, "[e]nergy production refers to forms of primary energy—petroleum (crude oil, natural gas liquids, and oil from nonconventional sources), natural gas, solid fuels (coal, lignite, and other derived fuels), and combustible renewables and waste—and primary electricity, all converted into oil equivalents."[101] The values range from 29 to 2,084,935 thousand tons in this data set.

I examined ninety-two countries of the world. Countries that were excluded were missing data for one of the variables. To ensure that a relatively large number of countries with a significant state economic intervention legacy were included, I imputed the legacy variable values for post-Soviet states. The 1975 data include only a value for the Soviet Union, zero. Because of the uniformity of Soviet economic policies, it is reasonable to assign the value of zero for 1975 to each of the states that emerged from the Soviet Union. With this adaptation, the data set covers all regions of the world and all income levels, as shown in Table 4.12. This indicates that excluding countries for which data were not available most likely did not introduce bias. However, the data set does exclude the 13 most corrupt countries in the 168 countries measured by the CPI, because they lack data on one or more other variables. The absence of these cases can make a relationship that I find in the data set appear stronger or weaker than it actually is if the relationship is not constant across all the cases. Extrapolating results to those missing cases would also be problematic. Overall, the data set appears representative with the exception of the most corrupt countries of the world.

---

100. For postcommunist countries, the CPI measure uses a survey that asks experts a question that is similar to this state regulation measure: "Is the government free from excessive bureaucratic regulations, registration requirements, and other controls that increase opportunities for corruption?" Transparency International, "Corruption Perceptions Index 2011: Long Methodological Brief," transparency.ee/cm/files/lisad/pikk_metoodika.pdf (accessed December 19, 2013), 3. However the correlation between the state regulation measure and the CPI is not statistically significant for postcommunist countries, indicating that this measure is not problematic for these cases.

101. World Bank, "World Databank."

TABLE 4.12. Number of countries in different regions and with different income levels

REGION	NUMBER	INCOME LEVEL	NUMBER
East Asia and the Pacific	11	Low income	9
East Europe and Central Asia	18	Lower middle income	20
Western Europe	19	Upper middle income	24
Latin America and Caribbean	11	High income	39
Middle East and North Africa	11		
North America	2		
South Asia	5		
Sub-Saharan Africa	15		

Analysis

Using this data set, I conducted a series of statistical analyses, which I describe in detail in the appendix. Here let us consider the general conclusions. Because my argument focuses on the influence of market reform under the two conditions, it is important to consider market reform's effect on corruption under the four possible configurations of conditions: a legacy of significant state economic intervention with no or weak market-enhancing institutions, no legacy with no or weak market-enhancing institutions, a legacy with effective market-enhancing institutions, and no legacy with effective market-enhancing institutions.

The findings, summarized in Table 4.13,[102] strongly support my claim that market-enhancing institutions are important to reducing corruption. When effective market-enhancing institutions are present, market reform decreases corruption. This has important policy implications, which will be discussed in the final chapter. The analysis does not illustrate my claim that market reform increases corruption when there is a legacy of significant state economic intervention but no effective market-enhancing institutions. Instead, this analysis shows that market reform reduces corruption under these conditions. This negative finding is most likely because the CPI combines grand and petty corruption. When a legacy is present, market reform reduces the opportunities for grand corruption by trimming officials' extensive responsibilities, and this likely masks how market reform can promote petty corruption by limiting where individuals can turn for assistance to meet everyday needs.

The inclusion of grand corruption in the CPI likely plays a role in the effect of market reform in other ways as well. Its inclusion may help to explain why

---

102. For readers who have studied the appendix, note that while we cannot discern the effect of market reform on corruption when effective market-enhancing institutions exist (in model 3), we can discern it from models 4 and 5.

TABLE 4.13. Market reform's effect on corruption under different conditions for countries of the world

	NO OR WEAK MARKET-ENHANCING INSTITUTIONS	EFFECTIVE MARKET-ENHANCING INSTITUTIONS
Legacy	decreases corruption	decreases corruption
No legacy	increases corruption	decreases corruption

market reform increases corruption when a significant intervention legacy and effective market-enhancing institutions do not exist. Specifically, under these conditions the new illicit opportunities that market reform offers politicians outweigh the relatively small number of opportunities it eradicated. Moreover, market reform may decrease corruption when market-enhancing institutions are present because government officials may be restrained in their ability to take advantage of new market opportunities to engage in corruption. To the extent that market-enhancing institutions that restrain government officials' behavior, such as independent judiciaries, develop alongside credit registries, market reform will present fewer occasions for officials to engage in grand corruption.

The inclusion of the alternative explanations in the statistical analysis provides strong evidence that the argument is not spurious. These tests are also described in detail in the appendix. None of the alternative explanations can account for all of my explanatory factors. Poverty, specifically lower levels of GDP, and greater numbers of state regulations do increase corruption. However, this is consistent with my expectation that the factors I identified are sufficient, but not necessary, to promote corruption. Natural resource endowments did not have an effect on corruption levels.

The statistical analysis supports my argument about petty corruption as well as theories of grand corruption. The results highlight the importance of market-enhancing institutions to reduce corruption, as the argument in this book claims. In addition, the findings suggest that market reform is likely to decrease corruption in countries with a history of significant state economic intervention, as theories of grand corruption assert. Including the alternative explanations in the analysis showed that the argument was not likely spurious and, as expected, that my explanatory factors are only sufficient, not necessary, for corruption. After all, corruption has multiple causes.

Overall, the evidence in this chapter illustrates the causal argument I make and some of the correlations predicted by my argument and theories of grand corruption. From the Central Asian cases it is clear that market actors do not offer an alternative to corruption. Market reform in the context of a history of significant state economic intervention and absent or weak market-enhancing institutions limits market actors' abilities to provide the goods and services that individuals need. Individuals instead turn to government officials but find that market reform has reduced state resources and thus increased the competition for them. Individuals offer bribes, use personal connections, and promise political support in order to try to gain an advantage in this competition. The next chapter considers how societal groups' limited resources also contribute to corruption.

ISLAMIC INSTITUTIONS AND SECULAR CHARITIES

Obstacles to Providing Substitute Resources

"The mosque? What kind of help could we get from it?" Marzhan, the villager in southern Kazakhstan, responded to my question about the local mosque as a source of assistance.[1] My exchange with her highlights how societal institutions that observers have expected to provide assistance in Kazakhstan and Kyrgyzstan to a large extent do not. Mosques, Islamic schools, and proselytizing Islamic groups along with local, secular charities have grown in number since the late Soviet era when restrictions on charity, religion, and organizing were reduced. This growth and the experiences of other countries in similar circumstances raised expectations among some observers that these organizations would provide substitute resources as the Soviet welfare state eroded. Yet in reality neither Islamic organizations nor secular charities can meet the basic needs of citizens because they lack the resources.

Just as a legacy of significant state economic intervention and an absence of market-enhancing institutions weaken markets, these two conditions also contribute to a lack of resources among groups in society. Historically, Islamic institutions and local charities had few resources because of the substantial economic intervention of the Soviet party-state. Market reform, coupled with political liberalization, offered the promise of enriching the religious and secular charitable sectors; however, their resource scarcity has continued. Because of the absence of effective market-enhancing institutions, few people have disposable income to contribute to Islamic institutions and secular charities, and charities have limited

---

1. Author's interview (#161), Kazakhstan, July 22, 2001.

possibilities for obtaining credit. Interviews I conducted with representatives of these groups and with ordinary citizens confirmed that these organizations provide limited material assistance. Further supporting this point, the survey data show that few citizens turn to them for assistance. Other societal groups that have not been the focus of previous studies and speculation also do not provide substitutes for state resources. These include foreign charities, foreign companies, local businesses, professional associations, political parties, *aksakals*, and secular educational establishments. The paucity of resources available from societal groups encourages citizens to seek assistance from government officials, and to use illicit means when doing so.

The Growth of Islamic Institutions and Secular Charities

Citizens' minimal reliance on Islamic institutions and secular charities for assistance in Kazakhstan and Kyrgyzstan is surprising at first glance, considering that their numbers have increased dramatically in the independence era. The Islamic institutions include mosques, educational establishments, and proselytizing groups; secular charities have a variety of structures and missions. The growth began in the late Soviet era as the government relaxed restrictions on charity, religion, and organizing. The rate of growth increased with the collapse of the Soviet Union and thus the end to the communist party-state's regulation of these spheres of life. Over time the governments of Kazakhstan and Kyrgyzstan have imposed restrictions on religious institutions and secular charities, but overall, the restrictions and the implementation of these restrictions are not nearly as severe as they were in the Soviet era.

Mosques, Educational Establishments, and Proselytizing Groups

Mosques, followed in number by Islamic educational establishments and proselytizing groups, have proliferated in Kazakhstan and Kyrgyzstan. The increase in mosques has occurred throughout the territories, but especially in the southern part of each country. The southern part of each country is home to a larger percentage of ethnic Uzbeks, who generally observe Islam to a greater extent than their Kazakh and Kyrgyz counterparts. Members of the titular ethnicity in the south of each country also tend to be more observant, perhaps because of the Uzbek presence.

The number of mosques in Kazakhstan and Kyrgyzstan has grown to thousands today from double digits in the Soviet era. At the time of the Soviet Union's collapse the Kyrgyz republic had thirty-nine mosques, whereas today the country of Kyrgyzstan has more than three thousand.[2] In one of Kyrgyzstan's seven oblasts, Osh Oblast in the south, officials estimate that there are seven hundred mosques. The numbers are inexact because they include both official mosques, meaning those that have registered with the state, and unofficial ones, meaning those that have not. Estimates suggest that there is one unregistered mosque for approximately every registered one. If this were correct it would mean that there was one mosque, registered or unregistered, for every 750 Muslims in Kyrgyzstan.[3] Kazakhstan had approximately twenty-six mosques from 1944 until the political liberalization under Gorbachev.[4] Now it has 2,228 registered mosques and about seventy that are not registered.[5] This represents one mosque for every 4,400 Muslims in Kazakhstan.[6]

New mosques have emerged from numerous sources. In rural areas residents have turned village buildings into places of worship. For example, in the village where I lived in southern Kazakhstan an elderly man in the village went to the mufti in Almaty in order to found a mosque from a Soviet-era prayer group. An existing building was designated as the mosque. Mosques have also been constructed in rural areas using government funds. In more densely populated areas, communities have pooled resources to build mosques, and foreign donors provided funds in the early 1990s for the construction of mosques. Saudi Arabia,

---

2. Farideh Heyat, "Re-Islamisation in Kyrgyzstan: Gender, New Poverty and the Moral Dimension," *Central Asian Survey* 23, no. 3–4 (2004): 275–87, here 276; International Crisis Group, "Central Asia: Islam and the State" (Brussels: International Crisis Group, 2003), 25n102.

3. International Crisis Group, "Central Asia: Islam and the State," 25n102. This calculation uses 2009 data for total population and percentage of Kyrgyz and Uzbeks in the country, and it is an estimate. It assumes that all ethnic Kyrgyz and Uzbeks identify as Muslim, and it does not include Muslim minorities other than Uzbeks, although their numbers are small. World Bank, "World Databank," http://databank.worldbank.org/ddp/home.do; National Statistics Committee of the Kyrgyz Republic, "Natsional'nyi sostav naseleniia" [National Composition of the Population] (in possession of author).

4. Yaacov Ro'i, *Islam in the Soviet Union: From World War II to Perestroika* (New York: Columbia University Press, 2000), 182.

5. The former number is from Radio Free Europe/Radio Liberty, "List of Kazakh Religious Groups Curbed," 2012, http://www.rferl.org/content/list-of-religious-groups-in-kazakhstan-curbed/24750920.html (accessed December 19, 2013). The latter number is from U.S. Department of State, "International Religious Freedom Report: Kazakhstan" (Washington, DC, 2009).

6. This calculation uses 2009 data for total population and percentages of Kazakhs and Uzbeks in the country, and it is an estimate. It assumes that all ethnic Kazakhs and Uzbeks identify as Muslim, and it does not include Muslim minorities other than Uzbeks, although their numbers are small. Agency of Statistics of the Republic of Kazakhstan, "The Results of the National Population Census in 2009," 2010, http://www.eng.stat.kz/perepis_nasl (accessed December 19, 2013).

Pakistan, Turkey, and to a lesser extent Iran have provided funds.[7] Informal leaders of prison inmates have established mosques in the prisons in each country—in almost all prisons in Kyrgyzstan. The leaders supervise the prisoners in building them and prison directors typically donate construction materials.[8] Whereas citizens' and foreign donors' involvement reflects religious expression, state sponsorship has also been a sign of government officials' attempts to increase their legitimacy and promote nationalism.

The donations from foreign countries and foreign individuals almost completely subsided with the increase in government restrictions beginning in the mid-1990s. The start of the civil war in Tajikistan in 1992, the Taliban's seizure of Kabul in 1996, the 1999 bombings in Tashkent, and the September 11, 2001, terrorist attacks in the United States prompted these restrictions.[9] Government officials feared strains of Islam that were unfamiliar in Central Asia, such as Wahhabism and Shiism. Only a small amount of foreign funding for mosque construction has continued; countries have sometimes linked their economic and technical assistance to acceptance of funds for the construction of new mosques. For example, Oman, Saudi Arabia, and Iran provided assistance in the oil and financial sectors but also insisted on the acceptance of donations for the construction of new mosques.[10] Kazakhstan imposed additional restrictions on worship following a string of violent attacks in 2011, which the government attributed to Islamic extremist groups. The new regulations ban prayer rooms in public institutions and make it more difficult for religious communities to register with the state and thus to operate legally.[11]

The number of Islamic educational establishments has also grown in Kazakhstan and Kyrgyzstan, although not to the extents that mosques have. In Kyrgyzstan the number of Islamic higher educational institutions and madrassas increased from zero in the Soviet era to nine and fifty, respectively, in recent years. The number of madrassas encompasses those registered with the muftiate, but this does not capture small, neighborhood madrassas, which would push the

---

7. Igor Lipovsky, "The Awakening of Central Asian Islam," *Middle Eastern Studies* 32, no. 3 (1996): 14; Ghoncheh Tazmini, "The Islamic Revival in Central Asia: A Potent Force or a Misconception?," *Central Asian Survey* 20, no. 1 (2001): 1–21, here 16.

8. International Crisis Group, "Central Asia: Islamists in Prison" (Brussels: International Crisis Group, 2009).

9. Adeeb Khalid, *Islam after Communism: Religion and Politics in Central Asia* (Berkeley: University of California Press, 2007), 119, 123.

10. Martha Brill Olcott, *Central Asia's New States: Independence, Foreign Policy, and Regional Security* (Washington, DC: United States Institute of Peace Press, 1996), 32.

11. Nate Schenkkan, "Kazakhstan: Government Pressure on Devout Muslims Generates Resentment," EurasiaNet, March 20, 2012, http://www.eurasianet.org/node/65156 (accessed December 19, 2013).

number higher.[12] The pattern is similar in Kazakhstan, with an increase to nine madrassas and numerous unregistered ones.[13]

Many of the new Islamic educational institutions in Kazakhstan and Kyrgyzstan have been started from scratch with the assistance of foreign funders. Foreign donations have helped found more prominent educational institutions, such as the International Islamic Center in Kyrgyzstan, which is independent of the state Islamic structure and is funded by Kuwait, Pakistan, and Saudi Arabia.[14] In Kazakhstan, Egypt funded the Nur-Mubarak Egyptian University of Islamic Culture.[15] The most extensive foreign funder of education establishments has been the Turkish Islamic movement Gülen. The movement has established twenty-seven schools in Kazakhstan and twenty-five schools and two universities in Kyrgyzstan since 1992.[16] The schools provide an environment supportive of religious observers, but not a religious education, according to staff and students whom I interviewed. Madrassas have been funded by foreigners and, especially in less populated areas, community members have donated to establish them. For example, the Kyrgyzstani foundation Adep Bashati was founded by a group of Kyrgyz graduates of Al-Azhar University in Cairo and is funded by businesspeople, among other locals. The foundation sponsors madrassas, courses about Islam, and hajj pilgrimages.[17]

Islamic proselytizing organizations have also emerged in Kazakhstan and Kyrgyzstan. The largest, Hizb ut-Tahrir, is an international group that aims to create a caliphate through peaceful means. Missionaries and foreign funders of mosques and Islamic schools likely brought the ideas of the group to Central

---

12. International Crisis Group, "Central Asia: Islam and the State," 29; "Islam Faces Hurdles in Bishkek," *Times of Central Asia*, January 29, 2008.

13. "President Nursultan Nazarbayev Received Chairman of the Spiritual Department of Muslims of Kazakhstan Absattar Kazhy Derbisali," Agency for Religious Affairs of the Republic of Kazakhstan, February 22, 2012, http://www.din.gov.kz/eng/novosti_i_sobytija/?cid=0&rid=108 (accessed November 28, 2012).

14. Shahram Akbarzadeh, "Political Islam in Kyrgyzstan and Turkmenistan," *Central Asian Survey* 20, no. 4 (2001): 451–65, here 459, 461–62.

15. Khalid, *Islam after Communism*, 185. The university renamed itself the Kazakh-Egyptian Islamic University "Nur" after the ouster of Egyptian President Hosni Mubarak in 2011.

16. Farangis Najibullah, "Turkish Schools Coming under Increasing Scrutiny in Central Asia," Radio Free Europe/Radio Liberty, 2009, http://www.rferl.org/content/Turkish_Schools_Coming_Under_Increasing_Scrutiny_In_Central_Asia/1616111.html (accessed December 19, 2013); Berna Turam, "The Politics of Engagement between Islam and the Secular State: Ambivalences of 'Civil Society,'" *British Journal of Sociology* 55, no. 2 (2004): 259–81, here 265.

17. Bruce De Cordier, "Kyrgyzstan: Fledgling Islamic Charity Reflects Growing Role for Religion," EurasiaNet, December 8, 2010, http://www.eurasianet.org/node/62529 (accessed December 19, 2013).

Asia in the early 1990s.[18] The group's activities primarily include distributing information through leaflets, books, magazines, videos, the Internet, and seminars.[19] The organization has hundreds or thousands of members in Kazakhstan and thousands of members in Kyrgyzstan.[20] The Kyrgyzstani government placed the number in Kyrgyzstan at fifteen thousand in 2008, but since then numbers seem to be on the decline as members have had to migrate to Russia and Kazakhstan in search of employment.[21] With the return of migrants to Kyrgyzstan during the global economic recession, it is possible that this trend will be reversed. A reasonable estimate for Kazakhstan is two thousand members, all in the south. The estimates are inexact because Hizb ut-Tahrir is banned in the countries and operates clandestinely. Regionally much of the group is made up of ethnic Uzbeks from the Ferghana Valley in Kyrgyzstan and neighboring countries. Members of nontitular groups, including Russians, Tatars, Chechens, Meskhetian Turks, and Kurds, make up one-fifth of the group in the region. Primarily people ages eighteen to thirty-five join, and recently the group has been most successful in recruiting women, former convicts, and those at the younger end of the spectrum. In Kyrgyzstan, members of parliament, government bureaucrats, and successful businesspeople have joined the organization, according to the head of the government agency on religious affairs.[22]

The Islamic Movement of Uzbekistan (IMU) and the Islamic Jihad Union (IJU) are smaller organizations. These groups also aim to create a caliphate but through violent means. Two residents of the Ferghana Valley city Namangan in Uzbekistan, Tahir Yuldashev and Juma Namangani, established the IMU in the 1990s. The IJU splintered off from the IMU approximately ten years ago as some members preferred to concentrate on overthrowing governments in post-Soviet Central Asia, whereas the IMU had turned its focus to supporting the Taliban in Afghanistan and Pakistan. The factions may have reunited because the new IMU leader, Usmon Odil, advocates refocusing efforts on post-Soviet Central Asia.[23]

---

18. Kathleen Collins, "Ideas, Networks, and Islamist Movements: Evidence from Central Asia and the Caucasus," *World Politics* 60 (2007): 64–96, here 83.

19. International Crisis Group, "Central Asia: Islamists in Prison," 7; Gulnoza Saidazimova, "Central Asia: Banned Islamic Group Hizb ut-Tahrir Continues to Gain Members," EurasiaNet, August 13, 2007, http://www.eurasianet.org/departments/insight/articles/pp081407.shtml (accessed December 19, 2013).

20. International Crisis Group, "Central Asia: Islamists in Prison," 3.

21. Alisher Khamidov, "Kyrgyzstan: Radical Islam Losing Its Appeal Amid Economic Distress and Government Repression," EurasiaNet, December 8, 2009, http://www.eurasianet.org/departments/civilsociety/articles/eav120909.shtml (accessed December 19, 2013).

22. Emmanuel Karagiannis, *Political Islam in Central Asia: The Challenge of Hizb ut-Tahrir* (London: Routledge, 2010), 65.

23. The previous leader was allegedly killed in a 2009 U.S. military drone attack in Afghanistan.

Primarily an ethnic Uzbek organization, the IMU has set its sights on the government of Kyrgyzstan, as a result of the ethnic violence in the southern part of the country in 2010. Greater numbers of Uzbeks than Kyrgyz died and saw their property destroyed, and almost all of those tried after the tragedy have been Uzbeks. Abuses against Uzbeks by local security forces in the south have driven some Uzbeks to join the IMU, according to the national government.[24] The IMU is estimated to have one thousand to five thousand fighters from post-Soviet Central Asia as well as from the Caucasus and Russia. The IJU is thought to have considerably fewer. Within post-Soviet Central Asia, most of these groups' operations have been in Kyrgyzstan, Tajikistan, and Uzbekistan.[25]

A fourth group, Tablighi Jamaat, is a missionary and revivalist group composed of Pakistanis. The group speaks with people on the street and goes door-to-door, teaching people how to observe Islam, for example, by attending mosque. An estimated ten thousand Central Asians are followers, with the majority living in Kyrgyzstan, especially in the Ferghana Valley.[26]

Following a series of violent attacks in both countries in 2011, the governments have claimed that additional Islamic groups exist and that they are responsible for the violence. The government of Kyrgyzstan named Jaishul Madhi, meaning the Army of the Righteous Ruler, as the perpetrator of bombings and attempted bombings of public buildings.[27] Its fifty members are followers of the deceased North Caucasian insurgent Said Buryatsky and they have received explosives training in Tajikistan and Afghanistan, the government claims.[28] The government of Kazakhstan identified the group Jund al-Khilafah or Soldiers of the Caliphate as responsible for attacks in its country. According to the government, Kazakhstanis fighting on the border of Afghanistan and Pakistan formed the group in 2011 to attack Kazakhstan.[29]

---

24. Bruce Pannier, "The Growing Threat of Militants in a Corner of Central Asia," EurasiaNet, April 23, 2011, http://www.eurasianet.org/node/63355 (accessed December 19, 2013).

25. International Crisis Group, "Central Asia: Islamists in Prison," 4; International Crisis Group, "Tajikistan: The Changing Insurgent Threats" (Brussels: International Crisis Group, 2011), here 1.

26. International Crisis Group, "Central Asia: Islamists in Prison," 4–5; Igor Rotar, "Pakistani Islamic Missionary Group Establishes a Strong Presence in Central Asia," EurasiaNet, July 22, 2007, http://www.eurasianet.org/departments/insight/articles/eav072307a.shtml (accessed December 19, 2013).

27. Pannier, "The Growing Threat of Militants in a Corner of Central Asia."

28. Deirdre Tynan, "Kyrgyzstan: Security Officials Blame Islamic Radical Group for Recent Violence," EurasiaNet, January 13, 2011, http://www.eurasianet.org/node/62708 (accessed December 19, 2013).

29. Joanna Lillis, "Kazakhstan: Astana Jolted by Terror Incidents," EurasiaNet, November 16, 2011, http://www.eurasianet.org/node/64529 (accessed December 19, 2013).

Secular Charities

In addition to mosques, Islamic educational establishments, and proselytizing groups, secular charities have proliferated in Kazakhstan and Kyrgyzstan since the collapse of the Soviet Union. Kazakhstan had 3,050 registered nongovernmental organizations (NGOs) as of January 1997, and Kyrgyzstan had seven hundred registered by January 1998.[30] This constitutes approximately one NGO for every five thousand people in Kazakhstan and one for every 6,800 people in Kyrgyzstan. By 2011, more than 9,851 in Kyrgyzstan and 36,815 had registered in Kazakhstan, representing approximately one organization for every five hundred people in each country.[31] Not all of these registered organizations have charitable missions; some are professional associations or sports clubs, for example. Moreover, not all of them are active or effective: one report indicates that only 1,500 to 2,000 actually operate in Kyrgyzstan, and another estimates that of those only five hundred "offer quality services to their target groups."[32] That said, the numbers do suggest that local charities have emerged and their number has increased significantly in both countries.

The most common path to the establishment of a charity has been that acquaintances in a locale perceived a problem and formed a group to resolve it. These individuals were typically acquainted through work, school, military service, or an ethnic minority network. For example, in central Kyrgyzstan two nongovernmental organizations were created by groups of teachers—one from a pedagogical college and another from a secondary school—to serve disadvantaged youth and women. In southern Kyrgyzstan one veteran contacted those in his town with whom he had served to establish a charity to help disabled and impoverished veterans and families of deceased veterans. The 1990 conflict in Osh, Kyrgyzstan, between Uzbeks and Kyrgyz encouraged local Uzbek notables there to work together to form an organization to provide material assistance and cultural support to local Uzbeks. In recent years many of these efforts have fallen into the new category of "mutual assistance groups," typically col-

---

30. Scott Horton and Alla Kazakina, "The Legal Regulation of NGOs: Central Asia at a Cross-roads," in *Civil Society in Central Asia*, ed. M. Holt Ruffin and Daniel Clarke Waugh (Seattle: University of Washington Press, 1999), 33–56, here 36.

31. The report describes the groups included in each count slightly differently, so these numbers should be treated as estimates. The number of organizations per person was calculated using total population data from the World Bank for 2011. World Bank, "World Databank," http://databank.worldbank.org/ddp/home.do (accessed December 19, 2013); United States Agency for International Development (USAID), "2011 CSO Sustainability Index for Central and Eastern Europe and Eurasia, 15th Anniversary Edition" (Washington, DC, 2012), 96, 100, 228.

32. USAID, "2011 CSO Sustainability Index for Central and Eastern Europe and Eurasia," 110. Charles Buxton and Kazbek Abraliev, "Leadership in Transition: Developing Civil Society Leaders in Kyrgyzstan" (International NGO Training and Research Centre, 2007), here 14.

laborations among ten to fifteen less affluent women to provide microcredit to the poorest in their community and to improve local infrastructure, such as roads.[33]

Two less common origins of charities are Soviet-era institutions or international organizations.[34] For instance, in central Kyrgyzstan an individual who had served as deputy chair for a Soviet-era *raion* committee for women left the position in order to create a charity to support women. As she noted, in her government position she had "became familiar with how women live here . . . [but] the committee worked in Soviet ways. . . . I decided to create my own organization. In the committee [we] could not really work."[35] In a case of international sponsorship, the nonprofit microcredit organization Bai Tushum in Kyrgyzstan began in 2000 with the assistance of the foreign economic development organization ACDI/VOCA and the charity Caritas Swiss. By numerous paths, secular charities as well as Islamic organizations have proliferated in the independence era.

Expectations of Islamic and Secular Assistance

Accounts of Kazakhstan and Kyrgyzstan and the experiences of other regions suggest that we could expect Islamic institutions and charitable NGOs to be a significant source of assistance for citizens. Eric McGlinchey argues that "Islamic charities have increasingly stepped in to deliver what central governments cannot."[36] Islamic social welfare tenets have been described as having "a high potential for the societies of Central Asia, particularly Kyrgyzstan, where according to World Bank data the poverty rate reached more than 40%. . . . Islam,

---

33. Alisher Khamidov, "Central Asia: Citizens Learning to Take the Initiative," EurasiaNet, May 23, 2012, http://www.eurasianet.org/node/65449 (accessed December 19, 2013).

34. Earlier studies of nongovernmental organizations in Central Asia described the preponderance of groups as government-organized or heavily influenced by international NGOs. They reached these conclusions because they conducted research primarily in the capital cities and relied largely on the accounts of representatives of international groups. By contrast, my findings are based on research not only in capital cities but also in other cities, towns, and villages, and I gathered information from domestic NGOs, local citizens, and government officials in addition to foreign representatives. For a more detailed analysis of this issue, see Kelly M. McMann, "The Civic Realm in Kyrgyzstan: Soviet Economic Legacies and Activists' Expectations," in *The Transformation of Central Asia: States and Societies from Soviet Rule to Independence*, ed. Pauline Jones Luong (Ithaca, NY: Cornell University Press, 2004), 213–45, here 216–17.

35. Author's interview (#14), Kyrgyzstan, July 10, 1997.

36. Eric M. McGlinchey, "Islamic Revivalism and State Failure in Kyrgyzstan," *Problems of Post-Communism* 56, no. 3 (2009), 16–28.

then seems to be the most accessible alternative to the demise of the Soviet social doctrines," another scholar concludes.[37] This poverty has encouraged a strengthening of Islamic belief in Kyrgyzstan,[38] as well as in Kazakhstan, so people may be more predisposed to turning to mosques and Islamic organizations for assistance. Moreover, the expansion of material assistance for Islamic institutions would mirror the situation in other predominantly Muslim countries. Millions of Muslims in other regions of the world regularly turn to their mosques and other Islamic institutions for assistance including material help and vocational training programs. As market reform has reduced government social services in the late twentieth and early twenty-first centuries, Islamic social services have proliferated in predominately Muslim countries of other regions of the world.[39]

The emergence of nongovernmental organizations has been one of the most popular topics among observers of Central Asia, thus leading one to believe that these groups may play a significant role in people's lives. In particular, local groups with foreign funding have received considerable attention. For example, Boris-Mathieu Pétric writes, "Nowadays, there is not one village in Kyrgyzstan that does not have one or several NGOs," and they are dependent on foreign aid for survival. He comments also on the direct involvement of foreign organizations in Kyrgyzstan, referring to it as a globalized protectorate: "As access to public services is declining, growing numbers are dependent on international NGOs for medical services. Higher education has been privatized and foreign foundations (Soros, Fatulla Gulan, etc.) are rushing in to fill the gap left by the state."[40]

---

37. Ioana Ban, "The Chance for Civil Society in Central Asia or the Role of Islamic Movements in Shaping Political Modernity," *Romanian Journal of Political Science* 6, no. 2 (2006): 117–28, here 121.

38. Heyat, "Re-Islamisation in Kyrgyzstan," 281.

39. Chaider S. Bamualim et al., eds., *Islamic Philanthropy and Social Development in Contemporary Indonesia*, 1st ed. (Jakarta: Center for the Study of Religion and Culture, State Islamic University Syarif Hidayatullah, 2006); Janine A. Clark, *Islam, Charity, and Activism: Middle-Class Networks and Social Welfare in Egypt, Jordan, and Yemen* (Bloomington: Indiana University Press, 2004); Denis Joseph Sullivan, *Private Voluntary Organizations in Egypt: Islamic Development, Private Initiative, and State Control* (Gainesville: University Press of Florida, 1994); Jenny B. White, *Islamist Mobilization in Turkey: A Study in Vernacular Politics* (Seattle: University of Washington Press, 2002); Carrie Rosefsky Wickham, *Mobilizing Islam: Religion, Activism, and Political Change in Egypt* (New York: Columbia University Press, 2002); Quintan Wiktorowicz, *The Management of Islamic Activism: Salafis, the Muslim Brotherhood, and State Power in Jordan* (Albany: State University of New York Press, 2001).

40. Boris-Mathieu Pétric, "Post-Soviet Kyrgyzstan or the Birth of a Globalized Protectorate," *Central Asian Survey* 24, no. 3 (2005): 319–32, here 323, 326. See also Lucy Earle et al., *Community Development in Kazakhstan, Kyrgyzstan and Uzbekistan: Lessons Learnt from Recent Experience, Occasional Papers Series No. 40* (Oxford: INTRAC, 2004), 18.

Evidence of Market Reform's Effect under the Two Conditions

Islamic institutions and secular charities, however, have been limited in their ability to assist individuals. The legacy of significant state economic intervention has meant that most Islamic institutions and secular charities are starting from scratch with no experience and no resources. Market reform without market-enhancing institutions has limited their ability to secure resources; when market actors cannot provide employment, income, and credit, people do not have the funds to make generous donations to Islamic institutions and secular charities. Furthermore, charities have difficulty obtaining credit to carry out their missions.

A Legacy of State Control of Charity

The Soviet party-state's control of the economy extended to religious and secular charity. Charity was effectively prohibited throughout most of the Soviet era because it was thought to impede efforts to establish communism. Charity was considered "one of the means the bourgeoisie uses to mask its parasitism and its exploitative face by means of hypocritical, demeaning 'aid to the poor' in order to deflect them from the class struggle"[41] that would result in communism. Charity was also banned because it was viewed as unnecessary in the Soviet economic system. The thinking was that the party-state provided for the welfare of the people, so the people did not require charitable assistance.[42] Moreover, under communism there should be no rich and no poor. So, in theory, no one was morally obligated to provide charity and no one required it. In the context of Muslim charity in Central Asia, the implication was that individuals did not have to pay *zakat*, an annual obligatory welfare contribution of surplus wealth, because, in theory, they did not have wealth in excess of their needs. And, Islamic institutions did not need to encourage either *zakat* or *sadaq*, voluntary contributions, because, in theory, there were no poor.[43]

In the early years, the Bolsheviks persecuted churches, which had been the main sources of charity, and closed charitable organizations not affiliated with their movement.[44] A decree in 1929 codified the anticharity campaign by pro-

---

41. A 1951 Soviet dictionary quoted in Adele Lindenmeyr, "The Big Impact of Small Deeds: Uncovering the Rich History of Russian Charity," Russia Profile, 2007, http://russiaprofile.org/culture _living/a3148.html (accessed December 19, 2013).

42. Ibid.; Anne White, "Charity, Self-Help and Politics in Russia, 1985–91," *Europe-Asia Studies* 45, no. 5 (1993): 787–810, here 788.

43. Ro'i, *Islam in the Soviet Union*, 141n159, 234.

44. Mervyn Matthews, "Perestroika and the Rebirth of Charity," in *Soviet Social Problems*, ed. Anthony Jones, Walter D. Connor, and David E. Powell (Boulder, CO: Westview Press, 1991), 154–

hibiting religious organizations from engaging in charitable activities.[45] This extended to mutual assistance funds, shelters, funeral funds, educational establishments, and any assistance to individuals.[46]

The campaign against philanthropy restricted the survival and development of Islamic organizations in the Soviet era. The state closed many mosques and subjected remaining and new ones to registration, strict guidelines, and monitoring.[47] The registered mosques represented only 1 percent of all Islamic organizations; worshipping illegally in unregistered organizations was more popular. In much of the Soviet Union, Muslims did not have a registered mosque nearby, so they could not worship there. Muslims who disagreed with the state's positions on Islam also did not attend the registered mosques. Instead, people worshipped in closed mosques, at shrines, in cemeteries, at private homes, in small structures constructed on private land plots and kolkhoz (collective farm) land, on threshing floors, and on the streets. For example, in the village where I lived in southern Kazakhstan a mullah met with ten people in a home that the participants viewed as a mosque. Neither the village nor even the *raion* had a mosque in the Soviet period. These meetings outside official mosques were illegal unless registered with the state. But the state granted approval only in eras when Islam was seen as less of a threat and only when a registered mosque was not accessible. Illegal worship was particularly common in Kazakhstan and Kyrgyzstan, which had a history of worshipping with mullahs outside of mosques because of the people's nomadic roots and the low population density.[48] Yet most illegal organizations met rarely. Many met just for a few main festivals, performance of life-cycle rites, and infrequent Fridays. Moreover, they had only small numbers of participants. And, the numbers of groups and participants rose and fell over time, with no steady increase into the late Soviet era.[49]

Financial restrictions limited the activities of both unregistered and registered Islamic organizations in the Soviet era. In an intentional effort to reduce funds to Muslim institutions, the state prohibited them from owning property and engaging in commercial ventures. The ban on property extended to *waqf*, religious endowments, which were seized by the state. The greatest blow to Islamic charity was the Soviet government's declaration that *fitr*, the main source

---

71, here 154.

45. White, "Charity, Self-Help and Politics in Russia," 788.

46. Ro'i, *Islam in the Soviet Union*, 27.

47. New mosques were mainly allowed to open during World War II in order to encourage support for the military effort.

48. In some cases local officials granted approval for worship outside registered mosques without the knowledge of higher state religious authorities, and thus provided some protection to worshippers. Ro'i, *Islam in the Soviet Union*, 185–86, 294, 300–301, 315, 317–18.

49. Ibid., 287–89, 291, 309–16.

of revenue for Islamic organizations, was not obligatory. Typically, every adult Muslim is obliged to make a payment to religious institutions or leaders during or at the end of *uraz*, the month-long feast concluding in the Uraz-Bayram celebration. The government did not outlaw *fitr* for fear of worsening relations with the Muslim population. However, donations were to be made only to registered mosques, which were then obligated to forward the money to the spiritual directorates, the official Islamic leadership, to use for salaries, maintenance of facilities, and other costs. During periods of greater religious repression donations dropped substantially. Overall, Soviet policies devastated Islamic charity.[50]

The challenges posed by government restrictions were even greater for secular charities. Few of them survived communism. When the Bolsheviks closed unaffiliated organizations, they allowed only branches of a few international charitable organizations to continue to operate. These included the Red Cross, the Society for Blind People, and the Society for Deaf People; however, they were controlled by the state throughout the Soviet era.[51] Their resources came from the state budget and through citizens' required purchase of membership stamps.[52] In sum, for six decades, organized charity was moribund in the Soviet Union.

Scarce Resources for Islamic Organizations and Secular Charities

In the 1980s, many secular charities and religious institutions emerged because legal changes enabled societal groups to form independently of the Communist Party and liberalized the practice of religion. However, they have been stymied in their missions to provide material help to average citizens because of the legacy of significant state economic intervention. Soviet prohibitions on charity meant that the new groups had no institutional history and few resources. Market reform in the absence of effective market-enhancing institutions has compounded this problem by limiting donations, endowments, and credit, which are key resources for societal groups.

---

50. Ibid., 27, 271, 486, 561. Despite the restrictions on religion, some charitable giving occurred. Although *fitr* and *sadaq* were only supposed to be given to a registered mosque, some individuals gave their donations directly to needy acquaintances or relatives. Furthermore, some evidence shows that registered mosques assisted destitute people who visited. And unofficial clergy, who received donations at the *mazars* (shrines) and in private homes when performing rites, kept the money and may have used it to help others.

51. Lindenmeyr, "The Big Impact of Small Deeds"; White, "Charity, Self-Help and Politics in Russia," 788.

52. Erkinbek Kasybekov, "Government and Nonprofit Sector Relations in the Kyrgyz Republic," in Ruffin and Waugh, *Civil Society in Central Asia*, 71–84.

Of the Islamic institutions, mosques are most relevant in terms of a mission of material assistance. Educational institutions and proselytizing groups are focused more on disseminating knowledge; some proselytizing groups also have the political objective of establishing a caliphate. Mosques, in contrast, aim to provide material assistance in addition to spiritual guidance.

Revenue for mosques from both foreign and domestic sources is now limited. As described above, the governments of Kazakhstan and Kyrgyzstan have restricted foreign funding of mosques since the mid-1990s, and, even when it was available, this funding was provided for mosque construction, not for operating expenses or welfare programs. Domestic sources of revenue include *fitr*, *zakat*, *sadaq*, and *waqf*. Yet with limited market opportunities, few individuals have become wealthy and are able to make generous donations. By one count 27 percent of Kyrgyzstanis and 21 percent of Kazakhstanis donate money or time to a religious organization;[53] however, the donations tend to be small. Consider, for example, the mosque in the village where I lived in southern Kazakhstan. It relies on the contributions of its members, but the villagers are in dire economic circumstances. Half of the able-bodied people are unemployed. Most people live off their garden plots and temporary seasonal employment. The few larger-scale private farms have not been able to expand and employ more people because of lack of credit and processing monopolies. With most villagers in poverty, the mosque has received no donations of land for an endowment and only limited donations of money and agricultural products. The imam interprets Sharia to require that people give 1 percent of their income each year. One percent of the income of impoverished villagers is little, assuming they can even afford that. The imam explained that his most reliable donation is sacks of flour once a year from the local miller.[54]

Like Islamic institutions, charities have indirectly been affected by market reform under the two conditions. With limited market opportunities it is difficult for citizens to earn income. Consequently, charities cannot rely on membership dues and donations. Only one of the many civic organizations I interviewed, a group to support the Russian diaspora in southern Kyrgyzstan, collected membership dues, but only those with positions inside the organization pay. Leaders of most organizations described how the amount that members—many of whom were unemployed or earning little—could possibly pay for membership was so small that it was not worth collecting. Mutual assistance groups have relied on monthly dues, typically 10 USD per month, in order to loan money to

---

53. This survey was conducted in 2008 by Beth Kolko et al. and the results appear in a book by Eric McGlinchey. The numbers are rounded. Eric McGlinchey, *Chaos, Violence, Dynasty: Politics and Islam in Central Asia* (Pittsburgh, PA: University of Pittsburgh Press, 2011), 38.

54. Incidentally, this is the miller who has the processing monopoly.

each other.[55] Donations to local charitable groups have been relatively rare: the veterans' group in southern Kyrgyzstan was able to secure some money to begin the organization by appealing to people's nostalgia for Soviet patriotism and respect for veterans. The fund for disabled children in central Kazakhstan relied on periodic assistance from private firms and individuals.

Unlike Islamic institutions, charities have also been directly affected by the difficulties of obtaining credit and engaging in successful business ventures. Laws on nongovernmental organizations do not prohibit charities from obtaining credit, and in other countries of the world credit has been important to the expansion of the nonprofit sector. Yet, none of the organizations I examined in Kazakhstan and Kyrgyzstan had obtained credit. Limited market opportunities also make it difficult for charities to fund their activities through business ventures. Of the groups I interviewed, only the veterans' organization in southern Kyrgyzstan engages in business, selling cotton and produce from southern Kyrgyzstan in Russia and purchasing metal there for resale at home.

With limited possibilities for membership dues, donations, credit, and business ventures, charities have been funded primarily through their leaderships' personal resources and secondarily by foreign grants and local governments. Leaders of charities typically use their own money to register their groups because winning a grant or finding a sponsor is difficult at this early stage. Yet even more mature organizations regularly rely on their leaders' and most dedicated members' personal resources. For example, one of the charities in central Kyrgyzstan collects used clothes, produce, and animal products from its members to distribute to others.

Only a minority of organizations receives foreign funds, and even those that do need to rely on other sources of funding as well. Foreign funds are available only for certain missions, such as civil society development or ethnic harmony, and for certain expenses, typically not rent or transportation. They are also usually in the form of grants, one-time windfalls instead of continuous support.[56] Finally, foreign donors are less accessible to local charities based outside of the countries' capitals. These limitations have meant that foreign funds are not a primary means of support for local charities. With few options for support, local charities often rely on local governments for office space, meeting places, utilities, and transportation.[57] Although an end to Soviet-era restrictions enabled

---

55. Khamidov, "Central Asia: Citizens Learning to Take the Initiative."

56. McMann, "The Civic Realm in Kyrgyzstan."

57. In reaction to the 2003 Rose Revolution in Georgia, the 2004 Orange Revolution in Ukraine, and the 2005 Tulip Revolution in Kyrgyzstan, where Western support for NGOs was seen as a precipitating factor, Kazakhstan has tried to discourage reliance on foreign organizations. In 2005, the government adopted a new Law on Social Contracts enabling local charities to apply for con-

Islamic organizations and secular charities to proliferate, market reform under the two conditions has limited their resources.

Limited Material Assistance from Islamic Organizations and Secular Charities

With their scant resources, Islamic and secular organizations do not provide the material assistance average citizens need.[58] Religious leaders and government officials confirmed that mosques generally do not provide employment, credit, or income. For example, in the village in southern Kazakhstan, the imam explained that the mosque neither helps people find work nor assists with credit. The only material assistance the mosques provide is to distribute small amounts of food or money to the poorest villagers during the observance of *uraz*, Uraz-Bayram, and Kurban-Bayram (a sacrificial festival). The village deputy *akim* placed the number of villagers who receive assistance during celebrations at ten to fifteen.

Islamic educational institutions in Kazakhstan and Kyrgyzstan may offer their students room and board, but they do not provide employment, credit, and money.[59] In fact, degrees from some of these Islamic higher education establishments do not even facilitate employment because these institutions are not recognized by the state.[60] Furthermore, they typically limit their material assistance to their own students. An exception is the Adep Bashti foundation in Kyrgyzstan, which provides stipends and materials to approximately two hundred students who are studying at institutions other than its madrassas in Bishkek and Osh.[61]

Hizb ut-Tahrir, the IMU/IJU, and Tablighi Jamaat have provided targeted, but not widespread, material assistance. Hizb ut-Tahrir offered emergency relief to earthquake victims in Naryn, Kyrgyzstan, and has organized community

---

tracts to provide social services. The result, however, was the creation of additional government-organized NGOs instead of support for existing independent charities. Armine Ishkanian, "Social Policy and Development in Central Asia and the Caucasus," *Central Asian Survey* 25, no. 4 (2006): 373–85, here 379; Vsevolod Ovcharenko, "Government Financing of NGOs in Kazakhstan: Overview of a Controversial Experience," *International Journal of Not-for-Profit Law* 8, no. 4 (2006), 21–29.

58. Other religions also provide only limited material assistance in Kazakhstan and Kyrgyzstan, typically through foreign missionaries. They are mostly of different Christian denominations, and they typically provide only periodic material assistance in small amounts to small numbers of people. An American Baptist organization in Kazakhstan was unusual in that it had a business credit program, but only five of seventy interested people received credit.

59. Eric McGlinchey offers examples from Osh, Kyrgyzstan. McGlinchey, "Islamic Revivalism and State Failure in Kyrgyzstan," 26.

60. International Crisis Group, "Central Asia: Islam and the State," 29.

61. De Cordier, "Kyrgyzstan: Fledgling Islamic Charity Reflects Growing Role for Religion."

projects, such as repairing irrigation canals, in a few locations in the country, particularly in the south.[62] The organization also provides material aid to its imprisoned members.[63] Hizb ut-Tahrir reportedly pays young adults to distribute leaflets. However, members are also expected to contribute 10 percent of their income to the organization and purchase every issue of the organization's Uzbek-language newspaper, *Ong-Al-Waie* (Awareness), so involvement in this organization is not a good means to support oneself.[64]

The IMU promised monthly salaries of 700–1,000 USD to its fighters, who have mounted incursions in Kyrgyzstan and Uzbekistan and battled U.S. forces in Afghanistan; however, former fighters reported that they were never paid.[65] There have not been reports of Tablighi Jamaat providing material assistance to its supporters.[66]

Secular charities are also not able to meet individuals' needs for employment, money, and credit. The most typical assistance provided by charities is infrequent or periodic provision of goods. Although this can significantly improve recipients' standard of living in the short-term, it does not address the long-term difficulties of lack of income or credit to create a business. Infrequent assistance includes the occasional pair of shoes or schoolbooks one of the charities in southern Kyrgyzstan is able to provide to disabled Uzbek children and the medicine and groceries that a charity in central Kyrgyzstan distributes to women and poor people. Periodic assistance typically coincides with special dates. For example, the veterans' organization in southern Kyrgyzstan provides poor veterans and deceased veterans' families with money and coal on December 28, when the war in Afghanistan began, and on February 15, when the troops left Afghanistan.

Local charities typically do not help with generating income. In none of the locations where I worked was there a charity that focused on finding or generating jobs for people. Credit programs by nongovernmental organizations did exist,

---

62. Similarly, the education foundation Adep Bashati provided bread and temporary financial assistance to victims of the 2010 violence in Osh. McGlinchey, "Islamic Revivalism and State Failure in Kyrgyzstan," 21–22. De Cordier, "Kyrgyzstan: Fledgling Islamic Charity Reflects Growing Role for Religion."

63. International Crisis Group, "Central Asia: Islamists in Prison."

64. Saidazimova, "Central Asia: Banned Islamic Group Hizb ut-Tahrir Continues to Gain Members."

65. Martha Brill Olcott, "Roots of Radical Islam in Central Asia" (Washington, DC: Carnegie Endowment for International Peace, 2007), here 33.

66. Neighborhood Islamic charities, or *jamiyats*, may be a growing presence in Osh, Kyrgyzstan. Evidence shows that they provided relief for refugees of the state violence in Andjian, Uzbekistan, in May 2005 and that local businesspeople support them financially. McGlinchey, "Islamic Revivalism and State Failure in Kyrgyzstan," 26. The role of local businesspeople in meeting people's basic needs directly and through religious or secular charities is further discussed later in a section on local businesses.

although they helped only a small number of people. For example, a charitable organization in central Kyrgyzstan was able to provide eight women with credit for ventures such as running a farm, operating a cafeteria, or making handcrafts. In one and a quarter years a charity aiming to help women and the poor in central Kyrgyzstan had provided approximately thirty individuals with credit to grow potatoes and wheat and make handcrafts. This assistance is significant for the recipients, but it helps relatively few people.

Even with the help of foreign organizations, local charities that provide credit have a limited effect. For example, through its Poverty Alleviation Project, the United Nations Development Programme (UNDP) granted ten local organizations the funds to create microcredit programs to support rural residents' small businesses in southern Kyrgyzstan. In three years several hundred people received loans of 1,000 to 11,000 som, or about 50 to 600 USD, for one year or less at approximately 40 percent to sew household goods, grow crops, or raise animals, among other ventures. However, this is in a province of 1.5 million people, with approximately 99,000 considered poor. Moreover, these loans, like bank credit, are only for the short term, which makes it difficult for people to escape poverty.

A promising exception is the Kyrgyzstani nonprofit microcredit company Bai Tushum and Partners, which had granted loans to more than 100,000 clients by 2010 and has offices in approximately half of the country's *raions*. International awards for transparency indicate that, unlike many of its for-profit counterparts, it does not engage in predatory lending. Thanks to its nonprofit status and support from international lending institutions like the EBRD, Bai Tushum can lend to a wider group of people and offer better terms. Farmers and potential entrepreneurs are eligible, and people without valuable collateral can obtain a guarantee from another person. The rates are nonetheless high, in part, due to the lack of credit histories. Bai Tushum has contributed information to the private credit bureaus and thus has helped to expand their coverage. Its further growth will be limited as long as its counterparts are hesitant to share information.[67]

Unlike Bai Tushum, most local charities do not have foreign financial support. Limited resources have forced most to have narrow target populations, further reducing their ability to provide substitutes for state goods and services. Irina, the Russian woman in the village where I lived in southern Kazakhstan, described how she and her family needed help desperately but had not turned to a charity for assistance. She is a veterinarian and her husband was a construction

---

67. Author's interview (#134), Kyrgyzstan, June 4, 2009. Bai-Tushum and Partners Microfinance Bank, http://www.baitushum.kg/en/ (accessed December 19, 2013); Myles G. Smith, "Kyrgyzstan: Could Microfinance Bubble Burst?" EurasiaNet, June 11, 2012, http://www.eurasianet.org/node/65527 (accessed December 19, 2013).

worker at the sovkhoz, but she has not received her salary for four years and her husband lost his job five years ago. They try to support themselves and their two teenage sons by living off their plot of land, pig, cow, and a few chickens. Sometimes her husband can find seasonal construction work, such as building a summer kitchen. Despite these difficult circumstances, she has not turned to local charities for help because, as she puts it, "I am not a pensioner or a mother with many children so no one helps me."[68] Her perception is accurate. Unlike religious institutions that are open to helping anyone, even nonbelievers in many cases, charitable organizations typically have a narrow focus. For example, in a region in southern Kyrgyzstan an organization helped veterans while another helped invalids or disadvantaged Uzbeks. This excluded much of the population. In a central province of Kyrgyzstan, one organization focused on mothers, single parents, and children and another group helped women and the poor. The category of poor is a broad mandate that a small number of charities have taken on, but this target typically refers only to those in the most dire circumstances—those who are physically unable to work or homeless.

Charities' limited geographic scope also reduces their influence. Unlike the Soviet party-state, which had representatives in each village and urban neighborhood, charities tend to form locally and many are based in urban areas.[69] For example, the village in southern Kazakhstan had no charitable organization. The *raion* where it is located had no local charities only foreign ones, which have their own limitations, as will be described later. Local charities had formed in the provincial capital but their work did not extend to the village. Neither secular charities nor Islamic organizations have managed to provide widespread material assistance in Kazakhstan and Kyrgyzstan.

Minimal Reliance on Islamic Institutions and Charitable Organizations

Because Islamic institutions and charitable groups have little material assistance to offer, few individuals in Kazakhstan and Kyrgyzstan seek their help in solving their everyday problems. This lack of reliance on Islamic institutions and charitable groups is evident from both the surveys and in-depth interviews.

---

68. Author's interview (#158), Kazakhstan, July 19, 2001.

69. Lucy Earle, "Community Development, 'Tradition' and the Civil Society Strengthening Agenda in Central Asia," *Central Asian Survey* 24, no. 3 (2005): 245–60, here 249; Earle et al., *Community Development in Kazakhstan, Kyrgyzstan and Uzbekistan*, 17.

TABLE 5.1. Societal actors and institutions from whom citizens have sought assistance in the past year in Kazakhstan and Kyrgyzstan (percentage of respondents, rounded)

	KAZAKHSTAN	KYRGYZSTAN
Religious institution or leader	1	2
Local, private charitable organization	1	2

Note: $n = 1,200$ for Kazakhstan and 1,199 for Kyrgyzstan. A portion of the 1,500 respondents in each country claimed that they had no problems or that describing their problems was too difficult and thus some respondents were not asked this question about seeking assistance.

No more than 2 percent of survey respondents in either country sought assistance from Islamic institutions or charities in the past year (see Table 5.1). At most, 2 percent of respondents in a country selected "religious institution or leader" or "local, private charitable organization."

Average citizens and representatives of Islamic institutions and charities I interviewed confirmed that individuals do not typically turn to these entities for material assistance. Not a single person I interviewed had turned to a mosque, Islamic educational establishment, or Islamic group, or secular charity for assistance.[70] These individuals were in need of assistance: they included urban residents who were unemployed and actively seeking work and villagers who had no income and were trying to survive on subsistence farming and odd jobs. In these interviews I asked people to describe the problems they faced in their everyday lives and how they tried to solve them. People often explained how they had considered different options for solving their problems. No one mentioned a mosque, Islamic school, or Islamic group in this context. Instead, I would have to prompt interviewees to discuss the possibility that Islamic institutions served as potential sources of assistance. The imam in the village in southern Kazakhstan corroborated these accounts, explaining that only one person in the village of 3,300 sought material assistance from the mosque each year. "People know the mosque does not have the means so therefore they do not seek assistance," he explained.[71] A few individuals I interviewed mentioned that they considered seeking help from charities, but they explained that the organizations could not provide them with the resources they needed.

---

70. Similarly, in her work in the late 1990s in Kyrgyzstan, Kathleen Collins did not find a single person who said they would turn to a mosque for a loan or financial assistance. Furthermore, not one indicated that a mosque was the most important factor in getting a job or being financially successful. Kathleen Collins, "The Political Role of Clans in Central Asia," *Comparative Politics* 35, no. 2 (2003): 171–90, here 178.

71. Author's interview (#173), Kazakhstan, July 30, 2001.

Not Averse to Islamic Institutions and Charitable Organizations

It is because of Islamic institutions' and secular charities' inabilities to meet material needs—not for other reasons—that people do not turn to them for assistance. The fact that people do use other services of Islamic institutions indicates that it is not an aversion to or suspicion of religion that keeps them from seeking material assistance. "For seventy years people were told religion was the opiate of the masses," the imam in Kazakhstan reminds us,[72] so it is plausible that people in Kazakhstan and Kyrgyzstan may be wary of associating with Islam. But, in fact, these countries have seen an Islamic revival, with people attending mosque, enrolling in religious classes, seeking spiritual guidance from religious leaders, reading religious literature, and making pilgrimages. Some people have also decided to pursue religious educations. The imam in southern Kazakhstan contrasted the limited material assistance his mosque could provide with the extensive work he was doing in the areas of spiritual guidance, conflict resolution, and youth courses on Islam and the Arabic language, as well as Kazakh culture. Aversion and suspicion explain only the limited contact with proselytizing groups, especially Hizb ut-Tahrir and the IMU/IJU. Most Kazakhstanis and Kyrgyzstanis prefer secular states[73]—likely a legacy of Soviet communism—and they are aware of their governments' bans of radical Islamist activity.[74] So, seeking material assistance from Hizb ut-Tahrir and the IMU/IJU would be not only unfruitful but also politically misguided. With the exception of these organizations,

---

72. Ibid.

73. International Crisis Group, "Is Radical Islam Inevitable in Central Asia? Priorities for Engagement" (Brussels, 2003); U.S. Department of State, "Central Asians Differ on Islam's Political Role, but Agree on a Secular State" (Washington, DC: U.S. Department of State, Office of Research, 2000), 5.

74. Government disapproval of certain Islamic groups is evident from Kazakhstan's 1993 law "On the Freedom of Religion and on Religious Associations," which initially prohibited religious political parties and then was broadened to prohibit the distribution of extremist or proselytizing materials without permission. Kazakhstan's 1995 constitution severely limited the activities of foreign religious organizations. In Kyrgyzstan, the registration of religious organizations was introduced in November 1996 as a means of discouraging extremism, although the requirement has not been effectively implemented. The government essentially banned foreign religious organizations beginning in 1999. A presidential decree and instructions to the National Security Service in 2004 banned extremist, fundamentalist, and Shiite missionaries. In both countries, government security agencies now meet with members of proselytizing organizations to try to discourage their involvement in them, and are increasingly incarcerating them and imprisoning them for longer. International Crisis Group, "Central Asia: Islam and the State," 25; International Crisis Group, "Central Asia: Islamists in Prison," 5–6; Karagiannis, *Political Islam in Central Asia*, 31, 32, 35; Khalid, *Islam after Communism*, 185.

Islamic institutions' lack of resources is the factor that discourages citizens from seeking material help from them.

Charities' limited resources are the only deterrent to seeking assistance from them. Some individuals have been suspicious of charitable organizations because they have believed leaders' true motives are personal gain and they were unfamiliar, at least in the early independence period, with practices such as traveling abroad for seminars and applying for grants.[75] However, people I interviewed mentioned the lack of assistance charities provide, not their suspicions, as the reason they did not turn to charities. Moreover, suspicion is unlikely to be an obstacle to seeking charitable assistance when many people have taken jobs that they were suspicious and ashamed of. In Kazakhstan and Kyrgyzstan, many people, including well-educated professionals, began buying and reselling goods to survive after the collapse of the Soviet Union. Yet people were suspicious of working in the bazaar because in the Soviet era they had been taught that "spekulatsia"—buying and reselling at a higher price—was amoral. "Teachers and doctors were ashamed to stand in the bazaar [and sell goods]," the head of an entrepreneurial association for central Kazakhstan explained.[76] Anara, an entrepreneur in a central city of Kazakhstan, recounted that when she left her job at a technical institute to work in the bazaar, "Many thought, 'How could a person with higher education work in the market?'" She explained to me how in the 1990s "prices doubled, and then increased five times, and when they increased ten times I woke up. We went to the store and prices had three more zeroes. I became fearful even though I had work and a salary. . . . But, I wondered how will we live if prices continue to increase."[77] These conditions led her to work in the bazaar. Considering that thousands of people in dire straits overcame their suspicion and shame to work in the bazaars, it is unlikely that fear and embarrassment prevent people from turning to charities for assistance. Instead, few people turn to charities or Islamic groups, because the organizations do not address the need to generate income.

Other Societal Groups and Individuals

Like Islamic institutions and secular charities, other groups and individuals in society cannot meet people's needs for income, employment, and credit. Foreign charities, foreign companies, local companies, labor unions or other profes-

---

75. McMann, "The Civic Realm in Kyrgyzstan."
76. Author's interview (#196), Kazakhstan, June 8, 2001.
77. Author's interview (#216), Kazakhstan, June 15, 2001.

sional associations, political parties, *aksakals*, and educational establishments do not serve as substitutes for the state. Their difficulties in meeting individuals' needs are reflected in the low numbers of people who have sought their help. No more than 4 percent of respondents turned to one of the groups.

Foreign Charities

Foreign organizations engaged in charitable work tend to work through local NGOs, so it is not surprising that less than 1 percent of citizens in Kazakhstan and only 1 percent in Kyrgyzstan would have turned directly to the foreign groups for assistance, as indicated in Table 5.2. Moreover, foreign organizations engaged in charitable work have many of the same limitations as local charities. Much foreign charitable assistance is narrowly targeted, infrequent or one-time, focused on goals other than generating income, and limited in geographic scope.[78]

One category of help is the distribution of goods to specific groups, such as refugees, disaster victims, and the poorest members of a community. In many cases this is one-time assistance. For example, the leader of a provincial branch of the Red Cross/Red Crescent in southern Kazakhstan explained that the organization tried to help each needy individual only once a year. She said that some people come repeatedly to the office and request help: "I ask, 'Why do you eternally come here? You came not long ago and ate at the cafeteria at a cost of $1.50. . . . Do you think you are alone? Let others receive help too.'"[79]

Other categories of foreign assistance—educational programs and community projects—might enable people to generate income in the future, but they do not provide an immediate solution. Educational programs, by the U.S. Peace Corps and the European Union's Technical Assistance to the Commonwealth of Independent States, for example, concentrate on teaching people foreign languages, agricultural techniques, and business skills. The community projects have local residents, typically in a rural area, improve infrastructure, such as sewer or water systems, with guidance and funds from the foreign organization.[80] A foundation in a foreign language or improved irrigation is helpful for generating income but only if jobs or credit are available.

Microcredit programs offer the most promising foreign assistance; however, they illustrate an additional constraint of foreign groups—limited geographic scope. Foreign organizations typically have a representative in place to monitor

---

78. Other foreign groups focus less on meeting material needs, concentrating instead on developing civil society and reducing ethnic tensions, for example.

79. Author's interview, Kazakhstan (#146), July 5, 2001.

80. Community projects aim to overcome an additional limitation of foreign assistance—poor knowledge of local needs.

TABLE 5.2.   Other societal actors and institutions from whom citizens have sought assistance in the past year in Kazakhstan and Kyrgyzstan

	KAZAKHSTAN	KYRGYZSTAN
Foreign charity	<1	1
Foreign company where you don't work	<1	0
Local company where you don't work[a]	3	<1
Labor union[a]	1	1
Respected male elder	1	4
Educational establishment	<1	2

Note: $n = 1,200$ for Kazakhstan and 1,199 for Kyrgyzstan. A portion of the 1,500 respondents in each country claimed that they had no problems or that describing their problems was too difficult and thus some respondents were not asked this question about seeking assistance.

[a] Some local companies and labor unions remain state institutions in these countries as a result of the communist period; however, market reforms have ensured that most are now nonstate entities. Counting them as market actors increases the difficulty of arguing that the reliance on the state is greater than reliance on nonstate actors.

credit recipients' use of funds. Only with such a monitoring system is it "apparent if the money was not used for the business—if [the entrepreneurs] bought a sheep for a wedding" instead, a regional manager of one foreign organization in southern Kyrgyzstan explained.[81] However, almost no groups have the human resources to operate such programs countrywide, particularly in larger countries like Kazakhstan. In Kyrgyzstan it is plausible to blanket the country. In the early part of the decade residents near urban areas and in provinces viewed by foreign representatives as easier to work in were the only people likely to have access to microcredit. More recently, foreign organizations have been able to open more offices by relying on locals to staff them. For example, the American organization FINCA has its headquarters in Bishkek but also has twenty-two branches and approximately 120,000 clients. Similarly, Kompanion, backed by the U.S. organization Mercy Corps, has offices in all regions of the country and has approximately 120,000 borrowers.[82]

With the exception of institutions like these, foreign organizations mainly help meet everyday needs by providing funds for credit programs run by local charities. Unlike Islamic institutions and local, secular charities, the limitations faced by foreign organizations are generally not because of lack of financial resources. Instead, mandates from their governments and boards limit their target populations and objectives. Preferences for immediate, concrete solutions encourage one-time or periodic assistance and the distribution of tangible goods

---

81. Author's interview, Kyrgyzstan (101), May 15, 1998.

82. FINCA, "Kyrgyzstan," http://www.finca.org/site/c.6fIGIXMFJnJ0H/b.6088573/k.348A/Kyr gyzstan.htm (accessed December 19, 2013); Kompanion, http://www.kompanion.kg/index.php ?lang=en (accessed December 19, 2013).

instead of ongoing assistance, the results of which are more difficult to measure. The difficulty of recruiting and retaining staff from the home country to work in remote locations causes programs to be concentrated in urban areas and places where it is considered easiest and most comfortable to work.

Foreign Companies

Scholars have identified foreign companies, even more than foreign NGOs, as holding the greatest promise for addressing everyday needs. For example, Pauline Jones Luong and Erika Weinthal note that "[a]n examination of several contracts with foreign companies active in the energy sector reveals a consistent pattern of foreign companies' adopting all the social and economic burdens in the regions, cities, towns, and villages surrounding the fields to which they have bought rights to explore and produce oil and gas," including maintaining full employment and paying back wages.[83] Not only on paper but also in practice, foreign companies can provide individuals with the income, employment, and other assistance that they need.[84] However, like charities, their assistance has limited target populations and limited geographic scope. They help employees of their operations and the city where they are based, but their operations do not blanket Kazakhstan and Kyrgyzstan. For these reasons, less than 1 percent of survey respondents in Kazakhstan and no respondents in Kyrgyzstan indicated that they had turned to a foreign company for assistance (see Table 5.2).

Let us explore these benefits and limitations by considering a foreign natural resource extraction firm working in Kazakhstan. From interviews I conducted with directors, employees, and residents of towns where it operates, I found that in many respects the foreign firm had taken over the welfare responsibilities of the enterprise and one large town. One director, one of many foreigners in upper management, began the story, saying, "What we perceived when we came was that the [Kazakhstani enterprise] maintains the entire town."[85] The enterprise had constructed homes and was providing free utilities and education, among other benefits. However, with the economic crisis of the early independence period, this system began to collapse. The Kazakhstani enterprise was relying on barter for inputs and for payment and was producing only 3 percent of

---

83. Erika Weinthal and Pauline Jones Luong, "Environmental NGOs in Kazakhstan: Democratic Goals and Nondemocratic Outcomes," in *The Power and Limits of NGOs*, ed. Sarah E. Mendelson and John K. Glenn (New York: Columbia University Press, 2002), 152–67, here 170.

84. See examples in Pauline Jones Luong and Erika Weinthal, *Oil Is Not a Curse: Ownership Structure and Institutions in Soviet Successor States* (Cambridge: Cambridge University Press, 2010), 288–90.

85. Author's interview (#218), Kazakhstan, June 16, 2001.

what it once had. "Without cash how could they pay the workers? Workers were paid in products and clothes," a current director explained.[86] Or, at times the employees were not paid at all. When the foreign firm purchased the enterprise in the 1990s, the workers had not been paid for five months and the decreased production at the enterprise meant that the town could no longer provide heat to people's homes at times. As a result, workers were finding excuses to stay at work to keep warm.

The foreign firm purchased not only the enterprise but its related facilities, including a children's cultural center, three children's summer camps, a textile plant that produced uniforms, and a cafeteria. It also eventually bought all the utility plants in the town as the local government was not effectively providing services, in part because of lack of investment in the facilities in recent decades. The firm also purchased a hospital and pays salaries at another one. Besides buying facilities, the firm has funded the city sports complex, schools, and children's camps. It also contributed 1 million USD for an oblast agricultural credit fund. The fund provides half of each loan and a bank provides the other half. In one year the fund provided credit to one hundred entrepreneurs.

The firm's direction and funding of these welfare services in this town has addressed the income and employment problems of its workers, but not of all residents.[87] Workers received their five months of back pay and now receive 150–200 USD per month on time. This money goes far because workers receive free medical care, one free meal at the cafeteria each day that they work, resort vacations at only 15 percent of cost, and subsidized university courses in their field. These benefits have an enormous effect on the town as approximately one in seven of the town's residents is employed at the firm. Moreover, an individual in an urban area typically lives in a household with four others—a spouse, two children, and a grandparent. However, as a worker at one of the firm's remote locations noted, while the firm's workers live well, other residents are trying to survive off their garden plots. Furthermore, although nonemployees in these foreign company towns have access to functioning and often improved infrastructure, such as utilities and public transportation, they may not be able to afford the prices charged by the foreign firms operating them according to market principles.

Foreign firms have in fact addressed the problems of income and employment for their own workers, but they cannot employ everyone in a location and they do not operate throughout a country. Instead, they tend to be based where

---

86. Ibid.

87. It is important to note that 23 percent of the enterprise's employees at the time of purchase lost their jobs, approximately 14 percent under early retirement plans and the rest through on-time retirement, migration, or layoffs.

extractive resources are available. For Kyrgyzstan, in particular, this is of little help because the country has few of these resources.

Local Businesses

Like foreign businesses, local businesses are limited in providing charity because of geographic scope, but also because of scant resources. Businesses, particularly large businesses, are more likely to be based in cities and thus more likely to help urban residents. But, whether they are based in urban or rural areas, most businesses do not have an excess of resources to use to help people. As a result, only 3 percent of respondents in Kazakhstan and less than 1 percent in Kyrgyzstan had sought help from a local company where they do not work. The local businesses that do manage to provide charity are those that were started at the end of the Soviet era by Communist Party leaders, specifically leaders of the Komsomol, a communist youth organization for people ages fourteen to twenty-eight. These businesses were built on the advantages of Communist-era connections and, in some cases, commandeering of state resources at the end of the Soviet era. Businesses developed by average citizens in later years face the limited opportunities resulting from market reform under the two conditions. The relatively few businesses that can afford to engage in charitable work fall into two categories: those that direct most of their assistance to their own employees and those that direct most of their assistance to local residents who are not employees.

Falling into the former category is a business in a city in central Kazakhstan. Ivan, the founder and a former Komsomol leader, established the company from a Komsomol housing program he began in 1987. At the time, his city had a shortage of apartments; young people had to wait ten years for the enterprise where they worked to provide them with a unit. The enterprises had a surfeit of cash but not the means or the mandate to build apartments. Ivan convinced the enterprise directors to let him use the cash to purchase construction materials. He and the employees waiting for apartments then built approximately 1,500 homes for their use. With market reform, Ivan transformed the business venture into his own private companies, one of which was the first private company in Kazakhstan. The companies continue to construct buildings as well as operate stores, produce bottled water, and expand into new areas.

Just as Ivan established the housing program with an eye to both meeting people's needs and making a profit, he provides welfare services to his employees today. His rationale for buying houses for employees today is that an employee "should not think about where to live, but about work."[88] He established

---

88. Author's interview (#217), Kazakhstan, June 15, 2001.

a cafeteria that provides free lunches to employees because he found that workers were getting sick from bringing in and eating poor quality food, and management was taking too long to go out to eat lunch. More generally, he explained why he provides extensive goods and services to his employees: "I want people to believe in the firm. That was a concern."[89] His philosophy has worked, as no employee has left voluntarily unless he or she has decided to emigrate. Ivan explained that his approach is also influenced by growing up in the Soviet era, when workplaces provided many benefits for employees.

In addition to providing houses and lunches for employees, Ivan established a day-care facility and school that are free for employee's children, and he pays for employees' care at the local hospital. Ivan also provides cars for employees; those who have worked well for a year or two are eligible. Finally, he makes small sums of money available for other purposes, such as an eye operation in Moscow for an employee's daughter.

Like other successful businesspeople, Ivan has focused on helping his own employees. People in the community are aware of this; as a result, nonemployees do not approach him for help. Ivan does, however, provide some support for the community. He subsidizes the school and hospital for nonemployees and distributes food to 366 pensioners in the *raion* on New Year's Day, Victory Day, and Pensioners' Day. Assistance three times a year is more frequent than typical. Businesses in Kazakhstan and Kyrgyzstan that make charitable donations at all typically do it only once a year, according to residents of each city and town where I lived.

Other businesspeople focus their charity primarily on the community. Consider, for example, a businessman in southern Kyrgyzstan. Bolotbek was active in the Komsomol in the Soviet era and he began his business ventures early. While a university student and a Komsomol leader, he opened small enterprises offering shoe shines and haircuts. In 1993, when he graduated from the university, Bolotbek used his accumulated capital and his Komsomol connections to purchase a restaurant through the privatization initiative. With a relatively small number of employees, most of his charity goes to members of the community who seek assistance with everyday problems. From zero to fifteen people approach him each month for help with different types of problems. To address legal problems, such as an unfair firing, he contacts government officials. For the problem of insufficient income, Bolotbek provides for individuals with his own money.

The two businesses above are exceptions; they are highly successful because they were started in the late Soviet era by well-connected people. As a result, they

---

89. Ibid.

are able to provide assistance to their employees and the community. Most businesspeople, however, lack excess income because of the legacy of significant state economic intervention and the weakness of market-enhancing institutions. Businesspeople explained to me that they could not help people by providing credit, other monetary handouts, or jobs because they did not have extra resources. For example, as one of four successful private farmers in a village in southern Kazakhstan, Muratkhan, explained, he does not help anybody outside his family because "You can only help when you have the means."[90] His tractor is too old to lend and he does not have surplus cash. His comments also highlight the point that extra resources go to household and extended family members, not to charitable giving.

Overall, charitable assistance from local businesses does not provide a substitute for state goods and services. Few businesses are successful enough to make charitable donations, and they tend not to be located in rural areas. The assistance is mainly targeted at each company's own employees. Help that does reach community members tends to be annual donations of goods.

Professional Associations

For potential entrepreneurs and businesspeople seeking to expand their ventures, professional associations would be a logical source of credit, yet in practice these associations do not serve in that capacity. Associations for farmers and for nonagricultural small businesspeople, such as traders, do "shorten the long path to becoming an entrepreneur," as the head of a businesswomen's association in Kazakhstan put it.[91] However, the groups focus on supplying information about inputs, potential buyers, and government laws and regulations, instead of providing credit. Associations typically offer seminars as well as one-on-one consultations. Some associations have begun to help attract buyers, for example, by serving as a central contact point for potential purchasers. Some have also begun to lobby the government.

While these associations provide information about credit—usually about the challenges of obtaining it or referral to a government credit program—it is rare for them to have credit programs themselves. The businesswomen's association is an exception; it has a small fund to supplement credit that female entrepreneurs have been able to obtain elsewhere. A farmers' association in central Kyrgyzstan was also able to provide credit during a two-year period thanks to a grant from the UNDP. It assisted thirty-five farmers; however, the terms allowed

---

90. Author's interview (#174), Kazakhstan, August 1, 2001.
91. Author's interview (#150), Kazakhstan, July 6, 2001.

only for purchasing seed or animals and for repayment six months later, so this credit did not enable expansion in terms of employment or processing. Like the other options for credit, this one has disadvantages: it helps only small numbers of people, has limited geographic coverage, and offers small amounts over short loan periods.

Another type of employment organization, the labor union, has been even less successful in assisting people. Labor unions were important welfare organizations in the Soviet era, but without the Communist Party's support and with the shift of workers from industry to bazaars, the old unions disintegrated and few new ones have formed. From the Soviet era to the present day, reliance on labor unions dropped from 18 percent to 1 percent in Kazakhstan and from 12 percent to 1 percent in Kyrgyzstan. Like charities, those new ones that have developed lack resources, in part, because of market reform under the two conditions.

Political Parties

Political parties also have not generally been a source of income, employment, and credit for people. Parties in Kazakhstan and Kyrgyzstan are not the party machines familiar in previous centuries in the United States. Parties are relatively small and short-lived because of government repression, unfavorable electoral rules, and divisions among elites. Like charities, they are also resource-poor, in part, because of market reform under the two conditions. The only exception to these generalizations are "parties of power," those parties established by sitting presidents to ensure that they remain in power. These parties do not lack resources because their leaders can draw on resources from their government positions.

Given this general landscape of parties, no survey respondent in either country reported turning to a political party for assistance.[92] In their capacity as government officials, some oblast and national deputies who are members of parties of power do provide material assistance, as described in chapter three. However, the resources are from the government, not the party organization, and individuals associate the assistance with the government officials, not with the party. Of the other parties in Kazakhstan and Kyrgyzstan, a couple of the larger, longer-lived parties reported receiving requests for assistance. One oblast division of a party in Kyrgyzstan reported that it received from zero to three requests per month. Bolotbek, the former Komsomol leader who began with shoe shine and

---

92. "Political party" was not an option on the survey, but respondents were encouraged to list anyone or any group they had turned to, even those that did not appear on the card provided.

haircut businesses, also headed an oblast division of a party. However, he used his profits from his successful businesses, not party funds, to assist people. Furthermore, those who requested assistance were targeting him, a well-known businessman, more than the party.

In general, parties that are not parties of power do not provide material assistance except for one-time handouts during elections. However, these resources come not from the political parties, but from state or personal resources. For example, the head doctor of a veterinary clinic distributed government veterinary medicine. A candidate in central Kyrgyzstan who worked on an oblast state property committee tasked with implementing privatization offered to tell voters "where they could profitably place their [privatization] coupons."[93] At other times, parties help people with legal or bureaucratic problems, such as an illegal firing or unreceived veterans' benefits, and they do this by contacting government officials. Political parties are not a source of employment, income, or credit.

Aksakals

Particularly in the early independence period local and foreign observers speculated that *aksakals* may be influential in Kazakhstan and Kyrgyzstan. *Aksakals*, literally white beards, are respected male elders in the community. Typically, *aksakals* are men who held positions of responsibility in the Soviet era, for example, as heads of industrial enterprises, sovkhozes, or local party divisions. The governments have granted them some formal authority, such as in the development of *aksakal* courts, which have been designated to resolve minor disputes in Kyrgyzstan. However, individuals do not turn to them for help with employment, income, or credit. Only 4 percent of survey respondents in Kyrgyzstan and 1 percent in Kazakhstan had sought help from them. In none of the rural or urban locations where I lived in either country did I find any evidence that *aksakals* help people obtain credit or employment. They are not sources of assistance because they no longer have access to the resources of their former posts, assuming those enterprises or offices even exist, and their influence has waned because they are more familiar with Soviet ways than contemporary ones. After all, they are accustomed to socialist, not marketizing, economies. As the editor of a newspaper in southern Kyrgyzstan observed in an interview with me, "There are young people now who can explain [survival in the market economy] to people. There are people who are prepared [to step in]. Most are businessmen."[94]

---

93. Author's interview (#22), Kyrgyzstan, July 2, 1997.
94. Author's interview (#56), Kyrgyzstan, April 29, 1998.

Educational Institutions

A more plausible source of assistance for young people who seek help in finding a job would be their educational institutions, but although the state no longer assigns jobs to graduating students, educational institutions have not stepped in to fill this void. Instead, graduating students tend to rely on connections to secure employment.

To illuminate the process I interviewed university staff and students graduating from a mining department in a university in central Kazakhstan. I focused on mining majors because they are some of the students most in need of assistance finding jobs. While the mining industry has enormous potential, it is a field that has gone through a period of layoffs during the independence phase. In this era, mining graduates have not always been in demand to the same extent as their counterparts in foreign language, economics, and computer science departments. Unfortunately, the help that their educational institution provides is limited.

The university staff and students have adapted to the end of the Soviet employment guarantee. The department chair commented, "When [job assignments were] centralized our heads did not hurt, but life dictates changes."[95] To help students find jobs, the department established an agreement with a foreign firm operating in Kazakhstan. The firm's management agreed to review students' files and test them; it typically employs ten to fifteen of the sixty who graduate each year. The department has also secured contracts for placement at a few other firms where department faculty members have made contacts through their research. The university sends letters to potential employers each year and holds a job fair.

The university makes a concerted effort; however, most students have to find jobs through connections, and these jobs are often not in their field. One student found work at a firm that produces iron bars for fences, where his neighbor is a director. The student explained, "I want to work in my field but the main consideration is that the salary is high and stable."[96] One fortunate student had three job offers, all secured through connections: an acquaintance proposed that he work as a mining technician in a nearby mine; an aunt secured a position for him as a mining safety engineer, which would allow him to travel around Kazakhstan; and a friend who is a Russian army general offered to help this student, an ethnic Russian, obtain a career in the Russian military.

As the director of a university office involved with placement explained, "The government's role is to make sure that enterprises operate. Nothing else is

---

95. Author's interview (#175), Kazakhstan, May 28, 2001.
96. Author's interview (#176), Kazakhstan, May 28, 2001.

needed. . . . Students should study well and find work on their own. This is normal and students are accepting of this."[97] The students, in fact, were divided on this issue. The two students described above were accepting. The first commented: "No one is guilty [for the poor economic situation]. Before, coal production was state-run. Now employers may decide how to run the business. . . . It is just the market . . . the economy."[98] Similarly, the second said: "There should not be an [employment] guarantee because enterprises are private now and take those whom they need. . . . Companies now pay more for a well-educated person."[99] On the other hand, another student who had neither a job nor connections in her field suggested, "The government should propose jobs for people but allow them to refuse . . . because many people now do not work in their fields."[100] While student opinion about the effects of market reform on job hunting was divided, all of the students were in the same position of relying more on connections than on their university to secure a job.

Societal institutions in Kazakhstan and Kyrgyzstan do not provide the employment, money, and credit that individuals need. They have not replaced the Soviet welfare state. The institutions some observers thought to be most likely to play this role, Islamic organizations and local charities, do not have the resources to help. Market reform in the context of a history of significant state economic intervention and absent or weak market-enhancing institutions has meant that few individuals are able to make generous donations and few opportunities exist for secular charities to obtain credit. For these and other reasons, foreign charities, foreign companies, local businesses, professional associations, political parties, *aksakals*, and secular educational establishments also do not offer substitutes for state goods and services. The next chapter examines one institution that has, in fact, been able to provide some individuals with the employment, income, and credit they need—families.

---

97. Author's interview (#180), Kazakhstan, May 29, 2001.
98. Author's interview (#177), Kazakhstan, May 28, 2001.
99. Author's interview (#179), Kazakhstan, May 28, 2001.
100. Author's interview (#182), Kazakhstan, May 29, 2001.

FAMILIES

The Uneven Effect of Market Reforms

"In difficult times I turn to Kanat," Marzhan said, referring to how she relied on her uncle, the successful private farmer, to resolve her problems and avoid engaging in corruption.[1] Like Marzhan, individuals in Kazakhstan and Kyrgyzstan turn primarily to family members for assistance, more so than to other personal contacts, such as friends and neighbors. Yet, only some people have relatively well-off members in their extended families who can provide the employment, income, or credit that they need. While market reform, as well as the economic chaos of the Soviet collapse, impoverished many people, some managed to adapt and prosper in the new economy. In this chapter evidence from a successful rural household and a successful urban household illustrates the type of support relatively well-off individuals can provide to their immediate and extended families and how members of these families rely on relatives as an alternative to engaging in corruption. Because of the small, dispersed nature of their families, reliance on relatives is less common among ethnic minorities than among members of titular ethnic groups.

The financial success of those individuals who are able to assist their relatives can be attributed to a constellation of factors. These individuals were relatively young and in leadership positions in the late Soviet era, and they became entrepreneurs either then or in the early independence period. They prospered as a result of market reform; whereas many people did not. This uneven effect of market reform provides an answer to the second puzzle of this book: Why do

---

1. Author's interview (#161), Kazakhstan, July 22, 2001.

some people rarely or never engage in corruption even in countries where it is pervasive? Market reform has made their extended families comparatively well-off so that these individuals can obtain the goods and services they need from relatives.

Significant Reliance on Family

Individuals in Kazakhstan and Kyrgyzstan turn primarily to family for assistance. In Kazakhstan 35 percent of survey respondents and in Kyrgyzstan 42 percent of survey respondents have sought assistance from a family member in the past year. These numbers are considerably higher than the figures for those who turned to any state, market, or societal actors, as indicated in Table 6.1. Of different family members, relatives inside the country but not in one's household are the most common targets of requests. In Kazakhstan 28 percent of survey respondents and in Kyrgyzstan 30 percent sought assistance from relatives in their country. This was followed by requests to household members, made by 13 percent and 19 percent, respectively. Many Kazakhs and Kyrgyz do not have kin outside their countries, so seeking help from such relatives was rare—3 percent and 2 percent, respectively. However, between the time of the survey and the global economic recession the number of Kyrgyz abroad grew when perhaps as many as 1 million people left Kyrgyzstan to work in Kazakhstan and Russia.[2] Turning to relatives outside the countries is more common for ethnic Slavs in Kazakhstan and Kyrgyzstan, but the percentages are still small. It is important to note that these relatives, as well as the friends, acquaintances, neighbors, and coworkers, and relatives described below, are not government officials, so their assistance does not constitute corrupt exchanges.

Evidence of Market Reform's Differential Influence

Although many people in Kazakhstan and Kyrgyzstan turn to family members for assistance, only a small percentage of relatives are able to provide the employment, income, and credit these individuals need. The numbers of impover-

---

2. The official numbers are between 350,000 and 500,000 but thought to be much higher. Mostly young men, and some young women, become labor migrants. Vanessa Ruget and Burul Usmanalieva, "Citizenship, Migration, and Loyalty Towards the State: A Case Study of the Kyrgyzstani Migrants Working in Russia and Kazakhstan," *Central Asian Survey* 27, no. 2 (2008): 129–41, here 130.

TABLE 6.1.   Family from whom citizens have sought assistance in the past year with comparisons to other actors in Kazakhstan and Kyrgyzstan

	KAZAKHSTAN	KYRGYZSTAN
Any family member[a]	35	42
Relative in country[b]	28	30
Member of household	13	19
Relative outside country	3	2
Any state actor[c]	19	24
Any market or societal actor[d]	16	14

Note: $n = 1{,}200$ for Kazakhstan and 1,199 for Kyrgyzstan. A portion of the 1,500 respondents in each country claimed that they had no problems or that describing their problems was too difficult and thus some respondents were not asked this question about seeking assistance.

[a] Included in this category were members of households, relatives living in one's own country, and relatives living in another country.
[b] The questionnaire specified a relative who is not a member of the household.
[c] This category includes government officials and the replies of a small number of respondents who specified law enforcement, social security, and government employment offices as separate from "government officials."
[d] This category includes banks, current and former employers, local and foreign companies where respondents do not work, religious institutions and leaders, foreign and local charitable organizations, labor unions, *aksakals*, and educational institutions.

ished, as recorded in Table 6.2, are staggering, considering that poverty was rare in the Soviet Union due to extensive state welfare services. The chaos of the Soviet collapse and market reform impoverished many, and although poverty has declined in recent years, it is still high in Kyrgyzstan. Substantial income inequality exists in both countries, indicating that while some families have become impoverished, others have thrived in the new market economies. The income inequality statistic in Table 6.2 is the Gini coefficient, which has a scale ranging from zero, indicating perfect equality, to 100, indicating perfect inequality. Most recently Kazakhstan had a score of 29 and Kyrgyzstan a score of 36. For comparison, Sweden, a country known for low income inequality, has a score of 25, and the United States, where recent media coverage indicates growing income inequality, has a score of 41.[3] In Kazakhstan and Kyrgyzstan the financially successful have been able to help members of their extended families. Let us consider an example from a village in Kazakhstan and a city in Kyrgyzstan.

A Successful Rural Household

The first case of someone who is thriving in the post-Soviet era is Kanat, Marzhan's uncle. He is one of four private farmers in the village and its environs who

---

3. Data are from World Bank, "World Databank," http://databank.worldbank.org/ddp/home .do (accessed December 19, 2013). The data are from 2009 for the Central Asian countries and from 2000 for the others. These are the latest data available.

TABLE 6.2. Poverty and inequality statistics from Kazakhstan and Kyrgyzstan

	POVERTY STATISTICS[a] (PERCENTAGE OF THE POPULATION LIVING ON LESS THAN 2 USD PER DAY)		INCOME INEQUALITY[b] (0 = PERFECT EQUALITY, 100 = PERFECT INEQUALITY)	
	KAZAKHSTAN	KYRGYZSTAN	KAZAKHSTAN	KYRGYZSTAN
1993	18	30	33	54
1996	19	NA	35	NA
1998	NA	61	NA	36
1999	NA	NA	NA	NA
2001	30	NA	41	NA
2002	22	67	35	32
2003	17	NA	34	NA
2004	14	39	32	35
2005	NA	46	NA	40
2006	3	32	31	39
2007	1	29	31	33
2008	1	21	29	37
2009	1	22	29	36

[a] Data are available online from World Bank, "World Databank," http://databank.worldbank.org/ddp/home.do. This poverty statistic is called the "Poverty headcount ratio at $2 per day." The latest data are presented. A missing year and NA indicate that data are not available for that year.

[b] The inequality statistics are the Gini index. The Gini index measures income inequality, with zero indicating perfect equality and 100 indicating perfect inequality. A description of the calculation can be found at the website above. NA indicates that data are not available for that year.

have succeeded, not only in subsisting but also in building an agriculture business. His work has changed dramatically since the Soviet era. As he put it, "Before, one worked to put in time; now, one works for oneself. Before, one worked 9 to 5 and had off Sundays. Now, one works to survive."[4]

In the Soviet era he was the head engineer and the second in command for production at the sovkhoz. His wife was working as an accountant at the sovkhoz. They had three children to support. After independence, as the economic crisis worsened, the sovkhoz began paying workers' salaries in grain instead of money. Kanat realized that his and his family's economic survival was at risk so he proposed to his brother, brother-in-law, and nephews—all working at the sovkhoz—that they begin a business together. The plan was to work together until each had sufficient capital to begin his own business. The initial business was to keep the grain the sovkhoz paid them and then sell the seeds back to the sovkhoz, which lacked them. In return for the seeds, the sovkhoz provided them with land and equipment and the family and sovkhoz split the profits from the harvest. Other sovkhoz workers sold their grain immediately for cash or other goods instead of providing seed to the sovkhoz.

---

4. Author's interview (#153), Kazakhstan, multiple dates in July and August 2001.

In the midst of this business venture, Kanat's wife left the sovkhoz because she was not being paid and there was no heat. She was concerned about ruining her health and not being able to care for their animals and home.[5] As she recounts, "There was no heat and often the electricity was turned off in the winter. We were freezing and people were getting bronchitis. . . . We put in a stove and we sat there in the smoke."[6] Kanat left the sovkhoz to pursue the family business full-time in 2001. At that point he had not received his salary—or even been paid in grain—for three years. Without a salary, he and his extended family had lived off profits from the business venture, his mother's pension, and food from their land and animals. He did not leave his job earlier because "there was the expectation that investors would come."[7]

Kanat and his relatives put together approximately 8,000 USD of capital to establish a private farm. The capital came from the seed venture and their long-term savings. They invested the capital immediately so they did not lose it to inflation and devaluation. They purchased combines and tractors and rented approximately 1,000 hectares from the sovkhoz to add to the 42 hectares the family had received through privatization. The business includes a 1,000 hectare grain field, 400 hectares of which are planted in wheat to sell, 100 of which are planted in barley for animal feed, and the remaining 500 that must rest every other year. The grain field brings in 5,000–10,000 USD per year depending on the snowfall and thus the moisture in the ground; the field is not irrigated.[8] This money is used to invest in the business: equipment to clean the grain and warehouses to store the grain have been purchased. It will be necessary to have pesticides sprayed from a plane because dust smut is slowly working its way across the

---

5. Their children were fourteen, eighteen, and nineteen at the time, so they did not require much care. However, she was responsible for preparing the food and maintaining the farmhouse, which today requires her to work from 7:00 each morning until 10:30 at night, except for a nap after lunch, which everyone takes. Those minimal conveniences that had existed to help her in the Soviet era are now worn out or shuttered. For example, her Soviet-era butter churn had broken and now twice a day, after milking the family's cows, she makes butter as well as sour cream and *kurut*, a hard-candy-sized cylinder of milk and salt, by hand. Preparing food takes most of her day because she begins almost every dish from the basic ingredients, such as freshly slaughtered chicken or lamb. Only bread is purchased. She also cares for thirteen chickens, many chicks, three mature cows, two calves, a turkey, two cats, and three dogs; burns the paper from the latrine; cleans chicken excrement from the breezeway, where the family eats and socializes; and maintains the many courtyards.

6. Author's interview (#154), Kazakhstan, multiple dates in July and August 2001

7. Author's interview (#153), Kazakhstan, multiple dates in July and August 2001.

8. In addition to harvesting grain, the farmer has cleaned grain for acquaintances in return for money or the promise of part of their future harvest. However, often the contract is broken, typically because the harvest is poor. In one case he is suing to get property from the person who owes him. The lawyer will get 10 percent of the claim whether he wins or loses. "Before people looked negatively at [lawsuits], but now it is just the times. . . . People are accustomed to it." Author's interview (#153), Kazakhstan, multiple dates in July and August 2001.

fields and reducing yield in those areas. Approximately 1,000 USD per year is spent to maintain a new livestock venture, designed to protect against bad grain harvests; however, this venture is not yet profitable.

SUPPORT FOR RELATIVES

In addition to the livestock venture, the earnings from the grain field must support a large number of people. The grain field provides income for Kanat, who manages the business, and the other four members of his household. The business also pays a salary to his brother who oversees the grain field, and it supports his brother-in-law who looks after the livestock, enabling them to provide for their own families. Kanat also employs five people to work in the fields, most of them relatives, including a nephew who works as a tractor operator. From March to November he employs another five people, including his nephew's wife. Relatives receive a salary and some of the profit, and nonrelatives are paid based on the number of hectares they work. In addition to his brother-in-law, two other people work with the livestock on an hourly basis.

The support of relatives only begins with regular employment of them. Kanat's wife emphasized his generosity, saying "It is best that I am not involved in the business because I would scold him for helping relatives."[9] This assistance has included paying off a past, steep debt incurred by his brother during a ten-year period when he left the family. With the wife's blessing their household has also given a cow to her sister-in-law who lives in another village and will provide room and board to her nephew who will attend a nearby technical school. She gives old clothes to her niece and her niece's family who live in a neighboring village. I also witnessed the farmer frequently giving relatives rides to and from the *raion* center twenty minutes away by car.

AVOIDING CORRUPTION

When assistance from a relative is in the form of income, credit, or employment, an individual can avoid engaging in corrupt practices with government officials. Let us consider in more detail the case of Marzhan, the farmer's niece, whose comment about not liking to give bribes began the book. In many ways, she is a typical rural resident: she and her husband Temir, ages forty and forty-two at the time of the interview, no longer work at the sovkhoz. Without their sovkhoz salaries, they are left with a small benefit of 470 tenge per month she receives for having many children. Temir has also been able to secure a state benefit of 750 tenge per month per child because he is unemployed; however, he has not received the payments for three months. So, in a month when they receive their

---

9. Author's interview (#154), Kazakhstan, multiple dates in July and August 2001.

benefit payments they have 3,000 tenge in income or approximately 23 USD.[10] This amount can buy them potatoes and low-quality flour and cover expenses for their one cow for the month. This does not cover many other expenses. A healthier, more varied diet would require additional funds. Their few chickens, from which they eat eggs and eventually meat, each cost 417 tenge per month to care for. A sheep, which they have not been able to afford, costs 7,000 tenge and the meat can last a month if stretched. Carrots for a month cost 120 tenge. Other household and personal goods must also be purchased periodically. The most basic adult shoes cost 1,500 tenge, boots 2,500 tenge, and a coat 1,000–2,500 tenge. A bar of soap costs 35–100 tenge.

Like all villagers, Marzhan and her family must pay for services that were free or highly subsidized in the Soviet era. Electricity and gas cost more.[11] Medical services are no longer free and food and linens typically must be brought from home to those who are hospitalized. Treatment for hepatitis B, a common ailment in the village, costs about 3 USD per day, according to my calculations.[12] The niece explained how she and her family avoid going to the hospital and doctor, and villagers go without teeth. "Now we are afraid of getting sick," she added.[13] Fear of the expense of falling ill was a common sentiment in the village.

Primary and secondary education is officially free, but parents, including Marzhan and her husband, must pay for textbooks as well as supply coal for heating buildings and paint for renovations. The sovkhoz no longer pays for graduates to study at universities and technical schools in Almaty. Those graduates with the highest scores on entrance examinations will be awarded a government grant, but most must pay for all the expenses of a higher education.

Entertainment, while not essential for survival, can be important to community relations and the fight against substance abuse, yet this also comes at a price now. The village club, subsidized by the sovkhoz, once offered shows, concerts,

---

10. They have slightly more money at their disposal in the spring when they sell extra milk from their cow.

11. The village does not have gas because some residents did not pay. The private gas company reacted by cutting service to the village as it is not profitable to provide only some residents with gas. Phone service is an additional expense, 250 tenge per month, or approximately 2 USD, plus the cost of calls outside the area. Marzhan and her husband opt to have phone service because their son will soon study in the provincial capital, an hour and a half away by car. Unlike other utilities, phone service was limited in the Soviet era because of a shortage and thus long waits for service. Water was free in the Soviet era and it is basically free now. Water from household pumps, used for animals and people, is free. Water from the village canal, which is used to water gardens, comes at nominal cost. Residents order canal water in advance for a certain time and the canal is opened. The fee goes to the salary of the man who operates the canal.

12. Kanat's son received a diagnosis of hepatitis B the day after I arrived. I was privy to discussions about purchasing medications and I witnessed the food preparation.

13. Author's interview (#161), Kazakhstan, July 22, 2001.

and films but has now been turned into a private disco that charges for admission. The sovkhoz also no longer provides vacations.

One expense residents do not have to worry about is rent or mortgages. Through the privatization program people could buy their own homes for low prices and most were able to do so. However, the sovkhoz no longer pays for home repairs as it did in the Soviet era.

Like typical villagers, Marzhan, her husband, and their four children have coped with the lack of employment and sufficient income by living off their land. Besides a cow and some chickens, they have a calf and a horse, although the latter is too old to provide milk or transportation.[14] They also have a garden. However, this approach is not adequate for covering all of their expenses, so, like other villagers, Marzhan looked for help outside their household. As described in the preceding chapter, the mosque does not have resources to help her, no charities exist in the village, charities in the *raion* capital neither provide the assistance she needs nor include her in the target population, and the village *akim* turned her away. Then she decided to apply to the *raion* credit program, which could enable her to begin an entrepreneurial venture. However, she learned that others in the *raion* had been offering a bribe in order to obtain credit.

Unlike many villagers, Marzhan, however, did not have to engage in corruption because she had a financially successful relative to whom she could turn for help. Her uncle Kanat hired her husband Temir to do seasonal work, the money from which will enable her son to obtain a higher education. When Marzhan's household expenses exceed her income, Kanat helps out by giving her some money. "My husband does not love that,"[15] she explains, but it has enabled them to survive. Kanat has also indirectly helped them with employment and income by offering advice. He advised her to try to secure an early pension for her husband because he did dangerous work during the Soviet era. He also recommended that she and her husband sue for their salaries from the sovkhoz, as approximately fifteen former employees have done.

A Successful Urban Household

The second example of thriving in the post-Soviet era is a family living in a city in Kyrgyzstan. The father, Omurbek, had made a career in the Soviet party-government, serving as a town leader and later a republic-level official. As the economy began to change under Mikhail Gorbachev, Omurbek became involved in business, acting as a middleman between farmers and bazaar merchants. His

---

14. Kazakhs drink horse milk as well as cow milk.
15. Author's interview (#161), Kazakhstan, July 22, 2001.

wife, Ainura, initially continued to work as a manager in a state-run service industry. She lost her job when the firm where she was working was purchased by a foreign investor who downsized. Ainura searched for work for two months, but because she lived in a city, she was eventually able to find a job again, even in the same industry. Most recently she invested the capital they had accrued to leave her post as a manager and become the owner and operator of a business in the same industry. The family accumulated capital from their pensions and salaries as well as another venture; they renovated two apartments, which they rent, often to foreigners, for a relatively high price.

SUPPORT FOR RELATIVES

Over the years, Omurbek and Ainura's financial success has enabled them to support their own four children, now grown, as well as their extended family. Recently they have provided money to a daughter whose husband was not physically able to work. Another way they have indirectly boosted the income of extended family is by providing free or subsidized housing in the city. Many rural and small-town residents in Kazakhstan and Kyrgyzstan have sought work in the cities, but finding housing can be difficult. As the villager Marzhan explained, "To move to the city you need money for a home and connections to get a job."[16] Omurbek and Ainura provided a room to a niece who came from a small town for employment; orders dried up at the factory where she was working because state purchasing guarantees had ended. The couple will allow a grandson to live in one of their apartments when he studies at the university in the city. His own town does not offer higher education.

AVOIDING CORRUPTION

The effect of the family's resources on decisions about corruption is particularly evident from the behavior of one of their daughters, Cholpon. In her twenties Cholpon was hunting for a job. She had purposely narrowed her search to positions that did not require paying a bribe or using a connection. She avoided government divisions where applicants bought their jobs. She even rejected the idea of asking for a position from one of her brothers, who managed a type of government office notorious for selling positions in the former Soviet Union and, before his tenure, in Kyrgyzstan. Cholpon also did not apply to international organizations where locals had control of hiring and had decided to hire based on bribes and connections instead of qualifications. Those who worked in or with this sector could easily identify these organizations, and she sought their advice. In one case, an international organization was establishing a new pro-

---

16. Author's interview (#161), Kazakhstan, July 22, 2001.

gram and the head, a local man, hired only his relatives to fill the second-tier positions. A woman in her forties with significant experience working in the Kyrgyzstani government with international organizations recounted a similar revelation. After losing her government job following the ouster of President Askar Akavev in 2005, she considered applying for positions with international organizations. In one case where the job description essentially matched her résumé, a friend who worked with the organization revealed to her that the search was bogus and the director, a local, had already designated relatives to hire.

How could Cholpon manage to avoid corruption in her job search? She had a back-up position that she had obtained legitimately but with the help of her family's resources. In the early independence period her parents had used their growing capital to send her to one of the best schools in the city and provide her with extra instruction in English. This preparation made it possible for Cholpon to gain admission to a well-respected European university. Her family's resources made it possible for her to cover the expenses of attending. With this education, Cholpon then secured a position with a multinational based in the European country. A family tragedy brought her home to consider the possibility of living and working in Kyrgyzstan; however, she could be selective in her search because the multinational was encouraging her to return. Furthermore, her language skills, European education, and impressive experience—resulting from her family's resources (as well as her own hard work)—made it likely that Cholpon would be a top contender for a job where qualifications matter.

Values and Corruption

A closer examination of the situations of Marzhan and Cholpon reveals that they avoid corruption because they have the resources to do so; they are not morally superior to the average person in their country. Describing the distribution of sovkhoz equipment as the farm was failing, Marzhan commented, "We do not have such money," to explain why she would not offer a bribe.[17] She would consider giving a bribe if she had the money, but her uncle does not provide money for bribes, only seasonal work for her husband and emergency funds for their household. Although willing to engage in corruption, Marzhan can usually avoid it because of her uncle's financial success and generosity. Cholpon is also like the average person in that she will engage in corruption when no other options exist. In one situation corruption was the family's only option, but they did not realize it at the time and later regretted not having offered a bribe. Cholpon did not

---

17. Ibid.

make the final cut for a study-abroad program because the locals managing the process for the foreign organization switched the list of finalists based on who paid bribes and had connections. Her mother, Ainura, explained that she would have paid a bribe but she did not realize one was required because it was a Western program. In her current job search, however, Cholpon can act on her preference not to engage in corruption because she has other options thanks to her family's resources.

Ethnic Minorities

To what extent do members of ethnic minority groups, particularly the relatively large number of Slavs in each country, rely on family assistance and, more broadly, how do they fit into this argument about corruption? Slavs depend less on family and informal government assistance because they have small, dispersed families and few connections with government officials. With fewer kin, they are less likely to have a well-off family member who can provide them with resources. However, they also lack an ethnic connection to government officials, so they are less likely to approach them for assistance in the first place and thus less likely to engage in corruption. Instead, Slavs rely on their own individual efforts to meet their basic needs.

Slavs constitute a significant portion of the populations in each country. Slavs make up 27 percent of Kazakhstan's population and 9 percent of Kyrgyzstan's. The category includes Russians, Germans, and Ukrainians. Russians are most numerous, composing 24 percent and 8 percent of the populations of Kazakhstan and Kyrgyzstan, respectively.[18]

Family assistance is less common among Slavs because they have smaller households and fewer relatives nearby. As Irina, a Russian woman in the southern village of Kazakhstan, explained, "Kazakhs have many relatives and help each other. Many businesses are family businesses so they hire their relatives and help each other. Kazakhs have an advantage because of these relative connections."[19]

---

18. The category includes only Russians, Ukrainians, and Germans, not other Slavs, due to the information available. Agency of Statistics of the Republic of Kazakhstan, "The Results of the National Population Census in 2009," 2010, http://www.eng.stat.kz/perepis_nasl (accessed December 19, 2013); National Statistical Committee of the Kyrgyz Republic, "Population and Housing Census of the Kyrgyz Republic of 2009 Book I: Main Social and Demographic Characteristics of Population and Number of Housing Units," 2009, http://unstats.un.org/unsd/demographic/sources/census /2010_phc/Kyrgyzstan/A5-2PopulationAndHousingCensusOfTheKyrgyzRepublicOf2009.pdf (accessed December 19, 2013).

19. Author's interview (#158), Kazakhstan, July 19, 2001.

By contrast, Slavic couples typically have fewer children than Kazakh or Kyrgyz couples, so Slavs have fewer offspring living at home or nearby. Moreover, because of Soviet job assignment policies that sent Slavs to work throughout the Soviet Union, especially in technical and managerial positions, only parts of Slavic families live in Kazakhstan or Kyrgyzstan, and the rest live in other post-Soviet republics. For example, a typical middle-aged Slav will have a spouse, one parent,[20] and two children in the country, but all her other relatives will be in other countries. The data in Table 6.3 reflect this situation, with smaller percentages of Slavs seeking assistance from household members and relatives within the countries.

The difference in reliance on family, between the titular group and Slavs, is greater in Kyrgyzstan because of the lower level of urbanization there. In Kyrgyzstan only 9 percent of Slavs, but 22 percent of Kyrgyz, turn to household members for help, and only 17 percent of Slavs, but 32 percent of Kyrgyz, turn to relatives inside their country. In Kazakhstan, we see almost no difference between Slavs (12 percent) and Kazakhs (14 percent) in terms of household members. The difference between Slavs (25 percent) and Kazakhs (31 percent) regarding relatives in the country is smaller than the difference in Kyrgyzstan. The dissimilarity between countries can be explained by the additional 20 percent of the population of Kyrgyzstan that lives in rural areas compared to the population of Kazakhstan. Rural titular families tend to be considerably larger than urban titular families. The higher proportion of large titular families in Kyrgyzstan accounts for the greater difference between Slavs and Kyrgyz and the smaller difference between Slavs and Kazakhs in terms of relying on household members. Overall, more Kyrgyz have a larger number of relatives from whom to seek assistance.

Migration accounts for another difference between the two countries—the smaller percentage of Slavs in Kyrgyzstan, compared to those in Kazakhstan, who seek assistance from relatives within the country.[21] In both Kazakhstan and Kyrgyzstan large numbers of Russians have migrated; however, more have left Kyrgyzstan. Ethnic violence in Kyrgyzstan in 1990 and 2010, and greater economic difficulties, as compared to Kazakhstan, have meant that a larger percentage of Russians have emigrated from Kyrgyzstan. Approximately 40 percent of the Russians who once lived in Kyrgyzstan but only 20 percent of the Russians who earlier lived in Kazakhstan have left. As a result Russians in Kyrgyzstan are

---

20. It is common for the middle-aged individual's mother, but not father, to be living because male life expectancy is significantly lower than female life expectancy in the former Soviet Union.

21. It cannot be attributed to greater rates of mixed parentage. For example, there are not more people of Russian and Kyrgyz heritage in Kyrgyzstan who are part of large extended Kyrgyz families. Of the survey respondents, only one Slav in Kyrgyzstan, and two in Kazakhstan, were of mixed ethnicity, also being members of the titular ethnicity.

TABLE 6.3.   Members of ethnic groups who have sought assistance from household members and relatives in the country in the past year in Kazakhstan and Kyrgyzstan (percentage of respondents, rounded)

| | KAZAKHSTAN | | KYRGYZSTAN | |
	KAZAKHS	SLAVS	KYRGYZ	SLAVS
Member of household	14	12	22	9
Relative in country[a]	31	25	32	17

Note: In Kazakhstan, 550 Kazakhs and 544 Slavs are included. The numbers for Kyrgyzstan are 742 Kyrgyz and 256 Slavs. Slavs included Russians, Belarusians, Germans, Poles, and Ukrainians. Most of the Slavs were Russian.

[a] The questionnaire specified a relative who is not a member of the household.

less likely than Russians in Kazakhstan to have a relative to turn to for assistance. In many cases not the entire family, but instead members of the younger generation, left in search of economic opportunities elsewhere. Older Russians felt that it was too late to begin a new life elsewhere.

As an illustration of migration in these countries, consider the situation in the village in southern Kazakhstan. In the Soviet era, seventeen ethnic groups were represented in the village of 3,850 residents. Today, of the 3,300 residents, only two German families remain, and Irina's family is the only Russian family I encountered. Irina described why Russians migrated from the village: "No one came and said, 'You are Russian and you should leave.' But people feared war and violence like there was in Tajikistan and Kyrgyzstan. . . . People were afraid that their children would be shot. . . . Sometimes when people are drunk they will say, 'You are living on my land.' . . . If there were work, people would not leave."[22] Irina and her family had decided not to migrate for the time being, in part, because they were under consideration for jobs in Almaty in the field of veterinary science. Like many other members of ethnic minority groups, Irina moved to the village on a job assignment. She grew up in Russia and obtained a degree in veterinary science there, and then was assigned to work in the village. Unusually, her Russian husband was born in the village; his father had settled there on his way home from fighting at the front against the Japanese. For the time being, Irina and her husband have opted to try to live on their land. As she explained, "When we went on vacation in Russia, we began to feel like it was time to go home. And, when we came back here, this felt like home."[23] So besides the job prospects, the family also has emotional reasons to stay. Yet, they have no relatives in the country.

---

22. Author's interview (#158), Kazakhstan, July 19, 2001.
23. Ibid.

Although Slavs in Kazakhstan and Kyrgyzstan do not have much extended family in the countries, few of them seek help from relatives in other countries. In fact, they do not rely on relatives outside their countries much more than ethnic Kazakhs and Kyrgyz do. In Kazakhstan 4 percent of Slavs and in Kyrgyzstan 5 percent sought assistance from relatives in the year prior to the survey compared to 1 percent of the titular ethnic groups in each country.[24] Slavs in Kazakhstan and Kyrgyzstan explained that, like them, their relatives outside of the countries were also struggling economically and that receiving material goods from them through the mail was difficult.

The reduced availability of assistance from relatives within Kazakhstan and Kyrgyzstan does not propel Slavs into corrupt exchanges. Policies in the Soviet and especially independence period promoted titular nationalities in government. As a result, ethnic minorities hold fewer government positions, so using connections based on ethnic identity is more difficult for Slavs. Also because Slavs have fewer relatives, a family member in a government position is a rarity. Nontitular groups are less likely to turn to government officials. Only 12 percent of non-Kazakh survey respondents sought assistance last year in Kazakhstan compared to 20 percent of Kazakh respondents. In Kyrgyzstan, the figures are 13 percent and 30 percent, respectively.

Lacking larger numbers of relatives and ethnic ties to government officials, Slavs rely more on themselves. Larger percentages of Slavic respondents, 38 percent in Kazakhstan and 49 percent in Kyrgyzstan, selected "myself" as a place to turn for assistance. Compared to members of the titular ethnic groups, 11 percent more Slavs in Kazakhstan and 18 percent more in Kyrgyzstan relied on themselves.

Friends, Acquaintances, Neighbors, Coworkers

The importance of family, even to ethnic minorities, is further underscored when we compare reliance on family with reliance on friends, acquaintances, neighbors, and coworkers. Individuals do seek assistance from friends, acquaintances, neighbors, and coworkers;[25] however, turning to nonrelatives for assistance is considerably less common than turning to relatives. This is evident from

---

24. The percentages of respondents were rounded. In Kazakhstan, 550 Kazakhs and 544 Slavs are included. The numbers for Kyrgyzstan are 742 Kyrgyz and 256 Slavs. Slavs included Russians, Belarusians, Germans, Poles, and Ukrainians. Most of the Slavs were Russian.

25. No significant differences are evident between members of titular and nontitular ethnicities in terms of seeking assistance from friends, acquaintances, neighbors, and coworkers.

the data in Table 6.4. In Kazakhstan 35 percent sought assistance from any family member, whereas only 12 percent sought help from a neighbor, friend, acquaintance, or coworker. The respective figures are 42 percent and 9 percent for Kyrgyzstan. Assistance from friends and acquaintances is most sought after and from coworkers least sought after, with help from neighbors falling in-between.

Some friends, acquaintances, neighbors, and coworkers can address the problem of lack of money. They typically provide employment or assistance with entrepreneurial ventures, sometimes including credit. Recall how the mining students at the university in central Kazakhstan had used friends, acquaintances, and neighbors, as well as relatives, to find work. Employment assistance is not limited to those fresh from university or technical school. A former mine administrator in the same province started a cable television company and hired many of his former workers from the mine. Finding employment through this approach, however, is not successful for those who do not have friends, acquaintances, and neighbors who can provide this type of help. Not having friends, acquaintances, and neighbors who could provide work was a common refrain I heard from the unemployed.[26] Furthermore, the unemployed do not have coworkers to whom they can turn for assistance.

When friends, acquaintances, and neighbors cannot provide a job, they may be able to help people start a business instead. Sulushash, the successful auto parts entrepreneur in central Kazakhstan, described how she and her husband began their business with the help of others. An acquaintance in the bazaar agreed to sell the husband some auto parts, which he could then resell at a slightly higher price. This work did not require any start-up capital, and it allowed him to learn which products would sell. Sulushash later joined him in working for the acquaintance. However, she noted that "You cannot earn real money working for someone else. With your own business you can earn more."[27] So with the help of their former boss and other acquaintances, they began their own auto parts distribution business. The former boss took the couple on buying trips to Russia and gave them advice. "We are like his graduates," Sulushash explained.[28] Other acquaintances lent them money at 5–7 percent per day. This was a steep

---

26. Another problem was that even friends, acquaintances, and neighbors who had the capacity to offer a job were unlikely to work in the sphere in which the unemployed person has been trained. For example, an unemployed music teacher in central Kazakhstan explained how her acquaintances and friends, as well as family, work in accounting and trade so they cannot help her. As she explained, "I do not have any relatives or acquaintances in other spheres of work. . . . All the good jobs are through acquaintances. Many are family businesses." The result is that many people work outside their area of expertise. From the employer's perspective, hiring friends, acquaintances, neighbors, and family can result in poor workers. Author's interview (#210), Kazakhstan, June 13, 2001.

27. Author's interview (#195), Kazakhstan, June 7, 2001.

28. Ibid.

TABLE 6.4.   Family and personal contacts from whom citizens have sought assistance in the past year in Kazakhstan and Kyrgyzstan

	KAZAKHSTAN	KYRGYZSTAN
FAMILY		
Any family	35	42
Relative in country[a]	28	30
Member of household	13	19
Relative outside country	3	2
PERSONAL CONTACT (NONFAMILY)		
Any personal contact (nonfamily)	12	9
Neighbor	3	5
Friend[b]	5	7
Acquaintance	5	7
Coworker	2	2

Note: $n = 1,200$ for Kazakhstan and 1,199 for Kyrgyzstan. A portion of the 1,500 respondents in each country claimed that they had no problems or that describing their problems was too difficult and thus some respondents were not asked this question about seeking assistance.

[a] The questionnaire specified a relative who is not a member of the household.
[b] The questionnaire specified friend who is not also a neighbor.

rate but the only way for them to obtain capital. Other entrepreneurs also described how they had obtained credit from acquaintances. The percentage is very high, but there is no collateral requirement—which is the main obstacle for urban entrepreneurs seeking loans from banks. A Russian acquaintance also helped Sulushash and her husband by letting them pay only 50 percent of the costs of goods and paying the rest on their next buying trip.

Sulushash described how this assistance to entrepreneurs is not unusual. "People help each other at the market, so money does not sit but grows.... If your car breaks down, you use a friend's and go together [to purchase goods]. When three or four people work together, everyone's position improves.... It is hard for one to improve alone."[29] This cooperation occurs among members of different ethnic groups, including Kazakhs, Russians, and Ukrainians, she explained. Sulushash and her husband have now begun to help other entrepreneurs. "We all began with nothing. It is hard to refuse people who have nothing, who have small children. A person may be good but cannot even earn a piece of bread.... I am not afraid of competition.... I do not need a private jet or a luxurious home."[30] They helped a neighbor who had three children and whose husband had lost his job and begun to drink. The couple set her up to distribute auto parts. In addition, Sulushash and her husband help those who have worked with them for about three years go out on their own.

---

29. Ibid.
30. Ibid.

Employment and business help more commonly comes from friends and acquaintances than from neighbors, particularly in rural areas where neighbors face the same financial challenges. As Irina, the Russian woman in the village in southern Kazakhstan, explained, "Life is more difficult in the village because it is hard to find work. In the city you can go to a person's home and ask to wash the floor. If you go to a neighbor here and ask to wash the floor, she would laugh."[31] Instead, neighbors provide a wide range of other assistance. Living on the farm in southern Kazakhstan, I saw neighbors sharing food, such as a delicacy made from pig fat, and providing free services, such as giving a ride to the *raion* capital, inoculating chickens, or cutting hair. Money and groceries are also common forms of assistance from neighbors. Irina explained, "There is a Russian proverb: 'You don't buy a home, you buy a neighbor.'"[32] At times she has lent 50 USD to a neighbor until he was able to harvest his grain or sell his goods at the bazaar. On other hand, she said, "There have been times when I could not lend someone 20 tenge . . . and we are not poor."[33] This assistance occurs in cities too. The urban couple, Omurbek and Ainura, frequently gave food to the children of an alcoholic neighbor in their apartment building and also provided money for the neighbor's burial later. This assistance among neighbors occurs among all nationalities. "Whether you lend to a person depends not on nationality, but on the decency of the person, on whether he will return it. There are no bad nationalities, but there are bad people," according to Irina.[34] Friends, acquaintances, neighbors, and coworkers do lend a helping hand to each other, even though family is the most common place to turn for assistance.

The Roots of Success

For family, friends, neighbors, or any individual to provide employment, credit, or money—especially significant sums of credit or money—they must have some means. This begs the question of how these individuals became financially successful in the first place. What is special about this small number of people who are thriving financially? Did they, by any chance, use corrupt means to become relatively wealthy? Use of illicit means would be ironic as it would mean that engaging in corruption enabled others to avoid it at a later date. What I found, however, is that corruption does not account for these individuals' eco-

---

31. Author's interview (#158), Kazakhstan, July 19, 2001.

32. Ibid.

33. Twenty tenge is approximately 15 U.S. cents. Author's interview (#158), Kazakhstan, July 19, 2001.

34. Ibid.

nomic ascendance. Instead, being relatively young, holding a leadership position in the late Soviet era, and entering business either then or in the early independence period were key factors.[35]

At the end of the Soviet era many of the people who are financially successful today were in their twenties to forties. The younger ones were in university, and the older ones were working in a variety of different fields. Age is an important characteristic in the sense that the people of these generations were beyond childhood and well before retirement age, so they could not rely on parents or pensions for support. They needed to figure out how to succeed in the new economic system.

Yet why did only a small number of those from these generations succeed financially? They were in positions of leadership in the late Soviet era, and these positions gave them resources, contacts, and experience that would be useful in the new economy.[36] The younger people were leaders of the Komsomol. For example, Sulushash, the auto parts distributor, was in her late twenties and head of her school's Komsomol organization when the Soviet Union collapsed. Other examples include the entrepreneurs Ivan, who began in construction, and Bolotbek, who began in shoe shining and haircutting. Those individuals at the older end of the age range held leadership positions at their workplaces. Muratkhan, the farmer described earlier in this chapter, worked as the head engineer and the

---

35. Interestingly, in addition to these factors, being female makes one more likely to be an entrepreneur, although it does not necessarily mean one will succeed in business. As a local employee of an EBRD small business program explained, "Many women are in business, whereas men have not adapted. . . . For men there is a kind of inertia. . . . In the East a woman is brought up to care for her children, so she will take any work to earn a single kopeck because she needs to feed her children." Sulushash, the auto parts distributor, described how concern for the children motivated her to build on her husband's experience working for someone in the bazaar to develop their own business. Talking about their three children, she explained "I needed to prepare the children, their education, their development, their psychological state." She has used their earnings to send their children to a better school, buy them a computer, and send them on trips to the United States and France. She contrasted her personality with her husband's: "I set a goal and fulfill it. I am not afraid." She described her husband as indecisive and risk averse. The idea of seeking credit upset him, she explained, because he was afraid they would lose their home. Author's interview (#193), Kazakhstan, June 5, 2001. Author's interview (#195), Kazakhstan, June 7, 2001.

36. Future generations will not have the benefit of these Soviet-era experiences to facilitate their entrepreneurial ventures and, in turn, support large numbers of relatives. One economic phenomenon that is new in the post-Soviet era is labor migration; however, this does not hold the same long-term promise of enriching households. Remittances do not endure in many cases. Migrants, typically young men, often establish new families in the countries where they work and abandon their wives and children in their homeland. Another common scenario is for migrants to return home after a relatively short period due to difficulties finding jobs or because of racial and ethnic harassment or legal problems abroad. Time will tell whether enough young men continue to send money home and overcome these obstacles so that remittances will be an alternative to corruption for a significant number of people. International Crisis Group, "Central Asia: Migrants and the Economic Crisis" (Bishkek: International Crisis Group, 2010).

second in command for production—positions he characterized as comparable to being a company vice president—at the sovkhoz. The three other successful farmers in the village also had vice-president-like positions in the sovkhoz. Omurbek, the father in the successful urban household, was a town leader and then a republic-level official. Successful entrepreneurs also emerged from industry. Nikolai, the successful store owner in a small town in central Kazakhstan was once a mine director.

The most clear-cut example of the use of resources from one's position is Ivan, the entrepreneur who built his construction business out of the Komsomol housing program when he was a Komsomol leader. For older entrepreneurs, the higher salaries of leadership posts, when coupled with good savings practices, also meant that these individuals had some of their own capital to begin a business, particularly if they began them before inflation hit in the independence period. Contacts were also important. Typically, the most helpful connections were not with government officials but with small traders who could offer market advice. Bolotbek, the former university Komsomol leader who began in shoe shining and haircutting, however, described how contact with local officials was beneficial to establishing his business: he knew all the local officials, including information about illegal and amoral things they had done, so he could make demands of them. In such leadership positions, these future businesspeople also gained some helpful experience, even though the economy had changed dramatically. For example, the former mine director explained his willingness to take a loan even on poor terms to begin his business, saying, "In the mines we were also borrowing. Credit is always advantageous."[37]

Another characteristic common to successful entrepreneurs is that many of them began their ventures early. Some started their businesses in the late Soviet or early independence era, whereas others began their businesses in later years but before they lost their formal employment. Sulushash, the auto parts distributor, Anara, the woman working in the bazaar, Ivan, the construction entrepreneur, and Muratkhan, the successful farmer, began their ventures in the late 1980s or early 1990s. Some others, including, for example, the store owner Nikolai, began their businesses in the late 1990s, but early in the sense that their formal employment had not yet dried up. This is significant because even though the economic crisis of the 1990s had not decimated their fields they were willing to take a risk with an entrepreneurial idea.

Entering business early meant that these individuals were the first to take advantage of opportunities. Ivan, the entrepreneur in central Kazakhstan who built apartment buildings, profited from the economic reforms in the late 1980s, as

---

37. Author's interview (#191), Kazakhstan, June 5, 2001.

well as his Komsomol position. He was the first to take advantage of the excess cash of enterprises and the need for housing. In the same region of Kazakhstan, Anara, described earlier as working at a technical institute, now has a successful business selling food in the bazaar because she seized an opportunity in the early 1990s. At the technical institute where she worked, employees had to pay a percentage of their salaries in order to receive their wages in cash instead of coupons to use at a store. She accepted coupons so as to not lose a percentage and then found that she could obtain goods that were in short supply at a store for miners. She then sold the goods at the end of the street near the institute and doubled her money. Anara expanded her business to sell in nearby sovkhozes and the city bazaar. Kanat's initial venture selling seeds back to the sovkhoz similarly took advantage of the state farm's financial crisis in order to earn income for his family.

Starting businesses relatively early and being the first to take advantage of new opportunities also indicate specific personality traits. These financially successful individuals seem to be more willing to take risks. Many people have suffered economically and some can identify opportunities, but only a smaller number have taken advantage of these opportunities, in part because of their leadership experience and resources but also because they were not risk averse. An official from a provincial small and medium-size business development office in Kazakhstan explained this well: "Many fell into business. Many lost work with the end of the union. . . . [However], the first wave of entrepreneurs left work on their own because they wanted to work independently. . . . They were the bravest individuals." This was in 1989 to 1993, and many created businesses related to their formal employment, as the construction entrepreneur, coupon schemer, and Kanat did. The official continued, "The second wave occurred after the disintegration of the union [in the mid-1990s] when people lost work and industry stopped. . . . People were forced into the bazaar."[38] Many of them struggled.

These successful entrepreneurs recounted how they were unusual in the risks that they took. They also contrasted themselves to others who are not risk-takers, who continued in their formal jobs, and are now in more difficult situations. Anara, the former employee of the technical institute, explained, "It is harder for those who stayed because now they cannot find different work."[39] Unlike most of his colleagues, Nikolai, the former mine director now store owner, chose to leave his job in 1998. Some had already been laid off but many continued to work at the mine, not receiving their salaries on time or receiving their salaries

---

38. The latest trend is the third wave. "The third wave of people have studied business and entrepreneurship. They are not forced into business. . . . These young people are studying with a particular goal in mind. . . . They know where they are going." Author's interview (#205), Kazakhstan, June 11, 2001.

39. Author's interview (#216), Kazakhstan, June 15, 2001.

in-kind. Nikolai, the former director, described how he is different: "In the mines most people were not initiators. There were few leaders. . . . The Soviet system discouraged leadership. . . . Workers were like screws. . . . Put them in their place and they work. . . . At the mine things were always changing, and I was always solving problems. . . . Therefore, I was more self-reliant and a person who takes initiative. . . . I also knew I should feed my family."[40] Nikolai added how he read an article about a business school in Japan where students were sent to different public places, like a store or the metro, and had to sing out loud. At first he thought, "What is the point of this? What if I cannot sing? Now that I am in business I understand. I should be able to sing a song and I should not have a complex. I can sing that song anywhere. . . . Few people can sing this song."[41] As a result of his willingness to take initiative and stand out, Nikolai is now in a better position than his former colleagues. "I am breathing different air. . . . I am much better off than my neighbor who continues to work in the mines. . . . I am one of the richest people in town," he explained.[42] One mine director who did not leave on his own has been demoted to cleaning work at the mine. Mining workers who were later laid off try to survive mostly by living off their small plots of land.

The personalities and experiences of these successful entrepreneurs can also be contrasted with those of unemployed people I interviewed. For example a teacher in her forties in central Kazakhstan lost her job at a music school and has been looking for work. She described how the end of the Soviet employment system and start of the new economy were not a good fit for her. "For me a job assignment would be better. But, some people have more initiative than me."[43]

Of the traits shared by the financially successful individuals, Soviet-era leadership positions offered the most potential for corruption. Studies have described how political and economic leaders in the Soviet era used their positions to enrich themselves.[44] Judging whether an economic behavior in this environment was corrupt, either by legal or cultural definitions, is difficult. In the late Soviet era when economic reforms were outpacing the legal changes, it often was

---

40. Author's interview (#191), Kazakhstan, June 5, 2001.

41. Ibid.

42. Ibid.

43. Author's interview (#210), Kazakhstan, June 13, 2001.

44. Andrew Scott Barnes, *Owning Russia: The Struggle over Factories, Farms, and Power* (Ithaca, NY: Cornell University Press, 2006); Marshall I. Goldman, *The Piratization of Russia: Russian Reform Goes Awry* (New York: Routledge, 2003); Olga Kryshtanovskaya and Stephen White, "From Soviet Nomenklatura to Russian Elite," *Europe-Asia Studies* 48, no. 5 (1996), 711–33. This is evoked by the term "nomenklatura privatization." The nomenklatura were the group of individuals in the Soviet Union who filled top positions.

not clear what economic behavior was illegal. From the perspective of Soviet citizens much of the new economic behavior, even that specifically allowed by law, violated ethics built upon decades of Soviet prohibitions against buying and selling for a profit. As individuals in post-Soviet countries have become more accustomed to new economic behaviors and more familiar with new laws, their assessments of what is corrupt have changed.

Whether by legal or cultural definitions of corruption, financially successful individuals in Kazakhstan and Kyrgyzstan did not accrue benefits from their positions illicitly in most cases. Spending one's salary or drawing on one's work experience to start a business is not corruption. By contrast, using state resources for private gain is evidence of corruption. The entrepreneur who began in housing might fall into this category; however, the legal framework at the time when this entrepreneur transformed the Komsomol housing program into his own private company was too murky to make a legal judgment about corruption. Culturally, the interpretation is clear-cut with locals not viewing the conversion as corrupt.[45] An unambiguous example of corruption is the former university Komsomol leader's use of blackmail threats to help build his business. The former example is more common than the latter, and overall, youth, Soviet-era leadership positions, and early ventures, not corruption, best explain the financial success of these individuals.

Relatively well-off individuals in Kazakhstan and Kyrgyzstan have offered others, mainly family members, an alternative to engaging in corruption. By assisting with employment, income, and credit, they enable their family members to meet their needs without approaching government officials with offers of bribes and other favors. Those who do not have financially successful relatives must resort to corruption. Markets, religious organizations, and secular charities also cannot provide them with the goods and services they need because market reform under the conditions of a legacy of significant state economic intervention and weak market-enhancing institutions has limited these institutions' resources. Market-enhancing institutions are particularly important to making alternative sources of essential goods and services available and stemming corruption: the analysis of ninety-two countries demonstrated that corruption is lower where market-enhancing institutions are effective. This global analysis also highlights that the problem of market reform promoting corruption is not specific to Central Asia; it exists wherever there is a history of substantial state

---

45. Of course, their evaluations are now colored by his generosity toward his employees and his charitable acts.

economic intervention and weak or absent market-enhancing institutions. Many countries of the world have these attributes, thus making a solution to petty corruption all the more critical. Establishing strong market-enhancing institutions as well as reducing restrictions on societal groups may be effective anticorruption strategies. Regrettably, it seems unlikely that Kazakhstan and Kyrgyzstan will implement these strategies.

REDUCING CORRUPTION

Policy Recommendations

Providing ordinary citizens with alternatives to corruption can be an effective anticorruption strategy. To the extent that markets, groups in society, and family members can meet individuals' basic needs, individuals are less likely to engage in corruption with government officials. Creating market-enhancing institutions and reducing restrictions on groups in society can increase the availability of essential goods and services from these other sources.

These recommendations for reducing corruption depart in vital ways from existing anticorruption strategies. The new recommendations rest on a fundamental observation: corruption is a two-party exchange that can be a coping strategy for citizens, not just a scheme for officials to boost their income. For these reasons, it is important to determine how to influence citizens', rather than just government officials', calculations about engaging in corruption. Other approaches propose reducing resources available to officials, decreasing their discretion, and increasing their accountability. However, these strategies do not address the root problem of corruption to meet everyday needs: citizens must be able to acquire essential resources through means other than illicit exchanges with government officials. Reducing the resources available to officials does not guarantee that substitute resources are available elsewhere. In fact, it only guarantees that competition, and thus incentives to engage in illicit exchanges for those remaining government resources, will be greater. Substitute resources need to be available from the market, groups in society, or extended family in order to stem corruption. Regarding the expansion of substitute resources, the outlook for Central Asia, the geographic focus of this book, remains rather bleak.

Acknowledge the Incentive of Ordinary Citizens

Because ordinary citizens, not just government officials, have an incentive to engage in corruption, an anticorruption strategy has to address each side's motivations. Focusing on both sets of incentives would enable a two-front attack on corruption. Unfortunately, existing recommendations concentrate exclusively on influencing the incentive of government officials.[1] The recommendations are directly or indirectly derived from scholar Robert Klitgaard's formula in Box 7.1.

Box 7.1 Robert Klitgaard's Formula

$$Corruption = Monopoly + Discretion - Accountability$$

Source: Robert E. Klitgaard, *Controlling Corruption* (Berkeley: University of California Press, 1988), 75.

Specifically, these approaches devise means to reduce officials' monopoly on resources, decrease their discretion, or increase their accountability.

Advocates of combating corruption by reducing government officials' monopoly on resources propose downsizing the state. Ideas include decreasing public spending, abolishing licenses, and reducing or eliminating government programs.[2] Advocates suggest that with fewer resources government officials will have fewer opportunities to engage in corruption. This approach is likely to be helpful in circumscribing grand corruption. In fact, the statistical finding in this book that market reform diminishes corruption to some extent supports this idea. However, these recommendations to downsize the state wrongly imply that citizens do not need government services. Governments have to provide certain regulatory and large-scale functions. Moreover, those who advocate downsizing the state overlook the fact that government officials still effectively have a monopoly if markets and groups in society cannot generate and distribute substitute resources. Downsizing the state will not reduce corruption to meet essential needs if people have no other sources for the goods and services they require. On the

---

1. Susan Rose-Ackerman advocates for this to be the focus, in *Corruption and Government: Causes, Consequences, and Reform* (Cambridge: Cambridge University Press, 1999), 5.

2. Anders Åslund, *How Capitalism Was Built: The Transformation of Central and Eastern Europe, Russia, and Central Asia* (Cambridge: Cambridge University Press, 2007), 252; Rose-Ackerman, *Corruption and Government*, 39.

contrary, downsizing will only increase competition and thus corruption for remaining state resources.

Recommendations to increase constraints on government officials aim to reduce their discretion and thus limit their opportunities to engage in corruption. These constraints include laws to combat corruption, effective law enforcement, an independent judiciary, a separation of powers, and anticorruption commissions or officials who report only to a legislature or an executive.[3] Yet this approach does not acknowledge that not only government officials but also ordinary citizens have an incentive to engage in corruption. This strategy does nothing to address the problem of limited substitute resources to meet everyday needs. Constraints are likely to discourage some government officials from accepting bribes and other favors that citizens offer, yet they are not likely to significantly reduce corruption.

Reducing officials' discretion is not even essential if they have no incentive to engage in corruption. For this reason, some scholars and policymakers have advocated increasing government officials' salaries as a way to reduce corruption.[4] The thinking is that economic need encourages government officials to demand and accept bribes and other favors, and if their needs are met, then they will not engage in corruption. This approach does not tackle ordinary citizens' economic needs and thus overlooks the fact that not only officials but also citizens can

---

3. Michael Johnston, *Syndromes of Corruption: Wealth, Power, and Democracy.* (Cambridge: Cambridge University Press, 2005), 200, 205, 208; Rasma Karklins, *The System Made Me Do It: Corruption in Post-Communist Societies* (Armonk, NY: M.E. Sharpe, 2005), 108; Goran Klemenčič and Janez Stusek, "Specialised Anti-Corruption Institutions: Review of Models" (Organization for Economic Cooperation and Development, 2007); Rose-Ackerman, *Corruption and Government*, 144–62; World Bank, "Anticorruption in Transition: A Contribution to the Policy Debate" (Washington, DC: World Bank 2000), 41–44.

Indonesia's Corruption Eradication Commission is an example of an anticorruption agency that has worked effectively. It has successfully prosecuted more than one hundred top government officials, and it has recovered significant state assets. Emil P. Bolongaita, "An Exception to the Rule? Why Indonesia's Anti-Corruption Commission Succeeds Where Others Don't—A Comparison with the Philippines' Ombudsman," U4 Anti-Corruption Resource Centre, Chr. Michelsen Institute, 2010, http://www.cmi.no/publications/file/3765-an-exception-to-the-rule.pdf (accessed December 19, 2013).

4. Michael Johnston, *Syndromes of Corruption*, 214; Karklins, *The System Made Me Do It*, 121; Rose-Ackerman, *Corruption and Government*, 72, 80.

Significantly increased salaries have been shown to reduce corruption among traffic police in Georgia, although other reforms, including replacing most officers, providing new equipment, and adapting training, were implemented at the same time. Lili di Puppo, "Police Reform in Georgia: Cracks in an Anti-Corruption Success Story," U4 Anti-Corruption Resource Centre, Chr. Michelsen Institute, 2010, http://www.u4.no/document/publication.cfm?3748=police-reform-in-georgia (accessed December 19, 2013); Lauren Horoschak, "Fighting Corruption in Saakashvili-Era Georgia: Successes, Challenges and Public Perceptions," U4 Anti-Corruption Resource Centre, Chr. Michelsen Institute, 2007, http://158.37.161.167/training/incountry-open/Georgia-materials/saakashvili-georgia -horoschak-2007.pdf (accessed December 19, 2013).

initiate illicit exchanges. Higher salaries could meet officials' economic needs, but greed may nonetheless encourage them to accept a bribe or other favor a citizen offers.

Unlike recommendations to reduce government monopolies and discretion, strategies that aim to increase officials' accountability do consider the role of citizens. However, they consider citizens only as watchdogs, not as individuals who may also have an incentive to engage in corruption. According to these recommendations, increased transparency helps citizens to uncover corruption. Measures to increase transparency include a free press, civic organizations, competitive elections, conflict of interest and financial disclosures, independent auditing, freedom of information acts, information about fees for government services, and monitoring of party financing.[5] Advocates of this approach add that educating citizens about their rights and establishing laws to protect whistle-blowers make people more likely to publicize corruption that they have discovered.[6] The underlying idea is that by enabling citizens to uncover corruption and punish their leaders for it, the officials will be less likely to engage in it. The evidence presented in this book, that citizens prefer not to engage in corruption and instead to search for other ways of meeting their needs, bodes both well and poorly for this anticorruption strategy. On the one hand, the evidence suggests that citizens are opposed to corruption and thus may be willing to serve as watchdogs. On the other hand, anticorruption campaigns that merely inform citizens that they have a right not to engage in corruption may have little effect as citizens already consider corruption repugnant. Most important, efforts to increase government accountability do not deal with the problem that citizens themselves have an incentive to engage in corruption, namely, to meet everyday needs. Increasing citizens' role as watchdogs can help in reducing grand corruption but it will be less useful in decreasing corruption to meet everyday needs.

---

5. Johnston, *Syndromes of Corruption*, 201–2, 204–6, 208, 212; Karklins, *The System Made Me Do It*, 109, 111–12; Rose-Ackerman, *Corruption and Government*, 162–74; World Bank, "Anticorruption in Transition," 40–41, 44–47.

Poor people in India have been able to use a freedom of information law, instead of corruption, to pressure government officials to distribute ration cards more efficiently, although bribery remains the quickest approach. Leonid Peisakhin and Paul Pinto, "Is Transparency an Effective Anti-Corruption Strategy? Evidence from a Field Experiment in India," *Regulation and Governance* 4 (2010), 261–80.

6. Johnston, *Syndromes of Corruption*, 208; Rose-Ackerman, *Corruption and Government*, 162. Michael Johnston's idea of deep democratization offers a framework for understanding how the political involvement of ordinary people can help combat corruption. Michael Johnston, *Corruption, Contention, and Reform: The Power of Deep Democratization* (Cambridge: Cambridge University Press, 2014).

A weakness of all of the existing recommendations is that officials often prefer not to change a system in which they personally benefit. Who is willing to implement the recommendations? Some advocates have suggested that international organizations and foreign countries can help. International anticorruption efforts independent of the target country seem most promising. Laws ending tax write-offs for bribes and prohibiting bribery outright can discourage foreign businesses from engaging in corruption. International efforts to reduce money-laundering can also be helpful.[7] Direct international pressure on countries to reduce corruption, through foreign aid conditionality,[8] is likely to meet with fewer successes because countries can refuse aid or hide corruption. For the same reason, it makes sense to focus attention on citizens, who would rather not engage in corruption and would instead prefer to meet their basic needs through other means.

Reduce the Incentive of Ordinary Citizens

For an anticorruption strategy to be effective it must not only acknowledge that ordinary citizens have an incentive to engage in corruption but also identify that incentive. This book found that meeting everyday needs is an incentive for citizens to engage in corruption and that an absence of resources from the market, groups in society, and family members strengthens that incentive. To reduce ordinary citizens' incentive to engage in corruption, it then follows that the market, groups in society, and extended family must be able to generate and distribute goods and services that individuals need. Creating effective market-enhancing institutions and reducing government restrictions on political groups are two ways to help achieve this.[9]

Market-enhancing institutions—"[r]ules, enforcement mechanisms, and organizations . . . [that] transmit information, enforce property rights and contracts, and manage competition"—can create substitute resources.[10] For example, credit registries facilitate lending by private banks and other financial institutions and thus meet the need for credit. This credit enables development and enlargement

---

7. Johnston, *Syndromes of Corruption*, 203; Rose-Ackerman, *Corruption and Government*, 185–93.

8. Johnston, *Syndromes of Corruption*, 212–13; Rose-Ackerman, *Corruption and Government*, 183.

9. Citizens' needs could also be met by introducing or reintroducing extensive state welfare programs. However, this approach expands opportunities for grand corruption. It is also not compatible with the market philosophy of international financial institutions, which can be important resources for anticorruption programs.

10. This definition comes from World Bank, *World Development Report 2002: Building Institutions for Markets* (New York: Oxford University Press, 2002), 4.

of private businesses and groups in societies, such as charities. Antimonopoly policies, another example of a market-enhancing institution, reduce the prices of inputs, freeing private businesses' capital for expansion. With expansion, private businesses hire more people, and thus meet their needs for employment and money. A successful entrepreneur or an employed individual is more capable of meeting the needs of his or her own household, providing for extended family, and making donations to groups in society. When the market, groups in society, and extended family can meet everyday needs, individuals do not need to offer bribes and other favors to government officials to try to obtain limited state resources.

Creating market-enhancing institutions is a plausible approach to combating corruption. International financial institutions began advocating the development of market-enhancing institutions in the early twenty-first century, as part of what has come to be termed the post-Washington Consensus.[11] This recommendation, and the broader idea of the necessity of state economic involvement, has endured and even strengthened through the global economic crisis beginning in 2008. According to a World Bank report, "[O]n the question of the respective roles of the market and state, the crisis reinforces the past decade's movement toward a balanced, less ideological approach. This approach gives primacy to the private sector as driver of growth, employment, and productivity, but recognizes that government may need to create the road network, metaphorically and literally, on which private firms can drive."[12] Although the primary goal is to increase economic growth, employment, and productivity, the development of market-enhancing institutions should also help generate substitute resources and thus reduce corruption.[13] Because campaigns to develop market-enhancing institutions have economic aims, they are likely more palatable to leaders who may take offense at outright foreign efforts to reduce corruption in their countries.

---

11. Washington Consensus originally referred to ten economic reform policies proposed by John Williamson of the Institute for International Economics in 1989. He believed politicians, bureaucrats, scholars, and technocrats with international financial institutions based in Washington, DC agreed that these were good policies for Latin America. The term has evolved to mean initial market reform. It has also been used pejoratively by critics of market reform and U.S. foreign policy. John Williamson, "A Short History of the Washington Consensus," in *The Washington Consensus Reconsidered: Towards a New Global Governance*, ed. Narcâis Serra and Joseph E. Stiglitz (New York: Oxford University Press, 2008), 14–30.

12. F. Halsey Rogers, "The Global Financial Crisis and Development Thinking," (Washington, DC: World Bank, 2010), 13.

13. One market-enhancing institution, an independent judiciary, has been identified as useful by those who call for constraints on officials. Karklins, *The System Made Me Do It*, 112; Rose-Ackerman, *Corruption and Government*, 151–59; World Bank, "Anticorruption in Transition," 41. Michael Johnston proposes establishing other market-enhancing institutions as a way to reduce political and economic elites' insecurity and, thus he argues, reduce corruption. Johnston, *Syndromes of Corruption*, 208.

For groups in society to reap the full benefits of market-enhancing institutions, an additional anticorruption strategy may be necessary in some countries. Governments will have to reduce restrictions on religious organizations and secular charities as well as other groups in society. Although not the main obstacle in Kazakhstan and Kyrgyzstan, laws and government harassment prevent individuals in other countries of the world from forming groups and providing essential goods and services. To the extent that the groups are simply charities and not also political groups, international development organizations can more effectively convince government leaders to allow them to operate. Advocating for freedom of organization in the name of poverty relief is less controversial than advocating for freedom of organization to combat corruption.

Citizens' preference to avoid corruption to meet everyday needs bodes well for these two anticorruption strategies. If the market, groups in society, and extended family can meet their needs, individuals will avoid illicit exchanges with government officials. However, this begs the question: Will individuals use similar techniques to secure goods and services from nongovernmental institutions, particularly markets and societal groups? Will reducing corrupt exchanges between citizens and government officials simply shift illicit practices to the private sector? Conceivably individuals could offer bribes and use personal connections, for example, to try to obtain credit from private banks or charitable organizations. Promises of political support, by contrast, would only be useful if market actors and representatives of societal groups sought political office. However, the risks and implications of corruption in the nongovernmental sphere are not as great. Citizens would have less incentive to use illicit strategies in their interactions with market actors and societal groups because of the existence of multiple sources for obtaining essential goods and services. This is in contrast to the present where limited alternatives to the state encourage citizens to use illicit techniques to gain an advantage in the competition for government goods and services. To the extent that corruption does occur in citizens' interactions with market actors and societal groups, the negative political consequences are minimized. Private financial institutions, religious organizations, and charities are not government bodies, so illicit exchanges with them are less likely to reduce government legitimacy and effectiveness, as political corruption typically does.

Because corruption to meet everyday needs is not the only form of corruption, strategies to create alternative sources of essential goods and services cannot eradicate all corruption. Some individuals, whether ordinary citizens or government officials, engage in corruption not to survive, but to gain an advantage. Moreover, corruption can be grand, involving exchanges of large amounts of money and goods between businesses and political elites. Corruption can also exist outside of the spheres of politics and basic needs, for example, in universities. Because of the varieties of corruption, other strategies are also needed.

In fact, even to combat corruption to meet everyday needs, a multipronged approach can be useful. Both citizens and officials can initiate corruption, so it is important that anticorruption programs address both parties. Prior anticorruption recommendations do not directly address the problem of corruption to meet everyday needs, and they focus on government officials' motivations, as described above. Some recommendations were developed with only grand corruption in mind, and some of these can actually promote petty corruption. Other recommendations are applicable to both types of corruption, and, by focusing on government officials' incentive, may serve as a useful complement to those presented in this book.

When multiple anticorruption strategies are used to reduce corruption to meet everyday needs, in what order should they be introduced? The strengthening of markets and groups in society should precede reforms of the government. This approach would address the root causes of this form of corruption. Changes to the government, such as further downsizing, can actually increase corruption for meeting everyday needs when substitute resources are not available. Moreover, increased salaries would be wasted, at least on government officials who seek income beyond their needs; they would continue to be receptive to citizens' offers of bribes and other favors. And citizens will not hold government officials accountable if, in order to survive, they need these officials to participate in illicit exchanges. Only once substitute resources are available to citizens should reform turn to decreasing the resources available to officials, reducing their discretion, and increasing their accountability.

Continued Corruption in Central Asia

The likelihood is slim that corruption to meet everyday needs in Kazakhstan and Kyrgyzstan will diminish in the near future. Efforts to develop market-enhancing institutions have been minimal: the governments have neither established public credit registries nor offered incentives for the development of private credit bureaus. Moreover, government competition policies have not improved. The growth of predatory lending has made credit available to a larger number of people but this will not be a long-term alternative to state assistance. Furthermore, neither government has made a genuine effort to tackle everyday corruption. Anticorruption efforts by the government of Kyrgyzstan have focused on grand corruption, and many anticorruption pronouncements have merely been plays to retain or acquire political power. The government of Kazakhstan has done even less to fight corruption.

Credit, which is important to meeting basic needs, has been more readily available in both countries thanks to predatory lending. Poor coverage by credit registries and credit bureaus and weak regulation of the microcredit industry has enabled this expansion. Unscrupulous microcredit companies lend to individuals who otherwise have not been able to obtain credit. They lend at exorbitant rates and often in a nontransparent manner. This credit is only a short-term alternative to state assistance, however. Microcredit industry watchers predict widespread loan defaults and microcredit company bankruptcy. Under this scenario borrowers not only lose their alternative to the state assistance but also face greater impoverishment.

Fortunately, a rosier scenario is imaginable because the governments of Kazakhstan and Kyrgyzstan have recognized the dangers of predatory lending. The Kazakhstani parliament is considering legislation to regulate the industry, and the Kyrgyzstani National Bank has closed some unscrupulous microfinance companies. These efforts may help the countries to avoid a bursting microfinance bubble. However, if government regulation increases, credit-lending will likely contract, also robbing many citizens of their alternative to state assistance.

The governments could compensate for the likely decrease in credit-lending by developing credit registries or offering incentives to lenders to do so. Credit information about potential borrowers would enable financial institutions to lend to more people responsibly. As people have borrowed through private and government microcredit programs, they have begun to develop credit histories. With this information, private banks can evaluate which individuals pose a sufficiently low risk to be worth lending to. Even with improved coverage, all individuals will not be eligible to obtain credit, as some potential borrowers may nonetheless be too risky. However, improved credit registry or credit bureau coverage would expand the number of eligible borrowers.

Unfortunately, little evidence indicates that the government will promote credit registries or credit bureaus. So far the governments have not developed public credit registries, even though officials have been aware that their absence has stymied economic growth, particularly in rural areas. The best hope is for private credit bureaus: private credit bureaus have begun to grow, covering approximately 46 percent and 32 percent of the adult populations of Kazakhstan and Kyrgyzstan, respectively, in 2013.[14] The nonprofit microcredit institutions

---

14. International Finance Corporation and Bank, "Doing Business: Measuring Business Regulations," http://www.doingbusiness.org/custom-query (accessed December 19, 2013).

have contributed to this growth; however, other players in the microcredit and banking industry, including the governments, have been reluctant to share information. A dramatic expansion of private credit bureaus coupled with sound government restrictions on predatory lending is the most likely way citizens will be able to obtain the credit they need to meet their everyday needs and thus to avoid engaging in corruption with government officials.

Whereas the slow development of market-enhancing institutions is discouraging, the trend of decreasing poverty bodes well for a reduction in corruption. People who are financially secure can help their extended families. From 2002 to 2009, the latest year for which statistics are available for both countries, the proportion of people living on less than 2 USD per day dropped from 22 percent to 1 percent in Kazakhstan and from 67 percent to 22 percent in Kyrgyzstan.[15]

The global economic recession may, however, reverse this trend, particularly in Kyrgyzstan. Farmers in Kyrgyzstan have had greater difficulty obtaining credit during the recession, even with the growth in predatory lending. Furthermore, prices for their products, particularly meat, fell, because people in Kazakhstan, a major market, began to eat less. Migrant workers lost their jobs in Russia and Kazakhstan and returned home to Kyrgyzstan. Even when Russia began to recover and job opportunities returned, migrant workers faced a new obstacle to finding employment in the country. Those who seek citizenship in order to work in Russia encounter additional paperwork and a year-long process, instead of three months. And applicants cannot leave Russia during that period.[16] Most recently Russia adopted a law requiring migrants to pass a Russian-language exam to work in service industries. With the decline of the education system after the collapse of the Soviet Union, rural Kazakhs and Kyrgyz receive inadequate or no Russian-language instruction in their home countries making this new work requirement daunting.[17] Even if they cannot mitigate the effects of the new Russian policies, the governments of Kazakhstan and Kyrgyzstan may be able to stem some of the gloomy effects of the global recession. Kazakhstan's government created an 18 billion USD stimulus package, mostly from its oil fund, and Kyrgyzstan's agreed to a 100 million USD stimulus package from the International Monetary Fund.[18]

---

15. This statistic is called the "Poverty headcount ratio at $2 per day," and it is expressed in U.S. dollars at 2005 international prices. World Bank, "World Databank," http://databank.worldbank .org/ddp/home.do (accessed December 19, 2013).

16. Chris Rickleton, "Kyrgyzstan: Russia Multiplying Citizenship Hurdles," EurasiaNet, December 1, 2011, http://www.eurasianet.org/node/64622 (accessed December 19, 2013).

17. "Kyrgyzstan: Labor Migrants Grapple with Russian-Language Requirement," EurasiaNet, February 1, 2013, http://www.eurasianet.org/node/66491 (accessed December 19, 2013).

18. Igor Gorbachev, "Kyrgyzstan Steels Itself for Slowdown," Institute for War and Peace Reporting, January 11, 2009, http://iwpr.net/report-news/kyrgyzstan-steels-itself-slowdown (accessed

The decrease in poverty, growth of private credit bureaus, and the expansion of credit have so far not been significant enough to reduce corruption, at least as measured by Transparency International's Corruption Perceptions Index. Since private credit bureaus emerged in the mid-2000s, Kazakhstan's corruption rating has hovered between 2.1 and 2.9, on a scale of zero to 10, or 21 to 29, as Transparency International began to present its scores in 2012 on a scale of zero to 100. Kyrgyzstan's has oscillated in the range of 1.8 to 2.4 (or 18 to 24).[19] It is important to keep in mind that Transparency International's ratings capture both grand and petty corruption.

Kyrgyzstan periodically undertakes national anticorruption efforts, but they have not yet reduced petty corruption. The target of the campaigns has been grand corruption, and the purpose often has been to undermine opponents of the regime as much as to actually reduce corruption. Frustration over political elites' corruption, as well as creeping authoritarianism, fueled the popular protests that ousted President Kurmanbek Bakiyev in 2010, as well as President Askar Akayev in 2005. In response, interim president Roza Otunbayeva initiated an anticorruption campaign. Criminal cases were opened against top officials in the Bakiyev administration for stealing state assets including hundreds of millions of dollars in Russian aid.[20] Anticorruption efforts in economic sectors with foreign investment, such as mining, show some signs of success. Foreign businesspeople have reported that bribes are less essential to negotiating and implementing transactions.[21] Two small glimmers of hope are evident for reducing both petty and grand corruption. First, a few public advisory councils, voluntary watchdog groups legislated by the government to monitor ministries and state agencies, have increased transparency and improved services, although most have had no effect.[22] Second, the government plans to fill positions in the state agency responsible for granting mining licenses with specialists instead of patronage appointees.[23] Connections to government officials would no longer guarantee positions in this agency.

December 19, 2013); Joanna Lillis, "Kazakhstan: Astana Acts to Bolster Banks and Contain Rising Unemployment," EurasiaNet, January 21, 2009, http://www.eurasianet.org/departments/insightb /articles/eav012209.shtml (accessed December 19, 2013).

19. Transparency International, "Corruption Perceptions Index," http://www.transparency.org (accessed December 19, 2013).

20. Deirdre Tynan, "Kyrgyzstan: Corruption Crackdown Intensifies in Bishkek," EurasiaNet, November 2, 2010, http://www.eurasianet.org/node/62287 (accessed December 19, 2013).

21. Chris Rickleton, "Kyrgyzstan: Bishkek Missing out on Gold Bonanza," EurasiaNet, September 12, 2011, http://www.eurasianet.org/node/64161 (accessed December 19, 2013).

22. Chris Rickleton, "Kyrgyzstan: Democratization Initiative Losing Steam?" EurasiaNet, August 13, 2013, http://www.eurasianet.org/node/67381 (accessed December 19, 2013).

23. Chris Rickleton, "Kyrgyzstan: Mining Sector in Nationalists' Crosshairs," EurasiaNet, October 9, 2012, http://www.eurasianet.org/node/66026 (accessed December 19, 2013).

The likelihood that these anticorruption measures or any others will enjoy great success is small, however. The corruption allegation as a political tool has returned in full force after a brief hiatus under Otunbayeva. Upon selection as interim president, Otunbayeva agreed not to compete for the regular position so anticorruption allegations were less useful to her. Since her administration, political elites have been slinging charges of corruption at one another once again. Their aim is to retain power or secure political positions in order to protect their business interests. Most recently, a flurry of corruption accusations brought down Prime Minister Omurbek Babanov in 2012. In Kyrgyzstan, the extent to which any anticorruption measure is genuine is questionable.

By contrast, in Kazakhstan anticorruption measures and allegations have been less common. Struggle among political elites has been minimized in part because President Nursultan Nazarbayev has managed to maintain relative ethnic harmony among Kazakhs and the significant Russian minority and has distributed some of the gains from the country's profitable oil industry. When carrots do not work, the administration has used sticks. For example, in 2012 the government seized the property of the only healthy opposition force, the Alga! political party, and sentenced its leader to jail. The alleged crimes were that the opposition sought to overthrow the government and incite protests among oil workers. Perhaps another political entrepreneur will try to harness growing discontent among oil workers as a means to secure power. In this scenario, competition among political elites could grow and anticorruption efforts as a political tool could become prominent. However, it is likely that before that came to pass the individuals would face prison time.

In Kazakhstan and Kyrgyzstan, as in other parts of the world, multiple factors can fuel corruption. However, in order to understand and combat corruption it is important to recognize that neither officials' demands, the absence of sanctions, convention, nor economic need automatically propels citizens into illicit exchanges with government officials. Rather, ordinary citizens engage in corruption when market actors, groups in society, and family members cannot provide the resources they need. When market reform occurs in countries with a legacy of significant state economic intervention and absent or weak market-enhancing institutions, goods and services from nonstate sources are limited. By creating these substitute resources we can reduce corruption.

STATISTICAL ANALYSIS

This appendix presents details about the statistical analysis that informed the conclusions described in the Rest of the World section of chapter four. Specifically, it explains how I tested for the influence of market reform, market-enhancing institutions, and a legacy of significant state economic intervention on corruption; market reform's effect on corruption conditional on the other two factors; and the effects of alternative explanations.

The first statistical analysis I conducted demonstrates strong support for the importance of the two conditions, a legacy of significant state economic intervention and market-enhancing institutions. Regression analysis suggests that countries with weaker legacies of state economic intervention and more effective market-enhancing institutions have less corruption. For the calculation, I regressed the Corruption Perceptions Index (CPI) variable on the legacy, market-enhancing institutions, and market reform variables. This model, in Table A.1, shows that legacy and market-enhancing institutions are significant at the .01 level, meaning that there is less than 1 percent chance of obtaining the result when no relationship exists. The magnitude of the effects is relatively small. A one-unit increase in the legacy and market-enhancing variables represent a 5 percent increase and approximately a .3 percent increase, respectively, in the range of actual CPI scores. The small size likely reflects the facts that the CPI score is only a rough proxy for petty corruption and that many factors influence corruption.

TABLE A.1. Corruption Perceptions Index regressed on legacy, market-enhancing institutions, and market reform variables for countries of the world

	MODEL 1 CPI	SE
Legacy	.410**	.069
Market-enhancing institutions	.020**	.005
Market reform	.158**	.064
Constant	1.764	.490
Observations	92	
R-squared	.520	

** = $p < .01$.

This regression also indicates that countries with more market reform have less corruption. The market reform variable is also significant at the .01 level. My argument, however, indicates that market reform's effect depends on the degree of state economic intervention historically and the extent of market-enhancing institutions currently. So, I conducted further tests that enable me to examine market reform's effect conditional on these two factors.

I conducted a series of four regressions. I first split the data set into two to explore how the degree of state economic intervention historically affects market reform's influence on corruption when market-enhancing institutions are absent or weak and when they are effective. One data set had only countries with no or weak market-enhancing institutions, meaning that less than 20 percent of the adult population was included in public credit registries or private credit bureaus. The other data set included countries where the proportion was 20 percent or higher. Then in each data set I regressed CPI on the legacy and market reform variables and a variable I created to measure the interaction between the two. Likewise, to explore how the extent of market-enhancing institutions influences market reform's effect on corruption when state economic intervention was historically strong and when it was weak, I split the data set in two. One data set contained only countries with significant state economic intervention, meaning they scored a zero on the index. The other data set included countries where the number was higher than zero. Then in each of these data sets I regressed CPI on the market-enhancing institutions and market reform variables and a variable I created to measure the interaction between the two.

The results of these four regressions are presented in Tables A.2 and A.3. These findings are also the basis for Table 4.13 in chapter four. The first table includes the analysis from the data sets that are split depending on the strength of market-enhancing institutions, and the second table includes the analysis from the data sets that are split depending on the presence or absence of a state intervention legacy. At the bottom of each table are predicted effects. Specifically, Table A.2 shows the effect of market reform conditional on whether market-enhancing institutions are effective or weak or absent, and Table A.3 shows the effect of market reform conditional on whether a legacy of significant state economic intervention is present or absent.

With the limited data, model 2 tests my argument that market reform increases corruption when market-enhancing institutions are weak or absent and a state economic intervention legacy is present. The results, however, are not as expected, most likely because the CPI measures both grand and petty corruption. The model shows that when market-enhancing institutions are weak, the result is an interaction effect between a legacy of state intervention and market reform, such that market reform reduces corruption when a state economic in-

TABLE A.2.   Corruption Perceptions Index regressed on legacy and market reform variables for countries of the world

MARKET-ENHANCING INSTITUTIONS	MODEL 2 NONE/WEAK	SE	MODEL 3 EFFECTIVE	SE
Legacy	.597**	.083	.337**	.138
Market reform	.123*	.071	.114	.143
Legacy × market reform	−.038†	.024	.016	.025
Constant	1.774	.444	3.581	1.123
Observations	40		52	
R-squared	.632		.214	

$** = p < .01$; $* = p < .05$; $^† = p < .10$.

The effect of market reform on corruption

When legacy = 0 (high intervention)	.123 (decrease)	NA
When legacy = 10 (low intervention)	−.257 (increase)	NA

("Increase" and "decrease" are expressed in terms of level of corruption not the CPI scale, where an increase in CPI means a decrease in corruption.)

TABLE A.3.   Corruption Perceptions Index regressed on market-enhancing (M-E) institutions and market reform variables for countries of the world

LEGACY	MODEL 4 PRESENT	SE	MODEL 5 ABSENT	SE
Market-enhancing institutions	.034**	.014	.014†	.009
Market reform	.095†	.060	−.308*	.146
M-E institutions × market reform	.000	.002	.004*	.002
Constant	2.089	.382	5.194	.629
Observations	33		59	
R-squared	.560	.250		

$** = p < .01$; $* = p < .05$; $^† = p < .10$.

The effect of market reform on corruption

When m-e institutions = 0 (absent or weak)	.095 (decrease)	−.308 (increase)
When m-e institutions = 134.4 (effective)	.095 (decrease)	.230 (decrease)

("Increase" and "decrease" are expressed in terms of level of corruption not the CPI scale, where an increase in CPI means a decrease in corruption.)

tervention legacy is present and increases it when a state economic intervention legacy is absent. Market reform most likely decreases corruption, as measured by the CPI, even when a legacy is present, because it reduces government officials' opportunities to engage in grand corruption, as the overbearing state theory would predict. As significant state economic intervention is reduced even without effective market-enhancing institutions, the net effect is to reduce the

CPI value because it includes grand corruption. The negative effect on petty corruption that my argument predicts is perhaps masked by the positive effect on grand corruption.

The additional finding from model 2 that market reform increases corruption when both a legacy and market-enhancing institutions are absent or weak is consistent with my argument and with grand corruption theories. My argument emphasizes the importance of market-enhancing institutions, and grand corruption theories highlight that market reform offers government officials new opportunities to engage in illicit exchanges, regardless of the history of state intervention.

More technically, model 2 shows that the legacy, market reform, and interaction effect variables are significant at the .01, .05, and .10 levels, respectively. When seven additional countries, which lack data on the natural resources variable, are included in this analysis these variables are significant at the .01 level. The results here indicate that with a maximum level of state economic intervention (legacy = 0) market reform has a positive effect, and a one-unit increase in market reform increases the CPI score by .123 (meaning slightly less corruption). With no legacy of state economic intervention (legacy = 10), market reform has a negative effect, and a one-unit increase in market reform reduces the CPI score by .257 (meaning somewhat more corruption). Remember, a higher number for CPI represents less corruption. In model 3, market reform is not statistically significant, meaning it has no influence on corruption when market-enhancing institutions are effective. So, I did not calculate predicted effects.

Now let us consider the analysis where the data set is split depending on whether a legacy of significant state economic intervention is present or absent. These results appear in Table A.3. They are consistent with the findings described above. Specifically, in model 4, where the legacy is present, the interactive term is not significant, so market-enhancing institutions do not influence market reform's effect on corruption when a legacy is present. Instead, market reform consistently decreases corruption when a legacy is present.[1] Model 5 again shows the importance of market-enhancing institutions to reducing corruption. With no market-enhancing institutions, a one-unit increase in market reform increases corruption, reducing the CPI score by .308. However, with the maximum number of market-enhancing institutions in the data set (a score of 134.4), each one-unit increase in market reform increases the CPI score by .230, indicating a reduction in corruption. When the additional seven countries are included, all three variables reach the .01 level of statistical significance.

---

1. With the inclusion of the additional seven countries, the market reform variable is significant at the .05 level.

TABLE A.4. Corruption Perceptions Index regressed on legacy, market-enhancing institutions, market reform, state regulation, poverty, and natural resource endowment variables for countries of the world

	MODEL 6 CPI	SE	MODEL 1 CPI	SE
Legacy	.079[†]	.052	.410**	.069
Market-enhancing institutions	.015**	.003	.020**	.005
Market reform	.015	.044	.158**	.064
State regulation	−.160**	.036	—	—
Poverty	.00006754**	.000	—	—
Natural resource endowment	−.00000001705	.000	—	—
Constant	3.850	.505	1.764	.490
Observations	92		92	
R-squared	.816		.520	

$** = p < .01; * = p < .05; † = p < .10.$

Including the alternative explanations in the statistical analysis indicates that the argument is not spurious. For the calculation, I regressed CPI on the legacy, market-enhancing institutions, market reform, state regulation, poverty, and natural resource endowment variables. Model 6 in Table A.4 shows that the market-enhancing variable remains significant at the .01 level. So, none of the three alternative explanations, even though they were the leading contenders, can account for all of my explanatory factors and corruption. This result offers strong evidence that my argument is not spurious. Moreover, the result shows that a weakness or absence of market-enhancing institutions does, in fact, contribute to a higher level of corruption. With a significance level of .10, the chance of obtaining the result when no relationship actually exists is less than 10 percent. The magnitude of the effects remains small, likely because the CPI score is only a rough proxy for petty corruption. A one-unit increase in the market-enhancing institutions variable represents a .2 percent increase in the range of actual CPI scores, so its effect did grow smaller.

The coefficient for the legacy variable drops substantially from .410 to .079, and the market reform variable loses significance, as a comparison of models 6 and 1 in Table A.4 indicates. A possible explanation for these changes is the introduction of the state regulation variable, which is significant at the .01 level. Logically, the legacy and state regulation variables could be related as they both measure state economic intervention. High state economic intervention, measured as deposits in state banks relative to private banks in 1975, could contribute to high state regulation, measured as the number of procedures to register a business in 2009. Including the intervening variable of state regulation in the analysis reduces the effect of the antecedent legacy variable. As models 2 through

4 demonstrated, the market reform and legacy variables interact, so market reform lost its significance once the legacy variable was included. Unfortunately, the data set has too few cases to test for additional interactions, such as between the state regulation and legacy variables.

More broadly, this model indicates that my explanatory factors are only sufficient, not necessary, for corruption. Besides state regulation, poverty is another factor that contributes to corruption. The results indicate that the more procedures required to start a business and the lower GDP per capita the higher the level of corruption. Remember that the higher the CPI score, the lower the level of corruption. Like state regulation, poverty is significant at the .01 level. The magnitude of the effects is small for state regulation and minuscule for poverty. A one-unit increase in the state regulation variable represents a 2 percent decrease in the range of actual CPI scores. A one-unit increase in the poverty variable, meaning an increase in GDP, represents a .0009 increase in the range of actual CPI scores. The natural resource endowment variable is not statistically significant, meaning that there is no evidence that this variable has an effect on the corruption variable.

Index